INTERPRETING
THE
LANDSCAPE

INTERPRETING THE LANDSCAPE

Landscape Archaeology in Local Studies

Michael Aston

B. T. Batsford   London

Acknowledgements

I am particularly grateful to Graham Webster, the General Editor, and Peter Kemmis Betty of Batsford for their encouragement during the writing of this book. At times they had more faith than I did.

Very many people have helped with the compilation of material, in discussion and aid with illustrations. My colleagues in the Extra-Mural Department of Bristol University – Joe Bettey, Michael Costen and Bob Machin – provided stimulating discussion, while David Bromwich (Local History Librarian, Somerset County Council) and John Chandler (Wiltshire County Council) went to great lengths to find references and bibliographical details for me. Joe Bettey also gave much useful advice on the final text.

Many people kindly gave me information and illustrations. I hope I have acknowledged them all in the text, but I would particularly like to mention Martin Bell, Andrew Fleming, Bob Croft, Desmond Bonney, James Bond, Chris Gerrard, John Hurst, Chris Taylor, David Hall, Dave Austin, Roy Canham, Ann Beard, Peter Wade-Martins, Rupert Bruce-Mitford, Barry Cunliffe, Chris Dyer, Stanley West, Oliver Rackham, David Wilson, Edward Price, Rob Iles, June Sheppard, Trevor Rowley, Brian Paul Hindle, Della Hooke, Jim Bolton and Nick Tweddle. Gordon Kelsey and his colleagues did sterling work on the photographs and line drawings.

I owe much to Carinne Allinson. Not only did she type from a nearly illegible manuscript, but her editorial skills contributed greatly to the completion of the book.

Finally, I would like to dedicate this book to my parents, who for so long have had to live with field archaeology and landscape history – perhaps this will give them some idea of what it is all about.

ISBN 0 7134 3649 2 (cased)
ISBN 0 7134 3650 6 (limp)

Typeset by Keyspools Ltd
and printed in Great Britain by
Courier International Ltd,
Tiptree, Essex
for the publishers
Batsford Academic and Educational
a division of B. T. Batsford Ltd
4 Fitzhardinge Street
London W1H 0AH

Contents

List of illustrations

Preface

This book is written for those who want to know about the English landscape, whether they are archaeologists, historians, geographers or anyone interested in our past, and for all those who may wish to do some local history research, a parish survey or a local study. It draws attention to recent research and studies in the English landscape and shows how these are relevant to the local researcher's own interests. It attempts not only to review recent literature and articles (sometimes published in obscure places) and to make available more widely and easily the ideas contained within them, but also to develop some new ideas, clarify current knowledge and ideas and show how research is proceeding. Its aim is to throw some light on the complicated processes that have shaped the English landscape.

Furthermore, it is hoped that it will make those engaged in all aspects of local research think more deeply about their studies and begin to see them against the wider background of landscape studies. There is a tendency to look at particular or individual landscape features and see only details, but we need to think more about involved historical and natural processes and look at examples of how other places have developed elsewhere. This may teach us something about our own area of study. Attention will also be drawn to those aspects of sites and features in the landscape which have not previously been fully appreciated – features which are common enough but generally overlooked in the text books, like pillow mounds and duck decoys.

Many text books published today tend to give the impression that the author has personally carried out the huge amount of research needed to compile the volume; alternatively, the reader is bombarded with pages of indigestible references. In this book I hope to have adopted a more honest approach. It is an amalgam of the research of many people and, wherever possible, I have credited individuals with their work in the text. In general, my own research has covered the Midlands (Worcestershire, Warwickshire and Oxfordshire) and the West Country (Somerset, Avon, Gloucestershire and Wiltshire); for other areas I have had to rely on the research of colleagues, for which I am most grateful.

The bibliographies for each chapter do not give all the relevant references on the subject. What I have tried to do is to direct the reader to the most significant and important books and articles, which will in turn lead to a multitude of further papers. These bibliographies should be regarded as a door to further, more detailed, studies.

Finally, I hope this book is written in a style most people can understand. I have tried to make it easy to read, but if at times it seems direct, personal or even colloquial, this is because it is my job to communicate by teaching and this is the way language is used today.

Introduction

Most people are interested in the past to some degree and almost everyone wants to know something about the locality in which they live. Most areas have local stories of Roman roads, ghosts, plagues, underground tunnels, civil war battles, and the comings and goings of medieval monks, Cromwell and Elizabeth I. There is usually little truth in these stories, but their recounting shows something of attitudes and concerns about the history of particular local environments.

Nearly everywhere in this country has a local history written about it, often in the nineteenth or early twentieth century, and frequently by the local vicar, schoolteacher, or landed worthy. Invariably, these histories are concerned with the church, the manor, and the important families but, whilst interesting in themselves, these studies do not answer some of the basic questions asked about a place today. Indeed, such questions were not even thought of in the past. So, something more rigorous is needed for those of us who are concerned about the history behind the familiar scene. We want to know how old the church is and at what period most of the buildings were constructed, or why the hedges look as they do or why the road takes the particular course it does. Other questions may seem more awkward: when and why was this village or that farm first built there; what do those bumps and hollows mean in that field, or even, where did earlier people find their water or what sort of agricultural system did they employ?

Such questions cannot be easily answered for most of the parishes and villages in Britain, but the fact that they are being asked shows that, over the last quarter of a century, a new way of looking at the landscape and our everyday surroundings, whether town or country, has developed. We owe our initial awareness of questions about the landscape to people like Professors William Hoskins and Maurice Beresford. A generation of research in archaeology, economic history, historical geography and local history, as well as related subjects like historical ecology and place names, is now beginning to put forward explanations for some of the features mentioned above. For a few places, the story

behind what we see around us is beginning to emerge and this will have clear implications for studies in other places. Over the next few decades much more will be learnt.

It is the aim of this book to put some of these questions about the landscape and its development into perspective by looking at research widely scattered over England. Where work has been done and ideas developed, these will be discussed. Some of these ideas will be useful and relevant elsewhere in the country, perhaps a village or parish under study locally, even if the place originally examined is many miles away. Frequently, it will not be possible to answer some of our questions at the moment. It is unlikely that the work done so far will be relevant everywhere, but two things are certain: that research carried out in Yorkshire will have important implications for the local historian or fieldworker in Somerset, and that an awareness of problems posed and work undertaken elsewhere may prompt inquiry into aspects of the landscape hitherto unsuspected or overlooked in our own locality. If this book succeeds in making us more aware, making us think and question, and putting our own 'Little Twittering' into some larger-than-local-history context, the future for landscape studies will indeed be fruitful and exciting.

If we look at our surroundings, we are confronted by a great variety of landscape features. Most of us now live in towns and much of our environment is urban or suburban. Yet until the nineteenth century, most of the towns and cities of Britain were small; even in the inner suburbs we may live in what was countryside until 80 or 90 years ago, and much of the framework of those areas is rural rather than urban.

Over the last ten years I have lived in five different environments. In Birmingham, the row of terraced houses, built around the turn of the century, was all that existed in a road which ran between fields in 1840 and was not built up until the 1930s, '50s and '60s. The last piece of infilling is just beginning. Even so, the rear fence of the garden there reflected an old (how old?) field boundary and opposite the front of the house was a nineteenth-century brickyard with its pit, later used as an orchard and then as a lorry-breaker's yard. Where was our medieval parish church, where were the farms working the fields, and why did the road, running as it did through fields, have such a sinuous S-shaped course?

At Milton under Wychwood in Oxfordshire I lived in a new bungalow in a village. It was a vast thriving place with many new housing estates, garages, schools and shops. The new estate was infilled in the rear of the older village properties and, when I came to dig the garden, quite some time after settling into the house, I came across the well-ploughed field soil of the former open field strips and a telltale scatter of medieval pottery sherds. My journey to work took me through a landscape created in the 1850s when the old open fields were enclosed and new farms, roads, field boundaries, and even stream courses were laid out. To me, the generally unattractive appearance of the village, and hence, I suspect, its rapid expansion, was largely due to this total landscape reorganisation just over 100 years ago (Fig. 84).

In Taunton I lived in a row of large fine terraced houses by the railway station, which had been at the edge of the town until the 1930s. This isolated row must have looked impressive across the fields. Indeed, the outline of the plots owed its shape to the pre-existing fields, although the buildings may have been generated by the Great Western Railway enterprise, begun in that part of the West Country by Brunel in the 1840s. My journey to work there took me over a pattern of medieval roads conditioned by the presence of a possible late Saxon bridge, Norman castle and medieval town.

For a year I lived on the edge of Oxford in a quarryman's house which had a small carved lion over the door. It was near Headington Quarry, famous for its quarrymen and morris dancers. The plot of land on which it stood was the result of 'squatting', or encroachment on a piece of waste or underused land, for across the end of the house ran the old road from Oxford to London. The road is now fixed by tarmac, but in earlier times it must have wandered amongst the mud and potholes between wide hedges. Nearby there were patches of woodland formerly used by Oxford colleges to supply their timber for building and firewood, and the hedges, with their great banks and rich botanical species, indicated old fields.

In Bristol I lived in the inner suburbs in an old stone house of Tudor date. This was part of a larger house, now demolished, which looks splendid on the old photographs and earlier nineteenth-century prints. Land for several miles around was attached to it in the eighteenth and nineteenth centuries, and outlines of fields and the stone walls of its gardens have con-

ditioned the plots built on in the 1890s and early 1900s and the road developments up to the 1930s.

I now live in Sandford, a small nondescript bungaloid village outside Bristol. The bungalow in which I live is only 20 years old, but it has an old holloway in front linking Sandford to the main village of Winscombe, and the plot on which it stands is very irregular in shape. One of the property boundaries is an old hedge on a stony bank and this forms part of a series of parallel boundaries running for miles across country linked to a hillfort 3 kilometres (2 miles) away.

The past is all around us then, a truism which deserves to be repeated because it *is* so true; whether we like it or not, in this country we *do* live in a museum. Yet how are we to disentangle and understand it? Some of the likely developments have been indicated above as well as some of the sources which can be used. We shall now look more closely at the landscape and see what we can make of it.

Let us go first to the countryside, because, as has already been mentioned, most of Britain was countryside until as little as 100 years ago, and also because the elements we are going to examine are more obvious to see, though not necessarily more easy to understand, than those in the towns and suburbs. On any car journey in the countryside, fields defined by hedges or walls form the dominant view. Roads run between fields; tracks, footpaths and bridleways cross and join, and every so often a farm is passed. In villages and hamlets we see buildings of all shapes, sizes, ages and functions, with yards, gardens, plots and paddocks around, behind and between them. At the end of the village the church frequently provides a focus for our attention; it may have a manor house next to it or stand alongside a stately mansion. If we have come any distance, we may have crossed streams or perhaps a river, and spent some time climbing up or down hills. We may have noticed areas of unenclosed commonland, old quarries, perhaps the ruins of a castle or abbey, or an old mill or factory in a deep valley. Signposts will tell us the names of the farms and villages and indicate the nearest towns.

What are we to make of all these features, where they are situated and how they are arranged? There are clearly many ways of subdividing them and each of us may have a logical way of ordering the study of such a landscape, but in this book we are going to look at the landscape more from how it has functioned than how it looks. As we shall see, this will clarify many of the problems of why the landscape looks like it does and thus make it easier for us to study the changes which have resulted in the present complex pattern.

The basic shape of the land has geological and geomorphological origins, but our concerns are with the activities of people over many generations. First

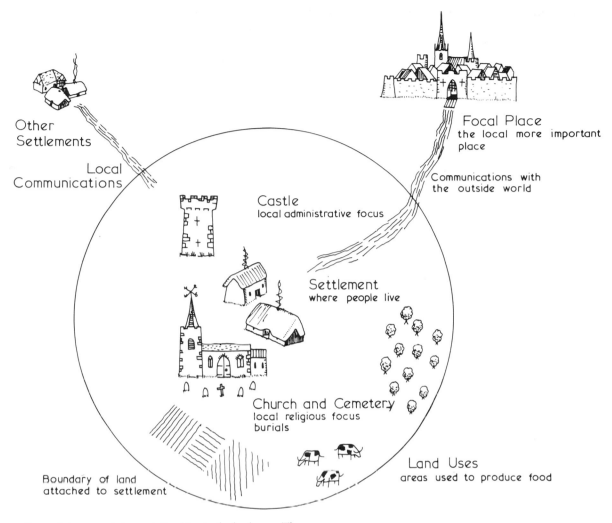

Other Settlements

Local Communications

Focal Place
the local more important place

Communications with the outside world

Castle
local administrative focus

Settlement
where people live

Church and Cemetery
local religious focus
burials

Boundary of land
attached to settlement

Land Uses
areas used to produce food

1 *Some of the more obvious relationships in the landscape. The example shown here is based on the medieval period, but the interrelationships depicted, between the settlement under study, its lands, other local settlements and the local town apply equally to all other periods.*

and foremost, people must have somewhere to live, even if it is only a temporary encampment, and so our main concern will be with settlements, a difficult word with many meanings. Here we shall consider villages, hamlets and farms: how they originate, what they consist of, how they change, and what they look like today. Secondly, people need to eat, and most of the landscape has been organised in the past to enable the maximum amount of food to be produced. Farming, fields and agricultural operations spring to mind and most land has been used for food production to a greater or lesser degree in the past. Land use is therefore a central theme, with discussion about how land has been used at different times, what field systems have been employed, and the ways of operating them, and how these patterns have changed through time.

The links between villages, farms and their fields, and between towns and the countryside are clearly evident in the landscape. Roads, tracks, rivers, and the small harbours and ports on rivers, estuaries and the coast were vital for moving goods about in the past. Towns often provided the points of exchange for these goods, and the fairs and markets with which we are so familiar today have a long history, although originally they were very different in character. So, focal places, where special goods or services could be obtained, form another less obvious, but equally important, element in the landscape.

Other aspects of earlier societies are not so obvious until a little thought is focused on them. Churches are a familiar element in the landscape, some of the most attractive and frequently the oldest buildings in any area. As burial places they were the successors to generations of earlier cemeteries and they provided the local religious focus, while the castle, manor house or stately home provided the administrative focus. Monasteries also had this latter administrative function in addition to their religious activities.

Recognition of these different aspects should help us to sort out what we see in the landscape. The obvious features of hedges, woods, buildings and fields are part of the way the landscape was *used*. Some aspects of the landscape have become specialised topics; buildings are the preserve of experts in vernacular architecture and historic buildings, but we can use the results of their research to help us understand our local landscape. Similarly, industrial archaeologists can point to the remains of early industrial activity and processes in the landscape and, even if we do not understand the mechanics or the chemistry, we can use their information in our studies also.

Finally, we must remember that the British landscape is very old in the sense that people have been living in it and using it for many thousands of years. It used to be thought that their influence before the Anglo-Saxon period was minimal and that prehistoric people had made little impact on their environment and left little trace of their activities. As we drive around much of the country this still appears to be true, but, over the last 30 years, fieldwork by archaeologists following motorway schemes, collecting pottery from fields, and looking for earthworks has shown that the landscape was very well developed even by 2000 BC, and air photographs taken by archaeologists show that

vast areas were covered by dense patterns of settlements and their fields well before the Roman conquest. In many areas little can be seen of this, but it certainly exists over wide areas. In any landscape study we need to be aware of what might lie hidden beneath the soil and how this may have influenced the layout of what we see around us, generally attributed to later periods. We shall, therefore, be looking at what we now know of prehistoric and Roman landscapes and how they might have influenced the framework of our present surroundings.

When Professor W. G. Hoskins wrote *The Making of the English Landscape* in 1955, he said (p. 14) 'The English landscape itself, to those who know how to read it aright, is the richest historical record we possess.' Since then, study after study has shown how much can be learnt. We now know that the landscape as created and used by people is much older than we ever thought, with perhaps as much as 12,000 years of intense activity represented. We know that its development has been more complex than we ever imagined, with many combinations of and interrelationships between the factors mentioned above. Change, rather than stability, has tended to be the order of the day. The idea of an unchanging landscape since time immemorial has had to be replaced now by one of great dynamism. If we could see the English landscape developing over the last 6000 years in a speeded-up film, it would certainly resemble an ants' nest, with not only the ants moving about at a great pace engaged in many jobs, but the nest itself being shifted constantly! This ants' nest which is the English landscape will be examined in this book to see how it has developed and what we can learn from it; but first we must look at the sources of information available to us to begin the investigation of the local landscape.

1

How do we know what we know?

The fact that there is likely to be an earlier local history of any particular parish has already been mentioned and will certainly be useful. What other sources are there for the history of the landscape? Where should we go to consult them or find out more, and what can we expect to learn from them? There are really five main categories of information – archaeology, aerial photography, maps, local history and related studies – and in this chapter we shall look at each of these and see what they can tell us.

ARCHAEOLOGY

A certain amount may be known about the archaeology of the area to be examined, and much else can be learnt from other sources discussed below. Most people do not realise that for most of the country no detailed archaeological fieldwork has ever been carried out and that there has usually been little, if any, recent excavation on any of the known archaeological sites in any area. The present lack of resources and the few archaeologists mean that this situation is not likely to alter in the near future and therefore a very real contribution can be made by the local fieldworker carrying out a parish survey or piece of landscape history research.

The Archaeology Division of the Ordnance Survey (which is now part of the Royal Commission on Historical Monuments (England)) has, over the years, compiled a monumental record of most of the known sites and finds in the country. If such archaeological features as hillforts, barrows, castle mounds or monastic sites exist in an area, these will be recorded on the OS Archaeology Division Record cards. The central repository is in Southampton, but there is another complete set in London (National Monuments Record) and there is usually a county set in the County Museum, Record Office, Local History Library, or with the County Archaeologist. The OS records, however, do not record extensive areas of earthworks or early landscape features associated with the post-Roman period, and they are not concerned with the

myriad odd features encountered in fieldwork which go so far to aid understanding of landscape development. Nevertheless, the record provides a good starting point if there are any major field monuments in the area under study.

Most counties now have some sort of Sites and Monuments Record, usually housed in the County Planning Department or the County Museum, and this tends to be based on the OS Archaeology Division records with further information added. Such records contain detailed 6-inch OS maps marked up with symbols of early sites and historic landscape features, together with collections of aerial photographs, ground surveys, references to museum collections, and so on. They provide a direct introduction to the existence of other material about the sites in an area and where this can be found, and the people in charge can often say how up-to-date parts of the record are and which areas of a county need more fieldwork, aerial survey and local history research.

How can these records aid our work of understanding the landscape? It is useful to know that there are field monuments of the Bronze or Iron Ages, or that a Roman villa has been found, or that there is a Norman church next to a motte and bailey castle, since each of these sites has implications for the landscape. Visits to them will often reveal further, less obvious, field evidence which has not so far been appreciated. Similarly, a collection of early pottery listed in such a record may indicate a site which can only be more fully understood when further investigation takes place. The record, then, can provide a beginning or base point for further work.

References to previous excavations contained in such records may be particularly useful. Even casual references to collections of pottery of a particular date or type, or the recorded depth of the bedrock in a certain spot, may help to indicate landscape changes. More detailed or large-scale recent excavations are likely to have revealed a great deal of information about the local landscape. This is particularly true where excavations have been accompanied by pollen or snail analysis or other environmental sampling, or where specialists have contributed reports on the local geology, soil or geomorphological changes or the botanical history of the area.

Palaeo-environmental evidence is becoming increasingly important and has great implications for the study of landscape history. Even though nothing may have been done on your area, it is important to appreciate the potential. Unless an expert is conducting research in your area it is unlikely that you will be able to learn much of the detail of local changes, although much more will be known of the environmental changes in the landscape in future from this type of data than from almost anything else, especially for the earlier periods. The chapter on prehistoric and Roman landscapes will show just how much can be found out.

The archaeological evidence so far discussed will provide a general background to the major field monuments and archaeological sites in the area and, if we are lucky, more detailed information from the occasional excavation or piece of environmental research will help. How can we supplement this, obtain a fuller picture and see the relationship of individual sites to the rest of the landscape? Various methods will be described below, and further excavation will add much new information. Fieldwork, simply and effectively carried out, will certainly provide one of the most cost-effective sources of additional information. Unlike excavation, it is non-destructive, leaving much of the evidence intact for future generations of researchers.

Fieldwork

Fieldwork at its most basic involves walking across the landscape recording features seen on the ground. In this section we are concerned with man-made features, but it is often difficult to separate these from natural aspects. It is thus advisable to record geological and botanical information as well; more will be said of this later.

Certain basic preparations need to be made before commencing fieldwork. Before work can begin, permission must be obtained from the farmer or landowner, and it is worth spending some time explaining to the owner what you are trying to achieve. Contacts and friendly introductions can smooth the path and gain access to some of the more private estates.

While compasses and survival kit are not generally necessary in this country, good footwear and warm waterproof clothing are essential. Since the best field-work is carried out in the winter (for reasons which will be explained below), rubber wellington boots with several layers of socks are the best footwear: it is inevitable that streams and boggy ground will be encountered and stout walking shoes are not adequate. Similarly, layered clothing is best, because with exertion and our unpredictable climate a well-padded

anorak is sometimes too heavy or too warm. A thin and a thick pullover, with a windproof and/or waterproof overlayer is best, enabling the maximum combination of layers for warmth and protection against wind or rain or both. Waterproof trousers that reduce to a pocket-sized parcel are also advisable.

Maps will be discussed below in more detail, but for fieldworking the 6-inch (1:10000) is the best widely available scale, although the $2\frac{1}{2}$-inch (1:25000) should be carried for the general locality and the 25-inch (1:2500) map for detail of a small area. With the wide availability of photocopying machines, it is useful to have copies of the relevant bits of the map to mark on in the field. With modern maps there are copyright problems and so, as will be explained below, the first edition OS 6-inch maps of the 1880s are generally used. It is a pity that the OS do not produce a 12-inch to the mile (i.e. 1:5000) map, since this would be ideal, combining the detail of the large-scale maps with the page size of the $2\frac{1}{2}$-inch or 1-inch maps. If you have access to map reducing or enlarging facilities, and particularly if you are working in an urban or suburban area, this is a scale well worth considering.

In order to protect such maps while working in the field, plastic dockets of A4 size or thereabouts should be carried, together with a board to write on. It is not worth buying anything expensive, because a piece of hardboard which can go in the plastic docket with some metal clips (foldback not bulldog) is cheaper and much better. A notebook, or better still sheets of paper which can be filed together or separately, with a selection of pencils, hard and soft, coloured crayons, a penknife and rubber, should also be carried. Plastic bags will be needed for finds of pottery and other objects picked up from ploughed areas. Driving to the area in which you are interested is quite acceptable, but there is no substitute for *walking* across the landscape.

Your records should be intelligible to anyone else if they are to be of any value. Always work as if you are about to drop dead – date and sign your work, put on scales, north signs and adequate keys; complete cross-referencing should be clearly marked. Days later you may not remember what it all means.

Earthworks

So, what are we looking for? Almost anything you see may be useful, but there are obvious categories of evidence. Earthworks provide perhaps the greatest source of information, particularly for the more recent periods. Almost any bump, lump or hollow has something to tell us, even if it is of little significance. There are, however, a few rules of thumb to remember. Firstly, even though the mound or feature you have found, recorded, and even surveyed, may look like a typical example of a certain type of site, without further research (or even excavation) it is usually impossible to tell. The few field archaeological manuals that are available lead one to think that every mound is explicable, although usually only four out of five features recognised on any reconnaissance are easily identifiable as particular types of archaeological feature.

Secondly, areas of earthworks, while looking homogeneous today, may in fact have originated at widely different times for varying reasons. A site which at first seems to be a monastic complex, with good quality earthworks but no standing building, may in fact have earthworks of an abandoned village which predate the monastery, and the terraces and gardens of a post-dissolution mansion all mixed up with the obvious monastic earthworks. The present view is like looking at the stars – in one view many ages are seen (*Fig. 26*).

Finally, to work in isolation from the field evidence alone is likely to prove misleading. Adequate preparation with the maps indicating field names, local geology and something of the local history of the area can help avoid some of the worst 'elephant traps' of explanation into which we are all liable to fall from time to time.

There are a number of text books which assist in the identification of archaeological field monuments and areas of early landscape and it is not a skill easily taught in a book like this one. The best advice for the fieldworker is to be persistent, visiting as many types of field monuments, in as many different seasons and parts of the country as possible. If sites are visited that are already well recorded and even fully excavated, it will prove easier to recognise similar features and landscapes in other areas. Later chapters will assist in such work, but without the acquired expertise and appropriate local background research, it is easy to be misled.

Round mounds

Let us take, as an example, the case of round mounds. Most archaeological textbooks and manuals on field techniques give the impression that all round earthen mounds that a fieldworker may encounter are round barrows of the prehistoric Bronze Age. This is partly because there are many of them, especially in the areas traditionally of interest to field archaeologists, such as the chalk uplands of Wessex and Sussex and other uplands like the Peak District and the North Yorkshire Moors. It is also a reflection of the interest of most fieldworkers (certainly until the 1950s) in the prehistoric and Roman evidence, almost to the exclusion of everything later, and also of the focus of attention on specific archaeological *sites* rather than wider landscape implications.

In fact, there are many features in the landscape which end up as round mounds and most of them are *not* prehistoric burial mounds! Indeed, since the work

of Leslie Grinsell (cataloguing barrows county by county across southern England), it is unlikely that large numbers of such sites will be found from now on; those that do turn up are likely to be degraded or damaged examples. What else, then, can round earthen mounds represent, and how can the fieldworker get clues to their original or previous use?

A host of recent activities has resulted in round mounds being constructed. In the Second World War, for example, 'decoy towns' were built to attract enemy bombers away from city targets. One of these remains at Black Down on the Mendips, south of Bristol. Here, parallel lines of small mounds about 1 m (39 in) in height run for long distances across the heathland. Nearby is a large air-raid shelter, and the lines of mounds run confusingly through a prominent prehistoric barrow cemetery! The site was one of a number of decoys in the West Country and fires were lit on the mounds to create the impression from above of pathfinders' flares and burning buildings. Not far away on North Hill at Minehead in Somerset another piece of moorland has many larger earthen mounds, some with hollows in the top. This looks like a large spread-out barrow cemetery, but there are triangular 'courses' and the remains of a tank turret and shells to indicate the site's real use as a Second World War tank-training range. The most prominent earthworks were mobile target tracks with underground blockhouses at one end. It is, thus, important to recognise that features from the 1939–45 war have now become 'archaeological', and care in interpretation needs to be applied by the fieldworker.

From earlier crises, and more primitive methods of solving them, came beacons. In the West Country many hilltops were used for signalling purposes and the fires or fire baskets were often placed on mounds. Confusingly, some barrows were used for this purpose, such as Cothelstone Beacon and Westbury Beacon in Somerset, and it is not clear how much, or little, of the earlier structure was disturbed. Frequently, the beacon use has entered the local folklore to the exclusion of earlier and later use of the sites.

This use and re-use of sites at all periods poses very real problems for the fieldworker. Without excavation it is impossible to say what, or how many, uses a round mound may have had. For example, in the Middle Ages round mounds were built for early castles and to support windmills. In either case, earlier barrows could have been used for the later structure. Thus, at Brinklow in Warwickshire there is a fine motte and bailey castle of Norman date, but its motte stands on a ridge and may originally have been the 'low' or burial mound of the place name. Many early mottes of small Norman castles were interpreted on early OS maps as barrows, and though it is impossible to tell without excavation, the *context* of some of these sites may be significant. Less substantial earthworks demarcating the bailey and other subsidiary enclosures may have gone unnoticed. Yet, even if they are disguised under later hedges or within present-day properties, they can often still be detected and recorded. Field names help, but the main feature is that many of them are near to early churches and sometimes associated with village earthworks. A small mound 1–2 metres (3–6 feet) high at Rochford in Worcestershire is almost certainly a small castle motte, even though it is nearly cut in half by the river Teme and has had fruit trees planted on it. It stands next to the local church, which has a fine 'Tree of Life' tympanum over the Norman doorway.

Similarly, windmills were invariably built on hills, or at least locally prominent spots – just the sort of places to find earlier barrows. At Stoke St Gregory in Somerset a fine mound on a hill overlooking the Levels could easily be a barrow. As at other windmill sites, the local field name Windmill Hill and the characteristic cross-shaped hollow in the top help in interpretation. The latter feature is the ghost of the 'cross-trees' used to support the post mills, but barrow-robbing, with treasure-hunting holes dug in earlier times into the centres, could result in a similar feature being formed.

The conversion to Christian use of earlier pagan sites often meant the incorporation of earlier features into churchyards. Maxey Church in Northamptonshire is almost certainly built on a barrow, one of several in the locality. The others are now ploughed out and appear as cropmarks, or have been dug away in gravel extraction. However, at Berwick in Sussex a round mound sits in the churchyard next to the medieval church – probably an earlier pagan feature taken over in early missionary activity.

A number of other mounds formed the meeting places of the hundred courts in the eleventh and twelfth centuries and perhaps earlier. Frequently, this fact is reflected in the later hundred names, such as Swanborough in Wiltshire and Secklow in Buckinghamshire (Fig. 18). Occasionally the mound remains, as at these sites, and also at King's Standing by Sutton Park on the outskirts of Birmingham.

Medieval fishponds are increasingly being recognised. Although usually dry, they remain as grassed hollows, sometimes with prominent dams. Again, the context is important, for a number have round mounds in the bottom which would have been islands when the pond was full of water. At Steeton in Yorkshire one such mound was dug in the mistaken belief that it was prehistoric in date! Such islands were used as refuges for ducks and other water birds.

Also from the Middle Ages there are instances of mounds being used as archery butts, as at Wold Newton in Yorkshire, or as gibbet mounds, as at Caxton in Cambridgeshire. Again, it is usually unclear whether this is a later use of an earlier site. Similarly, at

Low Ham in Somerset, a low mound with a slight ditch around it is shown on an eighteenth-century map as 'Dovehouse in decay' and evidently was the base of a circular medieval stone dovecote. Other mounds on village and major sites may also have been dovecotes, but this particular example may have persisted as a folly or gazebo for the nearby mansion.

In the sixteenth and seventeenth centuries very many mounds were built. The vogue for formal gardens necessitated the construction of prospect mounds, viewing platforms, and supports for seats, summerhouses, trees and shrubs (Fig. 26). A classic example is Lyveden in Northamptonshire, where the mounds are terraced with spiral paths. A more mundane example is Car Colston in Nottinghamshire, where two ordinary round mounds with a pond between form the prospect to a fine eighteenth-century house once lived in by Robert Thoroton, the county antiquarian. At Hatch Beauchamp in Somerset several mounds on a ridge mark the gardens of the lost Belmont House – it would be easy to interpret these mounds as prominent barrows. Elsewhere in landscaped parks other round mounds may be encountered. Ice houses, when ruined, look like barrows or small mottes, but the brick passages and domes of the ice chamber usually reveal their true purpose.

Industrial activity has also produced many intriguing earthworks. Early mining, in particular, was carried out via 'bell pits' and some of these again look like barrows. Confusion is easy, as the siting of much of this mining in upland Britain means that round mounds and hollow doughnut-shaped mounds can be prehistoric circular houses ('hut circles'), barrows, cairns, or mining activity – frequently a mixture of each! The Minnions area in Cornwall has extensive bell pits from copper and tin mining mixed up with the prehistoric Hurlers stone circles and accompanying barrows. In the Peak District many uplands, for example Bonsall, are pitted with lead workings which look like rows of robbed-out cairns. At Holcombe in Somerset a number of early coal mining bell pits remain from the thirteenth century onwards, while at Bentley Grange in Yorkshire iron mining bell pits of medieval date cover earlier ridge and furrow, providing superb field evidence for the relative dates.

The lesson with round mounds, as with other earthworks, is that great care and attention has to be given to them as features in the landscape whenever they are encountered. Without excavation, it may be impossible to say what they are definitely, but the context of them, their setting, and useful hints like field names, all help to decide what they might be. This examination of round mounds serves to demonstrate the problems in interpreting features which may look alike, but have very different origins.

Arable land and finds

Fieldwork on ploughed land is most likely to produce scatters of finds, especially pottery sherds. There are now several useful manuals explaining how to search fields systematically, carefully record the finds made, and understand what the finds mean. Initially, the new fieldworker looking for pottery tends to pick up only pieces of 'willow pattern' plate or blue and white Woolworth's crockery. Early pottery is much less obvious and the buff, grey and beige sherds take some identifying in plough soil. Studies have shown that dull, dry days after rain are likely to be the most productive.

Visits to local museums and reference to textbooks will show the sort of Roman and medieval pottery likely to be found. Prehistoric and Saxon pottery is much rarer and tends to be more friable; it is easily destroyed by plough action and weathering.

It is not possible here to explain all the types of pottery likely to be encountered, and a specialist in the pottery of the area will usually need to be consulted at the local museum to give more than an approximate guess at the age of any sherds found. However, a few points need to be mentioned. Firstly, the search should be systematic in 10 metre (33 feet) or so strips, with everything which is not natural being picked up and recorded. Secondly, the finds should be bagged up and properly identified with field reference, date, finder, location, and so on. Thirdly, the condition of the pot sherds found will be very important (*Figs. 42 and 43*). Large sherds of freshly broken pottery are more likely to indicate a former settlement site than small abraded sherds, which are more likely to have been ploughed over many times and must in many cases be the result of 'manuring' in earlier times, with domestic rubbish being brought out to the fields with dung, straw, and so on. Such small, broken, abraded sherds may thus represent the fields rather than the settlement, hence the archaeologist's great interest in the condition and number of sherds (you might expect more on a settlement), as well as the dating.

Pottery is not the only material found in plough soil. Metal objects are frequently picked up, including pieces of bronze and iron, as well as coins. Much, however, is often of recent date, representing bits of horse fittings and pieces of agricultural machinery. Since pottery and stone objects tell us most about previous human activity on a site, metal detectors are not likely to be very informative, unless one is only interested in valuable loot. Stone objects may include flint or chert flakes and implements and the same care needs to be applied as with pottery. Careful recording of all pieces found, waste flakes as well as implements, enables prehistorians to distinguish different types of sites from different periods, from settlements to camp-sites, with areas of arrowhead finds perhaps indicating hunting grounds.

Great familiarity with the locality is needed to record all that can be seen in plough soil and to interpret it correctly, but, as with other aspects of fieldwork, it is practice rather than teaching which achieves most. The secret is to separate out the 'natural' features, such as subsoil or drift-deposited material, from anything 'archaeological' (introduced by man), and then interpret what such material might mean. Areas of broken bricks might indicate former gate entrances, and darker soil may mark the sites of ditches or hedges of recently removed field boundaries; but equally, burnt clay or daub together with darker soil and patches of charcoal might indicate an earlier settlement or kiln site. It is often difficult to be certain, but the evidence should be carefully recorded and studied.

AERIAL PHOTOGRAPHS

It is difficult to emphasise enough how important aerial photographs are for the study of a landscape. Little real progress will be made without recourse to at least a few pictures and it is therefore important right from the outset to establish what air pictures are available for an area and how useful they are likely to be. There are basically two types of air picture (obliques and verticals) and two sources (those taken for archaeological reasons and those taken for other purposes). Vertical photographs provide a 'photographic map', taken looking down over a piece of country (e.g. *Fig. 26*), whereas obliques give a bird's-eye view (e.g. *Figs. 24 and 25*). Both are useful, obliques frequently showing sites in great detail, while verticals enable mapping of such features as ridge and furrow.

There are two national repositories of aerial photographs taken primarily for archaeological purposes. In Cambridge the collection built up by Professor St Joseph and continued by David Wilson includes hundreds of thousands of oblique views of most of the major field monuments and areas of archaeological interest. These are indexed by civil parish, and copies (and searches) can be made. The collection of the Air Photographs Unit of the National Monuments Record is indexed by OS grid squares and contains large numbers of cropmark sites and vertical pictures (e.g. *Fig. 66*). Again, copies can be ordered and searches made.

For any square mile of Britain, hundreds, if not thousands, of air photographs have probably been taken in the past. Certainly, since 1945, vertical air photograph coverage will exist for most areas, and there may be pre-war photographs for some areas. Some of the earliest and most useful material was taken by the RAF between 1944 and 1948. This series was taken for local government purposes and, because great areas were photographed in winter in low sunlight, it is particularly useful for landscape studies. Since that date, flights for local authorities (for planning and highways purposes) and by the statutory undertakers (gas, electricity, water boards, etc.), as well as map revision by the Ordnance Survey, have resulted in large numbers of vertical air pictures being taken. To begin any study such sources need to be located and access arranged. Frequently, such surveys can be seen by application to the above organisations or via the County Archaeologist, who will know of the local sources. The use to which all such photographs can be put will be indicated throughout this book. Principally, however, they are used to record changes in the landscape, and earthworks and features revealed by low sunlight, and cropmarks. Earlier photographs will, of course, show landscape changes that have taken place particularly well.

MAPS

After fieldwork and aerial photographs, maps form the third pillar on which successful landscape studies are built. Before the Ordnance Survey came into existence, there were few printed large-scale maps in Britain, but there are three major sources of early large-scale manuscript maps. The main Tithe Commutation Act of 1836 resulted in many parishes in Britain being surveyed on a large scale with a detailed accompanying 'award' being compiled, listing information about the parish, township or tithing. The tithe map, therefore, provides a good basic document for landscape study. It can be used to produce maps and information on land ownership, tenancy, land use and value, and, perhaps most importantly, it gives field and land parcel names and shows in detail a landscape before the effects of the nineteenth and twentieth centuries. It is useful to compile a 6-inch scale version of the tithe map on plastic tracing film for the area under study. This enables dyeline copies to be made, on which different classes of information can be plotted, and also tithe maps of different parishes can be more easily compared, since the originals occur at a variety of scales. For other areas, enclosure maps of the late eighteenth and nineteenth centuries can be used in the same way.

Estate maps, especially of pre-tithe date, can also be used in this way and, since they are available for some areas back to the sixteenth century, these are frequently extremely important sources (*Fig. 27*). Sometimes only small areas are shown, and 6-inch scale versions will help in comparison between different sources and dates.

From the early nineteenth century, mapmaking by the Ordnance Survey becomes of increasing importance. Even though the earliest maps at one inch to one mile are rather too small to give more than the major outlines, they can be compared with earlier maps at about the same scale (such as the Greenwood maps [1822] and Day and Masters maps [1782] for Somerset, and Andrews and Drury maps [1773] for Wiltshire); frequently, the two inches to one mile field sheets from which these first OS maps were compiled are accessible in local Record Offices. However, it is without doubt the larger scales that the landscape historian will find most interesting. In particular, the first edition OS 6-inch maps should be mentioned, which are by far the most useful maps to the fieldworker (*e.g. Figs. 39, 40 and 41*). There is usually a set of them in the local Record Office and copies can be made very cheaply without copyright infringement, enabling a complete coverage to be built up of the area under study. These maps are some of the finest produced, showing in great detail buildings, roads, hedges (often with tree species), stream courses, parish and other boundaries. Nothing the Ordnance Survey produces today on this scale is as good and so, as mentioned above, this is really the best basis for fieldwork and rural landscape history study in this country.

For more built-up areas and more detailed survey, the larger scale 25-inch (now 1:2500) and 50-inch (1:1250) maps are available from the late nineteenth century onwards. The modern versions of these maps give a wealth of detail, but again the older maps are more useful, with their record of places before the major changes of this century.

LOCAL HISTORY

There is a wealth of material published on the sources and use of local history material; Record Offices and Local History Libraries provide easy access to such material, and their staffs will readily give advice on the uses of the source material. However, a few general points need to be made on the use of local history material in any local landscape study. Firstly, much that is of interest to and forms the basis of the work of the local historian is often of little or no interest to the student of landscape history. Unless the documents refer to a feature or change in the landscape, they can probably be considered irrelevant. Documents which give good topographical detail, such as manorial court rolls, surveys and extents, are, however, of great importance. The stock-in-trade of many local historians – genealogical material, parish registers, and the mass of nineteenth-century documentation – tends, on the other hand, to be of very limited interest to those involved in the study of the history of the landscape.

Secondly, much local history, as carried out in the past, was rather more the magpie-like collection of facts than problem-orientated research. Proper landscape research needs to ask and, wherever possible, answer, questions. If a document or piece of local historical research helps in such work, then it should be used; if not, it should be put aside. An outstanding exception to the somewhat conventional approach to local history can be seen in the work of the editors of the Victoria County History (VCH) volumes at present underway. Working to a predetermined plan of manorial and estate history, economic history, church history, and these provide a wealth of easily accessible published material – a superb source of local landscape study, where they are available. Some counties are more advanced than others, but the student of landscape history is fortunate if he or she works in a region recently fully researched by the VCH.

A third source of documentation, and one of very great importance, is place names. Most place-name experts stress that this is a very difficult source of information to use and recent work by scholars in this field is dramatically altering our ideas on place names, so that books and articles written as recently as ten years ago are now likely to be out-of-date. As with the VCH, where there has been a recent volume published by the English Place Name Society (e.g. Berkshire or Cheshire), a mine of useful material becomes available, together with the latest assessment; but elsewhere there can be problems. In some counties, active work is being conducted by carefully supervised groups or PhD students. Clearly, as part of any landscape study, place names should be carefully collected, together with dates and sources of information. Assessment and interpretation should only be attempted, as with pottery sherds and earthwork interpretation, with the help of an expert if the worst mistakes are to be avoided.

Although oral history is important as a source of recent change, its use needs to be strictly vetted. Local knowledge of the landscape can be invaluable, and farmers in particular can usually give a wealth of advice on good and poor land, former cottage sites, alterations they have made, and finds that have been reported; all of this information should be collected and recorded. However, local people often have a fund of biased and poorly authenticated hearsay which, if too much note is taken of it, will confuse the serious researcher. In general, the local tradition concerning what has happened in the locality, particularly beyond a couple of generations ago, is the least reliable source of information and should be treated with great scepticism.

OTHER SOURCES

The study of the history of the landscape is much like other branches of the past. The student needs to read widely and to be skilled in several different disciplines. So far, we have considered archaeological, field and historical sources, but there are many other aspects of the landscape which are relevant to how people have used it in the past, and even a slight knowledge of them will aid understanding and interpretation of features discovered.

Change in the landscape has already been mentioned as a constant factor to be borne in mind. It might be assumed that any background material on the physical appearance of the landscape would be constant. One would expect the form of the countryside, the drainage pattern, soil types, climate and, to some extent, vegetation to be reliable over long periods. As with man's use of the landscape, however, these factors are changing all the time. Climate is perhaps the least influenced by people, but recent work has shown how even slight alterations in temperature or precipitation, hardly noticeable within a lifetime, may have brought about long-term changes in the way people used the landscape. This is a difficult field of study and the student is referred to the most recent publications in the bibliography.

While the overall appearance of the landscape based on the geology and geomorphological processes within it owes little to man, his interference with vegetation and drainage over the millennia has had widespread local effects. Prehistorians and palaeo-environmentalists have found evidence of increased erosion of soil from hilltops and valley sides as a result of clearance of woodland and soils left open to winter rains and frosts (*Fig. 3*). Many valleys have become filled with sediment, and river valleys have become choked with alluvium and colluvium brought down by streams running rapidly off vegetation-free slopes. Such changes can be shown over long periods in prehistory, and they are still happening. Only our changing technology is capable of initiating, diverting and preventing such 'natural' changes. It is well known that some rivers have less water in them now than in earlier times (*Fig. 54*) and formerly busy harbours are now choked with silt and alluvium (*Fig. 86*).

The type and condition of the soil is increasingly seen as the result of management or mismanagement by man. Following clearance of woodland and use for farming, many soils became degraded, and thus the modern soil map may not reflect the situation 500, 1000, or more years ago. When we use it to suggest areas of fertile land, well-drained country or boggy land, we need to be aware of change and to allow for this, if possible, in our reconstruction of earlier landscapes. Numerous excavations have shown better quality soil under, for example, Bronze Age barrows, showing that the present landscape is not like it was at all times in the past. As with climate, this is a difficult area to study, but some of the most useful books are referred to in the bibliography.

Mention of vegetation should remind us that it is

now difficult to envisage any part of the British Isles as undisturbed by the activities of people. It is now clear that there is *no* primeval woodland left; everywhere clearances, whether in Anglo-Saxon, medieval or seventeenth-century times, must be *re*clearances (*Fig. 92*). Pollen analysis demonstrates this very clearly. Nevertheless, the vegetation of a woodland, a hedge or a grassy field can, in the way Oliver Rackham has shown us, demonstrate man's use of the area in the recent past.

In summary, then, it can be seen that in order to understand our local landscape there is much we need to know before we start work. We can make our contacts with the County Record Office, the County Archaeologist, and any other experts we may know. We can find our sources of air photographs and old maps and get together our kit for fieldworking. But before we begin we should assess the problems of our locality and what information we are seeking. Only then will we know how to proceed.

The landscape itself is very complex – a series of interconnecting systems, with people at the centre. It has always been so and we need to become, very early on in our work, allergic to simplistic explanations for features we can see and changes we can infer. If we are prepared for complexity, we will make a more honest appraisal of how the piece of country we have chosen developed (*Fig. 93*).

Change and complexity are important concepts in studying our landscape, but we must also be aware of the great length of time any part of the British Isles has been occupied (*Fig. 92*). With the exception of periodic visits in interglacial periods, we are now dealing with about 12,000 years of continuous activity by people in Britain, and for about 10,000 years there is no known history. Even for the last 2000 years, only 100–200 years are adequately documented in some areas. Thus the importance of prehistory must be stressed if an honest landscape study is to be conducted. In that long period, perhaps only 3000–4000 years will have seen organised settlements, field systems, trackways and religious sites. We need to be aware of this long period when the framework of the landscape was being formed, and it is to this period that we now turn.

2

Early landscapes

Although Britain has been occupied by man for more than 25,000 years, in a form of intermittent visits over long periods between glaciations, it is only for the last 12,000 years or so that the country has been continuously occupied, with people moving into Britain permanently to exploit what resources were available. What sort of landscape did such Palaeolithic (Old Stone Age) and later Mesolithic (Middle Stone Age) people find and create, and what sort of economy did they practise?

With the retreat of the ice sheets, Britain was left as a landscape of glacial debris, alluvium and lakes, colonised initially by tundra vegetation. As the climate improved, woodland dominated by birch and pine developed, and by 8000 BC dense deciduous woodland covered almost all of the country. This very simplified picture has been worked out by the detailed work of pollen analysts studying fossil pollen grains from bogs, marshes and lakes. Of course, each of these landscapes of tundra, pine woodland and deciduous woodland was occupied by various types of animals, which in their turn were hunted by man. The archaeological evidence for this hunting activity over very long periods, from 12,000 to 4000 BC, consists of flint implements and a few bone objects from both open settlement sites and caves. Only rarely are other sites like hunting bases recognised, usually from scatters of flints, and very few have ever been scientifically examined.

THE EARLIEST LANDSCAPES

It is difficult to imagine in detail what such landscapes looked like, how they were used by people and in what sort of activities these people were engaged. Until recently, indeed, any impact on the landscape in such early times was considered to have been minimal. However, new assessments of the evidence are painting a radically different picture, emphasising the richness of the food and other resources available and the intensive and extensive use of the land by Upper Palaeolithic and Mesolithic communities (*Fig. 52*).

The range of equipment available to such people was very wide. A variety of flint implements included wood-, leather- and bone-working tools, and weapons, such as the microliths which formed parts of harpoons and possibly spears. Of greatest interest, perhaps, are the 'tranchet' axes (or 'Thames picks') which could be used for cutting down trees and preparing timber, leading to the possibility of extensive forest clearance even at this early date. (In this respect, fire was also of great importance.)

Such early communities were not only dependent on animals for food and raw materials, but their lifestyle was probably determined to a large extent by the seasonal movements of these animals between different grazing areas. Various authors have argued for seasonal camps and settlements based on the animal resources available – in the uplands in the summer and on the coast and lowlands in the winter. What is perhaps of greater interest is the suggested management of such herds, with men clearing areas to encourage browse and grassland formation in order to attract animals, and a more symbiotic relationship developing. It may well be, in fact, that clearance of woodland was taking place sporadically in the Mesolithic period (8000–4000 BC) to facilitate hunting by encouraging animals to frequent certain places and that this, together with the seasonal movements of herds, determined very early patterns of settlement, communication and territorial organisation of the landscape.

As will be indicated below, it is rarely wise to consider a single place in isolation. In this period, the recognition of early flint scatters on the uplands or the coast, or the location of a settlement site, whether in a cave or not, can rarely be divorced from other contemporary sites in the vicinity, even if widely separated. Professor Graham Clark has suggested, for example, that the dwellers on the Mesolithic site at Star Carr in Yorkshire were exploiting not only the lake on which it was situated, but also the lowland of the Vale of Pickering to the west, the Yorkshire wolds to the south, and the North Yorkshire Moors to the north. A wide range of habitats and resources was thus available within one or two hours' walk.

In Somerset, reconstruction of the earlier topography of the county has led Christopher Norman to suggest a range of rich resources available at different seasons, with men and animals moving from the rich pasture and woodland of the Somerset Levels in summer to the uplands of Exmoor, the Quantocks and the Mendips in spring and autumn. The woodlands everywhere would have provided game, animals for meat and other resources like bone and leather, fruit, berries, nuts, fungi, and so on, while the uplands may have provided natural or artificially created grazing for horses, deer, wild cattle, wild pigs, and a host of smaller animals. Roger Jacobi has described a vivid picture of hunters around Cheddar Gorge using the many shallow access valleys from the Levels to the top of the Mendips as ambush points for animals moving to and fro over the seasons, and it is noticeable how many of the Mesolithic sites located by Joan Taylor and Rebecca Smart are at the top end of shallow valleys in the front of the Mendips and close to former springs.

In such an economy, and also in the earlier phases of primitive agricultural communities, the coast and the larger river valleys provided very rich sources of food for small bands of people; many Mesolithic sites have been recognised in such areas. However, the coastline has altered drastically in the last 10,000 years. Britain finally became cut off from the Continent at the Straits of Dover around 6500 BC, although it may have been somewhat later between East Anglia and northern Europe via the Dogger Bank. Many of the Mesolithic coastal sites are now submerged in southern Britain or raised on 'raised beaches' in the north. This means that, although upland sites may be detectable everywhere, in the south only part of the early settlement pattern can be retrieved.

Thus it can be seen that the records of Upper Palaeolithic and Mesolithic flints, few and sparse as they may be to the local researcher, may, together with palaeo-environmental information and some idea of such early hunting, fishing and gathering life-styles, lead to a real appreciation of how the landscape was used by people in these early periods in the area under study. It is at least likely that this movement of people across the landscape, between favoured settlement sites and camps beside rivers, on the coast and in sheltered upland spots, may have determined many of the territorial and communication patterns more easily observed later on.

2 *Submerged forest off Minehead in Somerset. Well down the beach at low tide can be seen the bases of tree boles and the peat of the former forest floor. These provide dramatic evidence of sea level changes since Mesolithic times.*

The potential for the first management of the 'wildwood' may have been under-appreciated by researchers in the past, so that by the time the first people with a knowledge of agriculture arrived from Europe in the period before 4000 BC, the landscape may already have been greatly altered. As we have seen, there may have been extensive and managed clearances of grassland and scrub within the woods. It is also possible that seasonal meeting places had already been determined for the exchange of goods and people as well as social intercourse. Such places probably dominated recognised territories, over which certain groups exercised precedence in hunting and gathering, with leaders to reinforce the definition of such areas. Thus in some areas much of what we see in later landscapes may have been determined in outline before 4000 BC.

AGRICULTURAL LANDSCAPES

What is arguably the most significant event to affect the British landscape occurred some time before 4000 BC. The introduction of domesticated crops and animal husbandry from France and northern Europe marked the beginning of the Neolithic period (New Stone Age). This was to have a profound effect on the development of settlement, land use and the landscape. Improved polished stone implements, such as axes, meant that a greater impact could be made on the naturally forested wildwood landscape. The evidence from pollen analysis indicates phases of clearance, regeneration, and further clearance. In some cases, such clearance was followed by soil deterioration, but elsewhere the soil structure was not adversely affected and rich green grasslands with shrubs eventually prevailed. We can date the clearance of stable upland environments such as the chalklands of Wessex and Yorkshire and the Jurassic limestones of the Cotswolds and elsewhere to this period. In other places clearance was to begin a process of degradation which has never been reversed. In a real sense, the open moorlands of Cornwall, Devon, Somerset, Yorkshire and elsewhere are a product of man's mismanagement, particularly from the Bronze Age onwards; this will be discussed below.

The introduction of agriculture was accompanied by the first major 'engineering' works in the landscape. From 4000 BC, man radically altered the landscape by constructing large ceremonial, religious and burial monuments in clearings created in the wildwood. Numerous turf-built barrows and mortuary enclosures have been recognised on the chalk and limestone uplands, together with the enigmatic causewayed enclosures for which numerous uses have been suggested, ranging from settlement sites to vast necropolises. These tombs and enclosures belonged to and were used by specific groups of people who were also fully utilising the local countryside, partly for the new pursuits of crop-growing and animal husbandry, but also continuing the earlier hunting, fishing and gathering activities.

Few attempts have been made to set these earliest of monuments into any sort of context, but stimulating ideas of their contemporary landscapes have been proposed both by Colin Renfrew, who has argued that the tombs belonged to groups and therefore represent 'territories', very much as the medieval church related to parish communities, and Graeme Barker and Derrick Webley, who have argued for the inhabitants of causewayed enclosures exploiting a variety of different landscapes, much as Bronze Age and later Iron Age communities did. They discuss the contemporary environment from pollen and snail evidence, the technology for land clearance and working available to Neolithic people, and the implications of these aspects for local land use around such causewayed enclosures as Crickley Hill in Gloucestershire, Hambledon Hill and Maiden Castle in Dorset, and Whitesheet Hill in Wiltshire.

Despite some reservations, the model they propose suggests a rational use of the land in the period to 3000 BC and beyond, and, as in the Mesolithic discussion above, it implies changes in the development of the landscapes around these sites and at some distance from them, which may be important to the landscape student if there is a causewayed enclosure in the vicinity of his study. Since aerial photography of cropmarks has now shown that such sites are widespread, particularly beneath a number of later hillforts and in numerous river valleys, most parts of southern Britain may well have been within the territory of, and exploited by, one or other of these sites in Neolithic times.

The pollen record for the Neolithic period into the Bronze Age, approximately 4000 to 1500 BC, shows an even greater degree of woodland clearance with more extensive areas of grassland and some places tumbling down to scrub and waste. How was this achieved and what were the implications for the way men were using the landscape? What patterns were established of significance for the landscapes of later periods?

An extensive programme of geological thin-sectioning of stone implements in various universities over the last 30 years has shown quite clearly that between 3000 and 1500 BC there were a number of heavily exploited sources of stone and flint which were used to make axes and other implements. Great Langdale in the Lake District, the source of a hard fine-grained rock, perhaps produced most, but other important sources were western Cornwall, South Wales, Craig Llwydd in North Wales, and the Midlands. In the south-east, rich bands of flint nodules were extensively mined at sites in Wiltshire, Sussex and Norfolk – Grimes Graves being the most famous and accessible site today. The production of axes from these sites was on a prodigious scale, although we know nothing of how they were traded and distributed all over England and Wales. In a couple of cases, however, it seems that there were secondary centres for distribution: Humberside for Langdale axes and Essex for Cornish axes.

The implications of these patterns, elucidated principally by Bill Cummins and others, are only just beginning to be appreciated. In landscape terms, the effects were drastic and long-standing. Large areas were cleared and maintained in an open state. Even in modern experimental exercises, the inexperienced use of such axes in tree-felling shows just how effective they could have been. It is difficult to calculate comparative figures for how earlier people worked, but, in a recent experiment in Denmark, three men cleared 500 square metres (600 square yards) of birch forest in four hours and more than 100 trees were felled. The impact of clearance by men using stone axes can be appreciated from this, although we must consider that the use of fire may have been even more important.

SOIL CHANGES

Rather more important in the long term were the changes which could be initiated by such widespread forest clearance. In forested landscapes in temperate climate rain is intercepted by the tree cover and only reaches the ground slowly by percolation through the vegetation. It moves slowly through the soil and any minerals and salts essential to the soil structure, like calcium, which are leached out, are recycled via the root system back to the vegetation. Water is also delivered slowly and constantly to local streams, which consequently carry little sediment, since the soil is bound by tree roots. In such conditions, a brown forest soil seems to have developed widely from late glacial times through to the Bronze Age.

Several important changes begin after extensive clearance, and the effects can be exacerbated by man's use of the land for intensive agriculture. More open exposure of the cleared soil results in greater effects from heavy rain: much rain will run off open surfaces downslope, carrying soil with it, especially where the root structure cannot prevent this. This material is washed down into streams, which will consequently carry heavier loads of silt, vary more in their regime between swollen and normal, and deposit masses of alluvium elsewhere in their valleys as this material settles out. More water percolating through the soil is likely to leach out minerals which may not be easily replaced; calcium may be removed and, where the bedrock cannot replace the material essential to the soil 'crumb-structure', permanent damage and degradation may result. Heavy rainfall and the leaching out of iron salts may result in the formation of iron pans and podsolised soils; these are poorly drained and may lead to the formation of upland bogs and blanket peat.

Research by soil scientists, pollen analysts, geographers and archaeologists now indicates quite clearly that many areas of Britain owe not only their appearance but also their very soils to man's activities in the past. In North Yorkshire many barrows were built on a fertile rich brown-earth soil, which only later developed into the poor heathland podsol soil which covers the moors today, and similar changes occurred on other uplands. In Dartmoor, extensive clearance and exploitation by Bronze Age people from 2500 to 1000 BC (*Fig. 66*) accelerated natural changes which resulted in extensive poor soils and blanket bogs; this eventually, possibly under the impetus of heavier rainfall, necessitated the abandonment of the moor until the late Saxon period. The heathlands to the west and south-west of London were drastically affected by clearance of their natural woodland, and their thin, sandy, sterile soils are the result of the earlier soil being destroyed.

If such areas were damaged beyond recall in the

3 *Changes following woodland clearance (after John Evans, Martin Bell, and others)*

several millennia from 4000 BC onwards, why were all the areas cleared in the Neolithic and Bronze Ages not so affected? Areas such as the chalklands and the Jurassic limestones seem to show little evidence of soil degradation, while the field monuments indicate that they were densely settled. One answer seems to be that the subsoil, with its rich lime base, maintained the soil structure, preventing deterioration and loss of fertility and retaining the interest and yields of early farmers. Once cleared, these areas remained important, and are still fertile and valuable today.

LANDSCAPE CHANGES

Changes have occurred throughout prehistory, and there are important aspects for the local researcher to consider. Recent work in the chalk valleys of Sussex and Wessex by Martin Bell has shown how much change there has been. Soil erosion, run off, and soil movement downhill on the chalk uplands, together with solution of the chalk subsoil beneath, has resulted in major changes in soil quality and depth over the last few thousand years. Much of this material has ended up as the bedload of streams or as infill deposited along the valley bottoms. The cumulative effect has been to remove much of the archaeological evidence for settlement from the slopes and uplands, leaving behind only the remnants of flint implements and pottery and the deepest post holes. In the adjacent valleys infilling occurred, with the consequent gradual burial of any sites which may have existed there.

Martin Bell located settlements of the Beaker period of the Bronze Age in these sediments, suggesting that perhaps many more lie buried in valleys elsewhere. This is a possibility which has not previously been contemplated. The contemporary barrow groups of such valley settlements might be expected to be sited on the hills, where they do indeed survive in large numbers. Don Spratt's work in North Yorkshire has led him to suggest such an arrangement. Bob Smith's research in Wiltshire, developing some of the implications of the above, has begun to locate and define some of the valley settlements. He can show that silting and sediments over such sites, together with later erosion and obscuring by medieval sites, have removed many of the traces of such prehistoric valley settlements. For the local researcher, the implication is that the surviving field monuments of the prehistoric period are only a part, perhaps a small part, of the contemporary Neolithic and Bronze Age landscape, and that local topographical changes of soils, relief, and sedimentation might have buried or removed other more important parts of such settlement evidence. It is becoming more and more likely that the main centres of population exploiting the countryside were in the valleys and that the evidence is largely obscured by

4 *Kiln Combe, near Eastbourne in Sussex. A dry chalkland valley under excavation showing layers of hillwash overlying a series of occupation sites. The original valley floor lies at the bottom of the section; successive settlements have been buried by soil washed off the hills nearby into the valley. There are no surface indications of these settlements but many valleys must contain sites hidden in the same way; they can only be found by such large-scale trench digging. (Photograph by Brenda Westley, by permission of Dr Martin Bell)*

later (or continuously used?) settlements on roughly the same sites (*Fig. 57*).

The use of models, such as we have seen above, helps to clarify the relationship between what we can see and what we can only surmise. Models provide the possibility of predicting where we might find settlements and indicate some ways in which the contemporary landscape might have been exploited. The major field monuments, which are better documented, almost certainly provided the foci in the landscape, around which such subsistence settlements would have been placed and to which they would have looked for some specialised goods and services. Again, the local researcher needs to be aware of the potential evidence and relationships which may have existed in his area of study, whether the sites are well represented or not at all.

5 *The Sweet Track north of Wallway Farm, Meare parish in Somerset. Excavations by the Somerset Levels Project through the overlying peat have revealed the Sweet Track, a prehistoric trackway dating to around 4000 BC. It consists of a raised plank walkway supported by an underlying rail and angled pegs. It has been traced for over 3 kilometres (2 miles) between Westhay village and the Polden Hills to the south. Such structures imply considerable exploitation of the landscape at this early date. (Photograph copyright Somerset Levels Project)*

THE INTENSITY OF SETTLEMENT AND LAND USE – THE SOMERSET LEVELS

What other evidence is there of man's use of the landscape in these early periods, and what can it tell us? Research in the Somerset Levels over the last few decades has produced a mass of evidence of prehistoric timber trackways built to cross the lowlying marshy land between the uplands of the Mendips and Poldens and islands in the Levels. The earliest of these, the Sweet Track, is an elaborate plank walkway running from near Shapwick to Westhay. A variety of types of wood was used in its construction, ranging from small diameter poles to large pieces of split trees. John Coles, Bryony Orme, and members of the Somerset Levels Project have estimated that this must have involved the exploitation of extensive woodland from which

materials were taken out to be fitted into the track – planks from the same tree occur in different parts of the track. Later trackways involved large quantities of coppiced poles and rails (as in the hurdles used in the Walton Heath track) and, in the Meare Heath trackway, a reused timber structure – possibly a house. The former, according to Dr Oliver Rackham, indicates that areas of woodland were being carefully managed as coppices with standards in the Neolithic and Bronze Ages to produce the poles for rails and hurdles and the timber for the heavier tracks. Such sophisticated landscape management has hardly been contemplated before at this early date (*Fig. 63*).

What, then, if anything, is so special about the Somerset Levels? Firstly, we only know of the existence of these structures because of the waterlogged nature of the peat in which they are found, since without such conditions they would have rotted away and disappeared. Secondly, we have little information on the sites at each end of the trackways, since only scatters of flints have been found on the higher, drier, islands and uplands. The situation is like having a piece of the M1 motorway but no information about the existence of London or Birmingham. Thirdly, the Levels were clearly of great use to people with a limited technological and economic capacity. In the winter, the flooded areas provided abundant fish and wildfowl which could be hunted, and in the summer, in the drier areas, there was rich open grassland for cattle and sheep, reeds, wood and timber for building and construction, and wild animals and birds, as well as abundant fruits and seeds which could be hunted and collected.

In fact, the archaeology of the Levels is probably not exceptional in England, except in the state of preservation of the normally ephemeral wooden evidence. This is not to suggest that there were trackways everywhere (although they probably remain to be found elsewhere in Somerset, and records exist of others from the bogs of Lancashire), but that the exploitation of the landscape implied by them existed very widely. The elaborate construction of some of the trackways, the careful management of the landscape and organisation of both human and natural resources to produce them, certainly implies well-organised communities. Perhaps there was a much larger population in the area than has previously been supposed, with more intensive or extensive use of the landscape by 2000 BC than is generally assumed. It is unlikely that so much work would have gone into the construction of trackways for just casual hunting visits into the marshes. John Coles has suggested a model for this area demonstrating the variety of land uses available to prehistoric communities in the Levels region and, as we will see later, this implies a situation much in evidence and more easily proven in the Middle Ages.

By around 1500 BC we can construct a general picture of how the landscape may have been used, based on the work of pollen and environmental analysts, soil scientists, archaeologists, and 'prehistoric geographers'. Despite the survival of thousands of field monuments of this early prehistoric period, most of them represent burial, religious and ritual structures; there is little evidence for fields or settlements. As we have seen, some of this may be the result of not appreciating all the functions of the known sites until recently, but it seems mainly to be the result of landscape changes. Nevertheless, there is a consistency in the models suggested by John Coles, Don Spratt, Graeme Barker, Derrick Webley, and others. Each suggests the location of the settlements in favourable lowland situations with access to a variety of different types of land in different environments, with areas of upland, pasture or woodland at some distance, and the main areas of arable and pasture near to the settlements (*Fig. 59*). On wetter areas there was seasonal pasture, marsh for fish and wildfowl, and still plenty of provision for hunting and gathering of natural resources. In each case, the surviving field monuments are seen as only part of the original picture, with 'obvious' sites such as barrows probably occurring on the boundaries of territories attached to particular communities.

In any piece of country under study there will almost certainly be insufficient evidence to reconstruct the settlement and land use patterns of early prehistory, such as are described above. At the very least, these models suggest what might have existed and how the few sites that have been detected may be interpreted. More importantly, such ideas help to predict where other evidence should be sought.

For the later prehistoric period, rather more evidence is now available from Dartmoor and the major river valleys of what early landscapes looked like in the 2000 years or so before the Roman Conquest, and how such early arrangements conditioned the later, more easily recognised, post-Roman country-side.

DARTMOOR

Dartmoor is one of the few examples in Britain of an almost complete Bronze Age landscape. Various types of settlements have been distinguished, from isolated farmsteads in their own fields on the east side of the moor, through enclosed 'hamlets' with paddocks and 'gardens' (*Fig. 66*), to a few unenclosed and extensive settlements which look like villages. In addition to this settlement evidence, there is the suggestion of both pastoral areas – where few field boundaries have been recognised – and enclosed, presumably arable, areas where patterns of rectilinear fields can still be seen. In many parts of the moor contemporary burial and religious sites remain in the form of barrows, cists, stone circles and stone rows. As one walks over Dartmoor, a clear view of settlement and land use in the Bronze Age is possible.

In such a well studied and carefully recorded area, is there anything new that can be said about this Bronze Age landscape? We have already seen that the appearance of Dartmoor is man-made; following woodland clearance the soil degraded, and eventually blanket bog, and possibly a cooler and wetter climate, led people to abandon permanent settlements there and use the moor solely as temporary seasonal pasture (and later for mining).

What has not been appreciated until recently, however, is that it is possible to see many of the land boundaries of the territorial divisions and 'estates' of this period on Dartmoor. These are called *reaves* and, while they have been known for a long time, their age, extent and probable purpose have only recently been recognised. Research by Andrew Fleming, Geoffrey Wainwright and others has shown that there are several types of reaves. Some are built with stone, others with turf and peat, and some may originally have had timber fences on the top (and beneath). Some run across the moor, apparently randomly, but in fact outlining large areas which seem to relate to the major river valleys. Thus, they might have been defining 'territories' encompassing high moor, upland, valley land, and good land lower down, off the present moor itself.

Elsewhere it looks as if whole sections of the moor were divided up, in a very deliberate, possibly planned, way, with parallel boundaries running for miles across high tors and deeply cut valleys. This can be seen in the Dartmeet area especially. It is as if surveyors had worked out what they were going to do and then laid out the plan on the landscape, ignoring the difficult topography of the area.

In a number of cases, these parallel systems finish at terminal reaves (which also look deliberately laid out) at right angles to the rest. The areas beyond these terminal reaves contain burial and religious monuments which in some cases must be earlier; so perhaps some respect of older features is implied, an aspect which can be seen elsewhere where barrows and barrow cemeteries seem to have been avoided rather than ignored when the later fields were laid out.

Such large-scale, apparently planned and organised, land division has not been suggested before, but other examples are now being identified. Much of Wessex, for example, is covered with late prehistoric field systems, of perhaps late Bronze Age date, which are very regular in form, some clearly not related to their local topography. Also, air survey by Derek Riley over south Yorkshire and north Nottinghamshire has

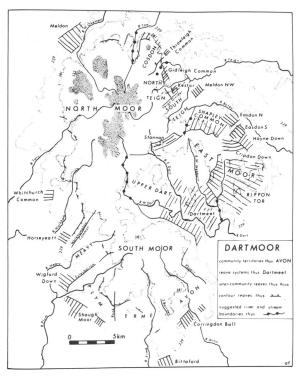

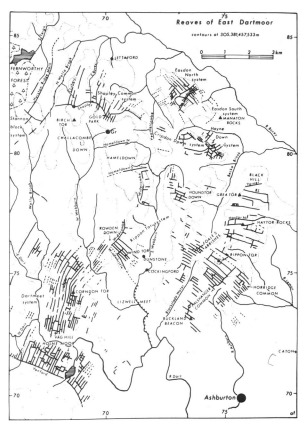

6 *Maps of Dartmoor showing reave systems. The left-hand map shows the main systems of land divisions from the second millennium BC around the moor, while the right-hand one shows in detail the systems on the east side of the moor near Dartmeet. These reaves survive in marginal land today but they can also be traced running off down into contemporary fields still used; how much of the rest of the landscape overlies such early land divisions? (By permission of Andrew Fleming and the Prehistoric Society)*

identified regular brickwork-like patterns of early fields over many square miles of country. Other examples exist in Essex, Sussex, and in some of the big river valleys.

Although most prehistoric settlements and field systems were less regular than these examples, they clearly predominate in some areas and were the normal way of subdividing the landscape. Do such areas represent prehistoric colonisation? Was the landscape planned and then the divisions built? And how much more can be recognised elsewhere of such systems? One thing seems clear, that such patterns did not exist only in the present largely abandoned marginal uplands, but also over great areas of the country. In some cases relatively modern fields can be seen to reflect these early arrangements and it seems, in areas of old (or continuously) enclosed land, that much of the basic framework of the landscape may be prehistoric. We must therefore allow for this even if we cannot always see it.

CROPMARKS AND RIVER VALLEYS

There are other aspects of early settlement not easily appreciated and these relate particularly to the major river valleys of the Thames, Severn, Warwickshire Avon and Trent which are the sources of extensive supplies of gravel. Here, aerial photography taken under drought conditions during the summer months is revealing hundreds of square miles of ploughed out prehistoric (and later) landscapes which survive below soil level, but which are only evident as marks in the growing crops. It is now wrong to think of such areas as having many individual sites, because, as with the uplands, what we are seeing and recording are complete landscapes.

Such cropmarks occur because soil moisture deficiency in gravel subsoils shows up the earlier features. Where the gravel ends and some other geological material begins which is not conducive to cropmark formation, the cropmarks do not appear. This does not mean that those areas were not occupied, however, and, although settlements were less densely packed away from the well-drained, easily-worked gravel, they certainly existed, as is shown by fieldwork and excavations in advance of road schemes. Again, the implication is clear – we have to think of buried sites in their landscapes, which will only be detected via redevelopment projects and cropmarks on air photographs. Some finds of flints and pottery may indicate

7 *Cropmarks at Foxley Farm, Eynsham in Oxfordshire. These cropmarks show at least three earlier landscapes before the enclosure landscape of 1802–7 produced the present pattern of roads and field boundaries. The circles are ditches of ploughed-out Bronze Age barrows. Around and between these are the ditches of late prehistoric farmsteads, roads and field boundaries. Overlying these are traces of ridge and furrow, the arable field systems of the Middle Ages which probably destroyed the prehistoric landscape. Some of the darker patches represent deeper topsoil and geological features. (Major Allen photograph No. 520 taken 10th June, 1933; copyright Ashmolean Museum)*

such sites, but more frequently the patterns of later hedges, boundaries and roads must reflect these earlier arrangements, even if we cannot be certain.

BEFORE THE ROMAN CONQUEST

The general impression of the prehistoric landscape (or landscapes, as there was much variety) in the centuries before the Roman Conquest is clear. We have to envisage a well-used and well-developed landscape with widespread settlement of farmsteads and hamlets, with well-defined fields and a range of land uses, including managed woodland and organised pasture. Settlement was denser in some areas than in others, although such a division may only be recognised, as suggested by Peter Fowler, from late Bronze Age times onwards. To gain the best impression of such a landscape, a visit to the Butser Ancient Farm Research

Project near Petersfield in Hampshire is advised. Here, all the archaeological evidence and vague cropmarks from air pictures have been transferred into a three-dimensional working model with buildings, structures, fields, crops and roads. It was into such a landscape that a foreign alien culture stepped in AD 43 when Claudius decided to send the Roman army into Britain.

ROMAN LANDSCAPES

It is still difficult to assess accurately what effect the Roman Conquest and the subsequent period of Roman occupation had on the development of the landscape. Clearly, large numbers of new features were introduced, new types of settlement were constructed and new activities were carried out, but 400 years is a relatively short period in the life of the English

8 *The experimental Iron Age farm at Butser in Hampshire. The reconstruction of the Iron Age round house at Butser and the replica farmstead attached to it gives a good impression of what a late prehistoric farm and its fields might have looked like. The research conducted there indicates great sophistication in farming and management of the landscape around 300 BC. Such a farmsteaa needed at least 48 hectares (120 acres), made up of 8–12 hectares (20–30 acres) grazing, 4–6 hectares (10–15 acres) for hay, 8 hectares (20 acres) of woodland, and the rest for arable, trackways and waste.*

landscape and to describe the Roman era as an interlude may, therefore, be correct in landscape terms.

For the first time, Britain saw properly constructed roads built with military precision – Watling Street, Foss Way, Icknield Street and Ermin Way. Recent studies, however, have shown that many of them must be later than the landscapes and minor roads they cross; in any case, they represent the motorways of the Roman period, and most of the country's land communication network was probably still in the form of lanes and tracks, as it had been before and would be again (*Fig. 90*).

Military forts were an innovation, but following the move of the Roman army to the west and north, they ceased to have their former landscape importance. Their status probably relates more closely to the major development in the Roman period – that of increased urbanisation with a very commercially-based economy. Most of the Roman towns and cities created seem to have been developed from earlier forts; in origin their sites represent strategic and tactical decisions taken by Roman military commanders.

In the countryside, life must have continued for a long time as it always had done. The basic framework of rural settlement was augmented and many farm-

steads were rebuilt and romanised, their people using Romano-British pottery, Roman coinage and other objects, and utilising the new features of dressed masonry, mortar, man-made roofing materials, heating systems, and mosaics – rectilinear planned buildings became the norm.

Although much of the economy was still at subsistence level, especially in the west and north, the monetary system and the existence of markets in towns meant that some estates could develop a more commercial economy, perhaps specialising in cattle or arable production. Such a situation is implied for some of the villas studied by Sarah Wool in the Cotswolds and by Ann Ellison and John Harriss in rural settlements in Sussex and Wiltshire.

Such a well-developed economy led to the greater exploitation of geological resources, and the English landscape witnessed quarrying of stone and ores on a scale not seen before – in the Forest of Dean (coal and iron), Derbyshire and the Mendips (lead), Cornwall (tin) and Dolaucothi in Wales (gold) – although most areas were worked and reworked later on and it is usually impossible to isolate the Roman element.

The high level of technical ability of Roman engineers, together with the well-developed commercial economy, meant that major civil engineering schemes could also be undertaken for the first time in the landscape. Some of the mining operations show this, and the Fens have Roman canals, embankments, and elaborate water systems. The same can now be seen in the Somerset Levels, and the aqueducts supplying Roman towns at Dorchester, Leicester and elsewhere. How many more Roman engineering schemes are there still to be recognised in the landscape?

In the late and post-Roman periods, this commercial economy was disrupted and abandoned, returning to its former subsistence level. The features which had distinguished the Roman interlude – the roads, towns, and villas – were abandoned or their functions were changed; industrial activities collapsed. Yet something very basic remained in the landscape which was of great importance in later periods. Increasingly in some areas it can be seen that settlement sites occupied in the Roman period continued through post-Roman times to form the basic framework of medieval and modern villages and hamlets. Of even greater importance is the fact that it seems that many of the Roman estates, the holdings belonging to villas and towns, continued into the post-Roman period and beyond to emerge as the basic administrative units of late Saxon and medieval England. This will be further discussed, but it is perhaps ironic that all the distinguishing, concrete features in the landscape from this period should disappear, but that the invisible ownership element should persist.

3

Estates and boundaries

In this book we will be discussing mainly features which are easily seen in the landscape, from deserted villages to fields and churches. Yet much of the historic landscape, and one very important element in particular, is not visible, though its influence is enormous. This is ownership. Who owns which bit of land and what they decide to do with it has always been of critical importance, and our landscape is the result of countless human decisions taken by individuals in the past. So land ownership and management are very relevant to our theme of landscape study and historical reconstruction: the estates belonging to particular individuals or corporate bodies, and the boundaries within which they lie are important factors to be elucidated for any area. Such considerations will apply at all periods, in prehistory as in documented history. It will probably be useful, therefore, to use the terminology of Fig. 93 and think of estates and territories, rather than the more familiar but restricted terms such as baronies, parishes, manors, tithings, hundreds, etc., although there is a clear relationship between them all.

It is important to define the estates and territories in the landscape under study, at different times, and to show how they have changed through time. We will need, therefore, to define estate arrangements and the units of land within them. In particular, and most importantly, we shall need to think about the origin of these blocks of land as cohesive units, and the date of definition of the boundaries. In most cases we will be asking when a particular parish or set of parish boundaries was first defined, and if that was the date of its origin or if it is older. Fortunately, there is a lot of research being conducted into this topic now and new ideas and information are constantly emerging.

ESTATES

The basic modern administrative units broadly correspond to the parishes, manors, tithings and townships of the medieval and later landscape. These occupy relatively small areas of land and are frequently associated with a village, several hamlets, or a scatter of farm-steads. They are usually clearly related to the parish church (*Fig. 17*).

Recent research, however, has drawn our attention increasingly to the larger units in the landscape. These are often difficult to define from earlier periods, but their importance as the basic building blocks of the administrative landscape can hardly be over-estimated. The first recent study showing the possibilities and implications of such 'estates' was that of Withington in Gloucestershire by Professor Finberg. In a masterful, seminal study he suggested that the parish of Withington, which occupies a large area in the Cotswolds, was in essence a Roman estate centred on a villa and several contemporary settlements. The land attached to the villa emerges as a seventh-century estate joined to a minster belonging to the See of Worcester, and its later history, with minor changes to the estate and its boundary, can be documented through the Middle Ages to the present modern civil parish.

This was considered revolutionary at the time it was written (1955), but case study after case study elsewhere in the country now suggest the same basic pattern of large estates. Peter Sawyer has suggested that some of the earliest surviving charters of the Anglo-Saxon period refer to such estates and hence for some areas in the seventh century the early estate structure can be defined. The counties with the most charters are Kent, Somerset and Worcestershire, and here large blocks of land were defined from the seventh century onwards, particularly when they were granted from kings to early monasteries.

Was the seventh century the date of origin of such estates, or were they in some way related to earlier land arrangements? Glanville Jones thinks that they may go back to pre-Roman times in many cases; June Sheppard has shown that the estate at Marden in Herefordshire, which has Roman settlements, a Saxon palace site, and a ninth-century minster on the site of the initial burial of St Ethelbert, was almost certainly the estate attached to Sutton Walls, the pre-Roman hillfort in the area which was reoccupied in post-Roman times (*Fig. 77*). At Brent in Somerset a piece of land was

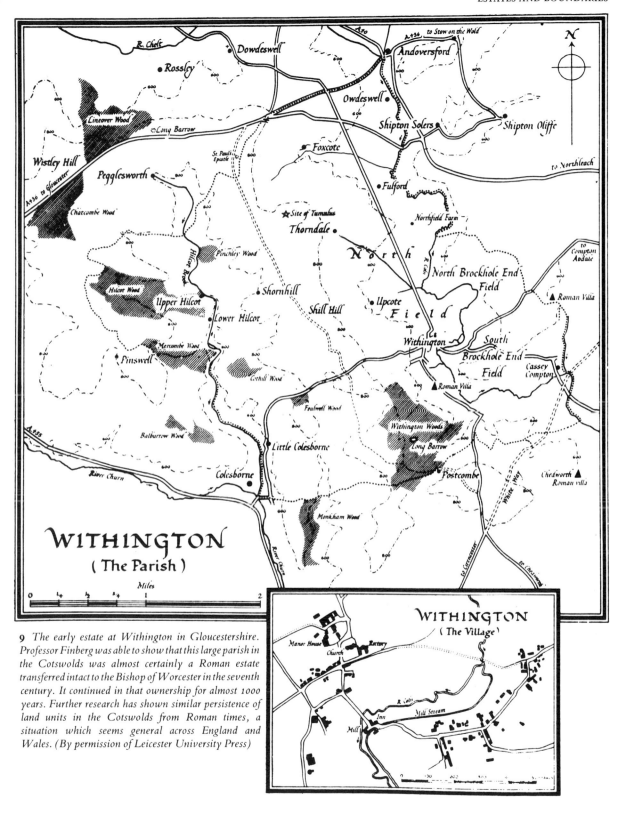

9 *The early estate at Withington in Gloucestershire. Professor Finberg was able to show that this large parish in the Cotswolds was almost certainly a Roman estate transferred intact to the Bishop of Worcester in the seventh century. It continued in that ownership for almost 1000 years. Further research has shown similar persistence of land units in the Cotswolds from Roman times, a situation which seems general across England and Wales. (By permission of Leicester University Press)*

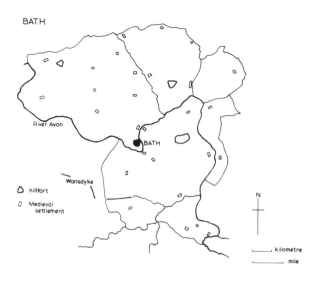

10 *Early estates at Bath and Brent in Somerset. Land at Bath was granted to a monastery by Osric in AD 676. The estate is probably reflected in the 100 hides of land of Bath hundred shown in the map.*

Brent was granted to Glastonbury Abbey in AD 663 or 693 by Ine, King of the West Saxons. The bounds are described as the Rivers Axe and Severn, the Termic stream and the River Siger. The unit of land persisted as a hundred into the Middle Ages. The Siger river can still be traced on the ground and from the air (see Fig. 54).

defined in the late seventh century when it was granted to Glastonbury Abbey. The bounds described include the former River Siger (*Fig. 54*) as well as the obvious topographical features of the Rivers Severn and Axe. This estate persisted into the Middle Ages as Brent Hundred, but there is an important Roman site at Lakehouse Farm and a magnificent hillfort on Brent Knoll. The theoretical territory attached to this hillfort, as suggested by Ian Burrow, is very similar to the land defined in the seventh-century charter, and it is thus possible that the estate of the hillfort persisted throughout the Roman period to emerge as a land unit belonging to Glastonbury Abbey until the sixteenth century. The long corporate ownership by the abbey enables us to see the early arrangement; the charter details survive and the 'focal place' of each period can be defined. This is true for the estates of other corporate bodies like abbeys and bishoprics, but we need to know how common this situation was.

Glanville Jones has conducted most research into the arrangement of early estates, and his work has enormous implications for any landscape studies if the basic administrative framework is to be understood. He draws attention to what he calls *multiple estates*, that is large areas of land made up of smaller units – the territories referred to later. Such estates were centred on a *caput* or head manor, and all other settlements on the estate were subsidiary to it. Their lower status is

shown in the customary services and goods they had to supply to the main caput – services including building and maintaining the lord's hall, bower, and possible defences, and goods rendered including lambs, wool, cattle and honey. Glanville Jones' ideas were based initially on studies of medieval Wales, where it was formerly assumed that a dispersed settlement pattern of pastoral farms had been the norm. However, his research, based on the *Book of Iorwerth* and other sources, suggests a very hierarchical society, with many bond hamlets engaged in arable farming as well as cattle raising, and dependent on a head 'court'.

Research on Yorkshire suggests the same sort of early arrangements, with the large estates there being called *shires* (the equivalent of the *maenor* in medieval Wales and what Glanville Jones terms the *discrete estate* or *federal manor* in England). Examples discussed by Glanville Jones are widespread: Wakefield and Aldborough in Yorkshire; Hitchin in Hertfordshire; Selsey and Findon in Sussex; Amesbury, Brokenborough, Cannings and Britford in Wiltshire; Cartmel in Cumberland; and Heighington in Durham.

What, then, are the characteristics of these early estates and what features must we look for if we are to define the landscape arrangements in the pre-Conquest period? Firstly, the whole estate was based on a *head place* or caput. What this would have looked like is sometimes difficult to imagine – it may have been no more than a larger-than-average farmstead, or it may have been a palace such as those found at Yeavering and Cheddar. Usually accompanied by a village or hamlet, such a caput may be called a *villa regalis*, but the terms *aula*, *mansio* and *maerdref* are also used. It is essentially the lord's hall. The name of this caput is usually the same as the whole estate and it is often recorded very early on. Characteristically, the name is topographical in form – referring to a river, hill, or

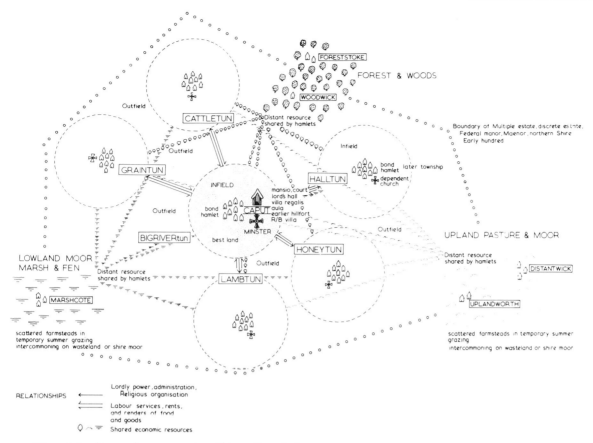

11 *The relationships and arrangements within a theoretical multiple estate (based largely on the research of Glanville Jones).*

major natural feature – although 'tun' may sometimes be added. Examples in Somerset include Chew and Chewton, both named after the River Chew; Frome, after the river of the same name; Taunton, after the River Tone; and North and South Petherton, after the River Parrett. In Wiltshire the old county capital, Wilton, is similar in form, named after the River Wylye.

Some caputs can be seen to be the logical successors to Roman and pre-Roman sites, the latter remaining as hillforts which may have been reoccupied in post-Roman times. Most caputs were in the lowlands, in river valleys surrounded by good quality fertile land, rather than in inhospitable uplands, and many were important manors by the time of *Domesday Book* (1086), usually in royal ownership or that of some other great body, such as a bishop or an ancient abbey. They were sometimes the heads of administrative units known as hundreds – hundredal manors with some of the characteristics of a town, and they may have had the minster church, upon which the churches elsewhere on the estate were dependent. These focal places will be discussed in the next chapter.

Around these caputs there would have been dependent settlements with bondmen to work the lord's land (called the Mayor settlements in Wales). Caputs were usually on the best land, initially with an infield/outfield system. The rest of the estate was made up of other bond settlements, each with its own infield/outfield system and dependent on the caput. This dependence is demonstrated in the subsidiary status of their churches, which were daughter churches to the minster. A much more important demonstration of this lower status, however, is the rents and services paid by dependent settlements to the caput. Customary dues recorded in the early Middle Ages sometimes give a clue to this.

Such discrete estates occupied large areas of land and included many settlements. Any particular settlement under study may have been a very minor place on such a large estate with the caput of the estate some distance away. Nevertheless, the English landscape is about status and hierarchies, and it is important to get some idea of which places were of greater or lesser importance locally

Many of these discrete estates made use of extensive

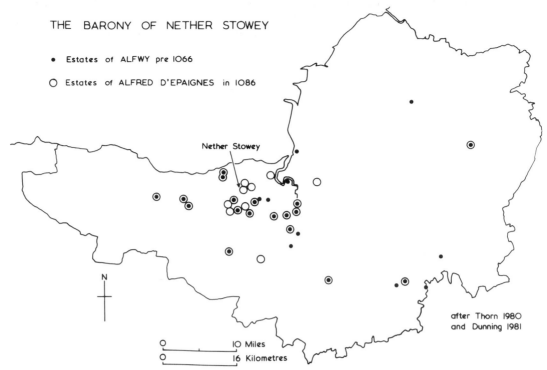

THE BARONY OF NETHER STOWEY

● Estates of ALFWY pre 1066

○ Estates of ALFRED D'EPAIGNES in 1086

Nether Stowey

N

after Thorn 1980
and Dunning 1981

0   10 Miles
0   16 Kilometres

12 *A caput and Saxo-Norman estate based on Nether Stowey in Somerset. The map shows the estates of Alfwy in the period before the Norman Conquest and those of Alfred d'Epaignes afterwards. There is a close correlation between the two. The estate was later* *called the Barony of Stowey and based on Nether Stowey castle (right), a massive Norman ringwork with the base of a keep and several baileys. Beneath this Norman castle may be the remains of an earlier fortified residence. (Photograph by Alan Wilson)*

areas of distant or upland resources of pasture or woodland. Glanville Jones cites a number of examples where scattered farmsteads existed in extensive temporary grazing in mountains and marshland, and where forest areas were shared between numerous vills. This intercommoning by a number of vills seems to be another indicative factor of early estates and has been used by Della Hooke and William Ford in their study of such estates in the Midlands. A good example in Somerset is Withiel Florey, granted to the Taunton estate in the tenth century as 'pasture' on Brendon Hill.

Thus we have to allow for a series of large units in the landscape from the seventh century onwards. These estates were centred on some of the most significant places in the landscape, with all other settlements dependent on them, and may be reflected later on in the lands of old established monasteries and bishoprics, or in some hundredal arrangements. Elsewhere, later changes will have obscured much of this early pattern, making it difficult to reconstruct the early framework.

Late Saxon developments in estates

By the tenth century we can see from the detailed boundary clauses contained in charters that the earlier estate arrangements are already becoming obscure.

The refounding of monasteries and the continual granting away of land by the crown resulted in fragmentation of the earlier large units and recombination of land under new ownership. An example of this has been discussed by Robert Dunning in Somerset. Within the ancient royal estates (and later hundreds) of Cannington and North Petherton, a large holding had been assembled by 1066 belonging to the Saxon Alfwy. It cut across the boundary between the two hundreds and was later centred on the Norman castle at Nether Stowey. Much of the holding was transferred to Alfred D'Epaignes after the Norman Conquest as a barony.

In general, estate development has not been studied for the pre-Conquest period – there are not enough documents and the field evidence is enigmatic. However, it would be useful if attempts could be made, as shown here, to relate later hundredal arrangements to early estates and then see if the disintegration of these can be shown before the Norman Conquest. Estates in the Church's ownership from an early date can be expected to have greater continuity, but there were still considerable changes before 1066. Lay estates, by contrast, are likely to show perhaps greater diversity, but there may be less information from which to reconstruct the pre-Conquest arrangements.

Early medieval estates – baronies

Following the Norman Conquest in 1066 there was one of the greatest reorganisations of estates this country has ever seen. Large numbers of Saxon landowners were replaced by new Norman lords, and their holdings were often, although as the above example shows not entirely, redistributed without reference to their previous arrangements. For the eleventh and twelfth centuries new estates developed centred on new caputs – the castles and monasteries of Norman England, with their lands spread across the landscape in manors and vills. With the exception of the estates of the anciently-established monasteries, these new baronies do not reflect the earlier estate arrangements. Yet, alongside the new ownership pattern, the arrangement of hundreds still persisted and, although there were changes in the early medieval period, the older pattern of estates is still often reflected in hundredal arrangements.

There have been a number of studies of the development of estates attached to monasteries which persisted through to the sixteenth century. However, baronies associated with castles or the greater landed lay families have not been studied other than from a legalistic or genealogical point of view. An exception is the estate of the Mortain family in the later eleventh century,

centred on Castle Neroche and their fortress at Montacute in Somerset, which was studied by Brian Davison.

With their abundant documentation, monastic estates are rather easier to study. James Bond, for example, has looked at the estates of both Abingdon and Evesham Abbeys, and clearly shown the variety of topographical features which can still be distinguished on their scattered estates. Such research can usually identify particular features such as barns, dovecotes or manor houses and show the distribution of estates in outline; but it will only be with very full documentation, or dogged persistence, that smaller pieces of land belonging to such estates can be distinguished. For Oxford and some other medieval towns where the documentation is particularly good this can be achieved, but it is usually very difficult in the countryside.

Post-medieval estates

Following the dissolution of the monasteries in the period 1530–1540, another wholesale redistribution of land took place and much of the post-medieval landscape, although by no means all, can be related to the estates created at that time. Some of today's well-known large estates were created then, like Longleat, from the land of an Augustinian Priory, and Lord

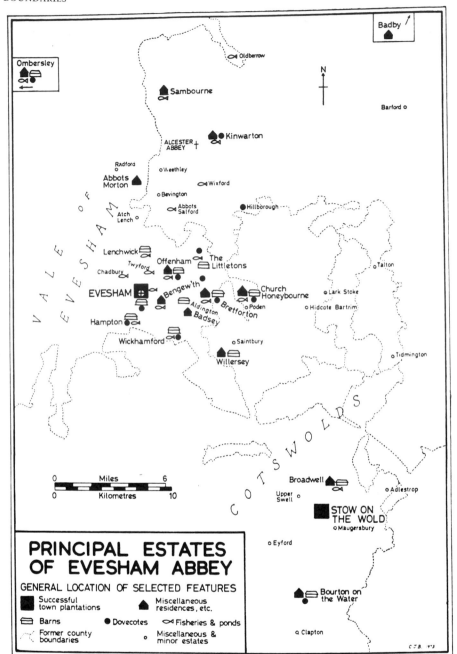

Badby

Ombersley

Oldberrow

Sambourne

Barford o

Kinwarton

ALCESTER
ABBEY

Radford
o
o Weethley

Abbots
Morton
Wixford

o Bevington
Abbots
Salford
Hillborough

Atch
Lench o

VALE

OF

EVESHAM

Lenchwick
The
Littletons

Talton o

Offenham

Twyford

Chadbury

EVESHAM

Bengew'th

Church
Honeybourne

Lark Stoke o

Bretforton

o Poden

Hidcote Bartrim o

Aldington
Badsey

Hampton

Wickhamford

o Saintbury

Willersey

o Tidmington

C

O

T

S

W

O

L

D

S

Miles   6

Kilometres   10

Broadwell

Upper
Swell

o Adlestrop

**STOW ON
THE WOLD**

o Maugersbury

o Eyford

Bourton on
the Water

o Clapton

PRINCIPAL ESTATES
OF EVESHAM ABBEY
GENERAL LOCATION OF SELECTED FEATURES

	Successful town plantations		Miscellaneous residences, etc.
	Barns	●	Dovecotes	Fisheries & ponds
	Former county boundaries	o	Miscellaneous & minor estates

C.J.B. '83

13 *The estates of Evesham Abbey in Worcestershire. The map shows the extent of the estates of the important ancient Benedictine Abbey at Evesham scattered over surrounding counties, and the principal features detectable on such estates. (Reproduced by permission of James Bond)*

Montague's property at Beaulieu, on the lands of a Cistercian monastery. In general, the abundant documentation for both these former monastic estates and the lands of the powerful late medieval families like the Hungerfords of Berkshire and Wiltshire means that the layout and arrangements of their estates can be re-constructed with relative ease and confidence. Maps in great quantity and superb detail become available from the sixteenth century onwards, and detailed estate records of the seventeenth, eighteenth and nineteenth centuries aid discussion of changing estate structure and policies which is impossible in earlier times. A good example of what can be achieved is Susanna Wade-Martin's research on the Holkham estate in Norfolk.

This section has attempted to show that more research is needed into the make-up of multiple estates in the earliest periods for which documents exist. The arrangement of these dictates so much of what we see in the landscape today. By comparison, the elucidation of ownership of estates in the late Saxon period (by 1066), the Norman period (1086 onwards), and the Middle Ages is relatively easy, especially for ecclesiastical estates. The abundant records and maps of post-medieval and modern times mean that much of the estate structure for these periods can be seen in great detail. By then, however, the main outlines have been in existence for a very long time, and it is these earlier arrangements about which we really need to know more and where future research should be concentrated.

BOUNDARIES

Dating the boundary

Within large estates, most of the administration of land, certainly in later periods, was conducted through parishes. A lot of parish boundaries were first defined in charters of the late Saxon period. Frequently, the boundaries of the areas of land are described and these refer to topographical features which can sometimes still be found in the landscape. These bounds often show that a particular parish, township, or tithing was the same in the tenth century as in the nineteenth, and we become aware of the remarkable persistence of boundaries

In the past, we have tended to assume that these first descriptions of blocks of land and their bounds were very close in date to the original definition of such estates or territories. As with place names, however, this may not be true. A discrete block of land may have been in existence for a long time before it was first described in a written document. Is there any way, then, that we can get any idea as to how old some of our boundaries might be? Clearly, where a boundary exists on the ground as a physical feature (a bank, ditch, or hedge) it can be examined archaeologically and some dating evidence may become available. It is more useful if the boundary feature can be related to a more closely datable field monument, so that the relative dates can be shown. So far, this has rarely been done. Similarly, considerations of a settlement's territory and associated land uses, which will be discussed later, may give circumstantial clues to the age of a block of land and indicate the possibility that current boundaries could be of Roman, late prehistoric, or even earlier origin.

The most interesting research so far, however, and that which points the way to the possibilities in other areas, is the work in Wessex by Desmond Bonney. He noted the incidence of barrows reused as Saxon cemeteries and other Saxon burials on or near parish boundaries in Wessex. The figure of over 40 per cent seems too high to be merely chance and he suggested

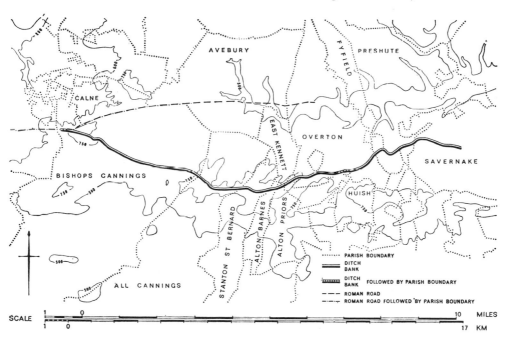

14 *The Wansdyke in Wiltshire. The Wansdyke probably dates from the seventh century AD and was a boundary between the Saxon kingdoms of Wessex to the south and Mercia. It cuts across parish boundaries leaving small areas of some parishes, such as Alton Priors and Barnes, isolated behind the dyke. It is unlikely* *that such boundaries were not defined by the time Wansdyke was built or it would probably have been used as a boundary feature: the boundaries may even be of prehistoric date. (By permission of Desmond Bonney – from Peter Fowler (ed)* Archaeology in the Landscape *Adam and Charles Black, 1972)*

that burials were being placed on boundaries, and that hence, because the dates of the burials were known from the types of grave goods, the boundaries must be of sixth- or seventh-century date at the latest. This would mean, in Wessex, that a large number of later parishes were already defined in the post-Roman period and that the well-known pattern of strip parishes was also there by that date (*Fig. 15*).

Further interesting relationships were noted when the Wansdyke, which runs across Wiltshire, was studied in relation to parish boundaries near Avebury and Bishops Cannings. This impressive linear earthwork running east-west is reckoned to be a division between the lands of Mercia to the north and Wessex to the south, and probably dates from the sixth or seventh century. Interestingly, it cuts across several parishes, so that in some cases very small areas of parish land are isolated behind the massive earthworks of the dyke. Surely, Desmond Bonney argued, if the parish boundaries had been defined *after* the construction of the earthwork, they would have used it as the 'natural' boundary – much like motorways and railways have been used more recently to define new local authority boundaries. The implication is that the parish boundaries were already there in the early Saxon period when the dyke was built. We are already beyond documentary description of such features in the early Saxon period.

Is it possible, however, to point to even earlier examples of boundaries? Desmond Bonney followed his initial research by an examination of parish boundaries associated with Roman roads and late prehistoric linear earthworks. He argued that the distribution of Iron Age and Roman sites on the Grovely ridge near Salisbury suggested territories which were reflected in the later parish boundaries. Along the crest of the ridge, the parish boundaries run between these earlier sites following one of the numerous Grims ditches, a bank and ditch of probable late prehistoric date. This *might* mean that the parish boundary was defined by later prehistory at least, but it might also indicate that definition occurred later using a well-defined pre-existing feature. Some support, however, is given to the former possibility by the fact that an equally well-defined Roman road also runs along the ridge, providing another possible line for the boundary 'surveyors' to use. Why did they choose the ditch and not the road? Was it because the boundaries were already laid out when the Roman road was built? Elsewhere in Wiltshire, particularly between the Roman towns of Verlucio (Sandy Lane) and Bath, parish boundaries follow the Roman road, so they could be Roman (possibly with a new area being colonised and estates being created) or later.

There are, however, instances where parish boundaries seem clearly to pre-date Roman roads. In Somer-set, Roger Leech has drawn attention to the patterns of parish boundaries and roads south of Ilchester on the Foss Way. The fact that virtually all of them cross the Roman road, which was created in the first century AD, suggests that at least some of these features were there in the landscape before the road was built; here, as elsewhere, it looks as if the road was put in arbitrarily across the landscape with little heed to existing features, much as when new roads and motorways are built today. A similar sort of picture emerges in Gloucestershire and Wiltshire, where the Foss Way cuts across parish boundaries in the Malmesbury area. Katherine Barker, who has invented the term *hercology* for the study of boundaries, suggests that a very regular pattern of boundaries was in existence before the Roman road was constructed.

It seems likely from this evidence, and by implication from studies discussed later, that many parish and other boundaries had already been defined by the later prehistoric, Roman and early post-Roman periods. How true is this generally? It is likely that further research will reveal more examples, and so close attention needs to be paid to the earlier certain boundaries of any territories and estates in the area under study.

Land units

We are accustomed to think of boundaries from an administrative and legal point of view. Thus, there are parish boundaries defining land attached to a particular church; more recently, civil parishes, which in many cases only vaguely now relate to religious parishes, have been defined for administrative purposes. These have a long and complex history of development, but no definitive book has yet been written on them – it is one of the great needs for students of the developing landscape.

It is clear, however, that these religious and civil boundaries are a lot older than any association with churches or local authorities. They relate in fact much more closely to economic and agricultural units, albeit often within larger estates and holdings. In many cases, what we see defined within these boundaries are units of land with a variety of land uses for the support of one or more settlements. In many areas, there were even more boundaries in the landscape than are used today, or were even apparent in the nineteenth century on tithe and other estate records. Desmond Bonney has been able to show this for the Enford area of Wiltshire, where the territory of each small settlement can be tentatively defined, even though most of their boundaries never emerge as more than tithing arrangements, if that. A similar case can be seen in Shrewton, where the identification of each separate vill within the estate begs the question as to the likely boundaries of each separate unit. Long linear field banks or persistent field

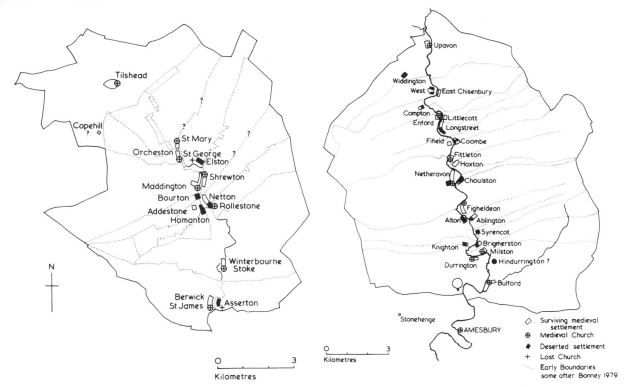

15 *Parish units in the Til and Avon river valleys in Wiltshire. Each of the medieval (and earlier?) settlements in this area has a long thin land unit attached. Such units are economic in origin,* *reflecting the allocation of different types of land – downland, meadow and arable – to each hamlet. Only later were some (but not all) adopted as parochial and manorial units.*

boundaries can often be suggested as something more than just divisions in the fields.

Because so many of our boundaries are economic rather than administrative, it is most important that the patterns of settlement at different periods are identified and the likely land uses within them postulated. Only then will it be possible to suggest that much of the invisible ownership landscape is there in the form of landscape features and is of greater antiquity than has been formerly thought.

There remains the problem of detached pieces of parishes (and, in some cases, of counties [*Fig. 13*]) or fragmented boundaries on the edges of some estates. Very often there seems to be no logical reason why small bits of one parish should be isolated, surrounded by the land of another. The explanation seems to be that of late ownership changes, but usually no plausible reason can be suggested. For larger areas and for more distant detached portions of parishes, a likely explanation is distant resources of either woodland or seasonal pasture shared with other villages. Much of the Somerset Levels and the Fens was shared out between the parishes around, and small blocks were allocated as detached portions at the time of enclosure or drainage (*Fig. 62*). Similar detached portions can be shown for land in the Arden Forest in Warwickshire belonging to parishes in the south of the county. The same can be

seen with the ownership of land in Neroche Forest in Somerset. A few examples remain of pieces of land still in no *single* ownership, such as meadowland shared between Axminster and Kilmington parishes in Devon alongside the river Axe near Newenham Abbey, common land on Dartmoor shared between Brides-towe and Sourton parishes, and meadow alongside the River Avon in Wiltshire shared between the parishes of Broughton Gifford and Melksham Without. No doubt there are others.

The course of the boundary

It is worth paying considerable attention to the physical remains of a parish boundary, especially if an Anglo-Saxon charter with boundary clauses exists or the piece of land can be defined in its present outline at an early date. River and stream courses are favourite lines, used extensively as boundaries in the past. Changes of stream course can sometimes be inferred where a meandering parish boundary leaves the present stream it is following but rejoins it further along its course. Straightening of water courses, together with mill and fishpond construction, may be an explanation, and occasionally the old course can be seen as a dry riverbed in the fields with the boundary still following it. This is the case at Gotherington in Gloucestershire, where examination of the present

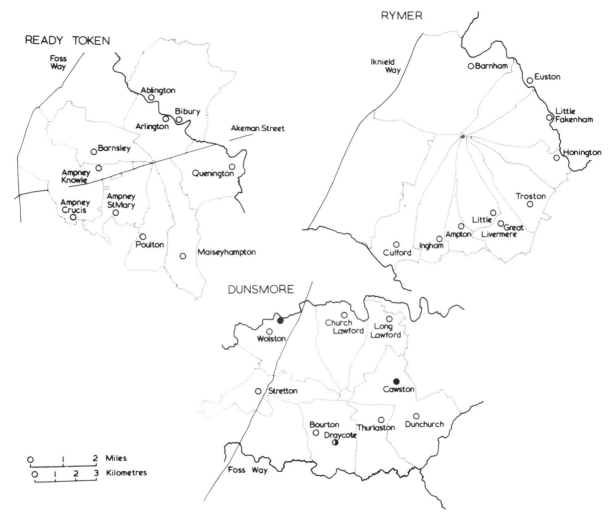

16 *Parish boundaries converging on Ready Token in Gloucester-shire, Rymer in Suffolk, and Dunsmore in Warwickshire. At each of these localities a resource is shared in common among several settlements. Access to the resource is reflected in the pattern of parish boundaries. Ready Token and Dunsmore were upland pastures, while Rymer was a mere or shared pond in the middle of common pasture and woodland in the Breckland. (After W. G. Hoskins and others)*

stream, in a straight gulley perched on the valleyside, led to the identification of an undocumented, previously unsuspected, water mill site.

The relationship between parish boundaries and water mill sites is an interesting one, since special arrangements are frequently made to incorporate a mill and its water courses within a particular land unit. A good example is the mill sites of Norton Malreward and Norton Hawkfield, south of Bristol, studied by Bob Williams, where a long tongue of land projects from Norton Malreward into the land of Norton Hawkfield to include the mill. Now that the mills have gone, only the parish boundary remains as evidence. In many cases, this association of boundaries with mills means either that the mills were in existence when the boundaries were defined (thus indicating an increased

number of Anglo-Saxon mill sites and a more extensive interference with river courses than we formerly thought), or that special arrangements were made to alter parish boundaries when new mills were built. Such changes should be documented, but few examples seem to be known.

Parish boundaries also tend to follow hilltop ridges, ridgeways, barrows and other earthworks. Sometimes, as in south-east Somerset, Dunsmore in Warwickshire, Ready Token in Gloucestershire, and Rymer, Breckland, in Norfolk, they come together at some common feature, such as an upland pond in a generally waterless area, an area of upland waste, or a piece of shared woodland.

We are accustomed from the literature to think of parish boundaries, particularly early ones, as being defined by huge banks and ditches. In this fieldworker's experience, boundaries between parishes are frequently very *un*impressive, often no different to general field boundaries in the vicinity, and were it not for the fact that the boundary line is *known*, the field evidence would in many cases not suggest it. Hedges with few shrub species, wire fences, or even no features at all, can all mark the edge of early documented parishes. However, considerable earthworks do sometimes exist and these are, of course, well worth recording.

In a number of instances, actual boundary stones remain, or have been recorded in the recent past. Sometimes, these are fine monuments with letters or numbers carved on them indicating the names of particular parishes or estates. On Dartmoor, they exist on the open moorland, demarcating not only parishes but also areas of grazing attached to particular villages. The early OS maps record them and they can often be retrieved from obscurity by fieldwork in examining the bottoms of hedges and the sides of ditches. Fred Aldsworth has drawn attention to the careful recording of such boundary features by the Ordnance Survey surveyors in the nineteenth century and the existence of their records as 'mere books'.

Where the boundary follows features like streams, ridgeways, Roman roads, or other clear features, there will be little problem in explaining the course of the boundary and the pattern of the parish's area. Nevertheless, there are usually many changes of direction and odd features which cry out for explanation. One pattern often referred to is the series of dog-legs many parish boundaries have, which shows that the boundaries follow existing or former blocks of strips in the open fields. Sometimes, earthworks of ridge and furrow or narrow early enclosed strips remain to give some clue to the course, but elsewhere the boundary itself must be the clue to the former existence of such an arrangement. If nothing else, such a pattern shows that the territory of a particular settlement was farmed to the limits when the boundary was defined, and again, if that boundary can be shown to be of a particular date, then something of early land use can be stated.

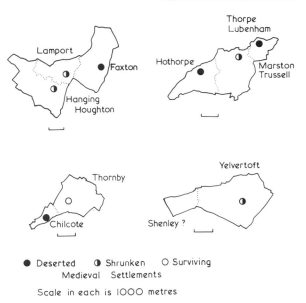

17 *Parishes with deserted settlements in Northamptonshire. In each case the present parish encompasses several medieval land units. Although numerous settlements are deserted or shrunken, their land is indicated by the obvious way pieces are 'tacked on' to main land units. (After Chris Taylor and Royal Commission on Historical Monuments (England))*

Long tongues of land reaching out to mills have already been mentioned, as have projections giving access to upland pasture or a pool, but other extensions may sometimes show the former existence of a settlement. This is particularly true where each parish was formerly a cohesive unit, but later amalgamations resulted in the 'stalk' of one on the side of another.

In general, then, we need to try to explain the earliest arrangement of the basic administrative land units in our study area and see if it can be identified as being of pre-Roman, Roman, or later date. The course of the boundary should be examined critically and questions asked as to why it follows the features it does, what sort of land is enclosed, and why the land unit is the shape it is. Detailed fieldwork around the boundary is rarely wasted.

4

Status in the landscape

As stated in the Introduction, this book is mainly concerned with ordinary settlements (be they villages or farmsteads) engaged in producing food from the land. However, it should be clear in looking at any landscape that some places are, or have been, more important than others. Today we see this in terms of which places have the shops, local school, or perhaps the parish church. By implication, we are suggesting that there is a hierarchy of places, or similarly that a particular place has a certain status in the local community. This chapter will therefore look at status in the landscape, since this hierarchy and the differences in status are so evident and mean so much in terms of why the landscape looks like it does.

At all times in the past, certainly as far back as the Neolithic period, there have been particular places to which surrounding settlements have looked for specialised goods and services. Though most rural settlements practised a predominantly subsistence economy, they needed certain goods and commodities from elsewhere which they could not provide themselves, and they were usually dependent on and subsidiary to somewhere else in terms of ownership, administration, and religious provision.

Geographers are familiar with the concept of the *central place* – a locally or regionally important centre fulfilling a number of functions for the settlements around. Such places always have a high status in the local settlement hierarchy and frequently occupy a central position geographically; they most obviously manifest themselves in the form of towns and cities. For long periods in the past, however, towns and cities did not exist, and yet many, if not most, of the functions which major urban centres fulfil today were still carried out in the landscape. We shall look at these functions in a moment, but it will be useful to think in terms of certain places in the landscape being the foci for single activities rather than a whole range of functions. Any one such focal place would thus have only one function, rather than the range of functions of the geographers' central place. Both focal and central places were important in the past and the concept is useful in explaining much in the landscape today.

FOCAL PLACES AND THEIR FUNCTIONS

Administrative

A number of distinctive functions can be recognised which certain places carried out instead of or in addition to the ubiquitous farming activities. Of these, control of the landscape is perhaps the most important, and hence at all times the administration or ordered management of the land was carried out from certain places, which may have been chiefs' residences, tribal capitals, kingly, lordly, or religious establishments. We can often recognise these sites in the landscape from which such administration may have been conducted. The control of resources by the landowner usually means that the sites are impressive, dominant, and have had a lot of labour and/or money invested in them. It is likely that the Neolithic causewayed enclosures and henges, late Bronze Age enclosures, and Iron Age hillforts of prehistory fulfilled this role to some extent. In Roman times the cities and major towns certainly did, and on a local scale many villas must have done so as well. In post-Roman times, reoccupied hillforts and hilltops were probably the focal administrative points for their regions, and by late Saxon times royal palaces such as Cheddar, Yeavering, and the newly-discovered site at Malmesbury were important royal centres, as were the old established monasteries.

In the medieval period many towns were administrative centres, especially the larger ones of the later Middle Ages, and this role has continued through to the present day with the county towns and district centres. However, the large number of castles erected in the eleventh and twelfth centuries (*Fig. 12*) and the hundreds of new monasteries founded during the same period also became the administrative centres of their estates, even if only for brief periods. Their extensive lands were organised and run from these focal places, which often appear relatively insignificant today. It is possible to see each monastery and castle, then, as the centre of operations within its area. Where excavations have been carried out, or detailed research conducted, we can see this central role manifested in the type and size of buildings on the site. The administrative function is demonstrated by the exchequers, book-rooms, and muniment stores of many sites, while produce from the estates was stored in large barns and granaries. Such aspects are the equivalent of the offices and warehouses of many organisations today.

In the seventeenth to nineteenth centuries large estates were usually run from the main residence of the landowner – particularly the large country house or stately home (*Fig. 23*). Nowadays, the administration of the landscape is increasingly carried out more centrally from office blocks in cities, controlling the extensive lands of pension fund and other estates, and locally from estate offices by agents.

This theme of administration in the landscape has not been studied to any great extent, and yet we have already seen that definition of estates is of critical importance in understanding the local landscape. In earlier times, each major estate would have been run by bailiffs and reeves, from a focal point on the estate. The *Domesday Book* gives a good indication of the status of certain places as caputs at the heads of estates in the eleventh century. In medieval times, each abbey and castle can be seen as the administrative head or caput of its scattered holdings.

Recently, several studies have tried to see such medieval sites in context. Brian Davison looked at the Count of Mortain's lands in the West Country based on the castles of Neroche and Montacute in Somerset; James Bond has examined the estates of Evesham Abbey in Worcestershire (*Fig. 13*) and Abingdon Abbey in Oxfordshire, and John Blair has discussed the endowments of Lewes Priory in Sussex before 1200. Monastic estates have thus received considerable attention, including those in foreign ownership, such as Marjorie Morgan's study of the English lands of Bec Abbey in Normandy, which were all administered from Ogbourne St George in Wiltshire. As John Blair says for Lewes, 'the creation of a group of holdings within a convenient radius and accessible from one manorial centre must have been an act of policy by the priory or its patrons'. We can see, therefore, by studying estates and their administrative caputs, deliberate acts of estate policy which have always had a dramatic effect on the landscape. Maps showing monastic estates or baronial holdings (although few of the latter have been attempted) serve to demonstrate the administrative focal place function of such sites as motte and bailey castles, ringworks, or small monastic complexes; at the same time the dependent or lower status of other settlements and surrounding lands is demonstrated by their relatively peripheral position.

Judicial

Many of these administrative caputs also had judicial functions, an arrangement with which we are not familiar today. For more recent times we have the evidence of county gaols, lock-ups, courthouses, prisons, particularly of the Victorian era, which are well documented and have generally survived. However, there is not much evidence of this judicial activity in the landscape before the Middle Ages, although it must have been there and some places were obviously more significant than others in its instigation. In medieval times well-documented court activities were carried out at the caputs already discussed.

In earlier times and into the twelfth and thirteenth centuries, many of the basic administrative and judicial activities were carried out through the arrangement of hundreds, hundred courts, and hundredal manors – courts being held at hundred meeting places, where three men for every tithing or vill had to attend at three-weekly intervals. The origin, arrangements and working of these hundreds are very complicated and the role of the hundred meeting place as a focal place, and the court as a central place, has hardly begun to be considered. Many hundred meeting places were at ancient sites in the landscape like barrows or stones, where they could have taken place for millennia, while others were at places which had other functions as well, such as centres of royal or ecclesiastical estates which coincided with hundredal arrangements. Yet others

18 *Secklow hundred meeting place, Milton Keynes in Buckinghamshire. This low mound was the hundred meeting place of Secklow hundred in Buckinghamshire. It is the only such site to have been excavated so far and has been shown to be of medieval date at least. (Reproduced by permission of Bob Croft and Milton Keynes Archaeology Unit)*

were situated in, or later moved to, places which eventually became towns with a full range of central place functions. The Secklow hundred mound in Milton Keynes is the only hundred meeting place which has been excavated, and no study has been carried out which might indicate that in addition to the courts other activities may have taken place, like markets and fairs, the collection of customs and dues, or religious ceremonies.

Local research can often locate the hundred meeting place for each hundred. In a recent study in Somerset, these included stones for Whitstone, Stone and Bempstone hundreds; trees for Catsash and Horethorne hundreds; and topographical features, such as Abdick hundred – probably Abbot's ditch. In Wiltshire, the mound at which Swanborough hundred met is still there, while outside Birmingham near Sutton Coldfield a low mound, significantly named King's Standing, marks the site of the local hundred meeting place.

The role of the hundred meeting point as a focal place in the late Saxon and early medieval landscape has remained largely unappreciated, although R. H. Britnell has recently discussed the potential. Hundreds and hundredal arrangements persisted in most areas for a long time, eventually emerging as the administrative units of the nineteenth and twentieth centuries (until 1974).

Exchange

The third important focal place function is exchange, currently a fashionable word in archaeological texts. It is used to encompass the whole range of activities whereby goods of one sort or another are moved about between sites in the landscape. Such exchange might take place by using money, by bartering for other goods, or as gifts, but in each case a change in ownership of the goods takes place. In our economy, where we are so familiar with money, it is difficult for us to envisage any other ways in which goods can be acquired, but in the past all sorts of mechanisms were employed and the same is true in the Third World today.

The definition of which places have previously been used for exchange activities will again lead to the identification of higher status sites. At all periods there must have been recognised places in a locality where goods could have been acquired or disposed of. It may be that causewayed enclosures and henges of the Neolithic period were used in this way, and current ideas about hillforts suggest that they should also be viewed in this light. Roman towns and cities clearly had the same role in the commercial, money-based economy of that time.

We should not, however, imagine that such exchange activities had to take place in a permanently occupied urban settlement. Indeed, early exchange activities could not have done, since towns did not exist before late prehistoric times, and in later times periodic markets and fairs provided many of the opportunities for trade. We do not know how early some of these markets and fairs were established or if there were equivalents in Roman and prehistoric times.

It is not the intention of this book to examine towns, but from the ninth century onwards, trade and commerce and the associated industrial and craft activities increasingly took place in or were controlled by towns. Richard Hodges has drawn attention to the beginnings of this process in the post-Roman period with the establishment of *emporia*. Following the collapse of the Roman economy, we can distinguish the re-emergence of commercial activity at these emporia, which were close to royal centres, connected to areas of production and consumption abroad, and based largely on luxury goods like gold, silver, jewels, furs and wine. Such sites are frequently on rivers, estuaries, or the coast, and examples include Southampton (Hamwih), York (Eorforwic), London (Londonwic), Fordwich in Kent, and Sandwich and Ipswich in Suffolk. They seem to have been under royal patronage and to have comprised industrial activities, craftsmen, and artisans, as well as merchants and traders. Such places were not really urban in this early period and possessed few other central place functions. More of them probably remain to be identified, particularly where there were important royal centres in Saxon times.

In the later Saxon period it was the royal estates, particularly the caputs, which developed exchange networks, especially when towns were developed. The king initially, and later other high-status landowners such as the bishops and major abbots, controlled the movement of goods between and within their estates, developing a number of markets and fairs. Some are recorded in *Domesday Book* (1086), while others may have existed but are unrecorded. Indeed, in the pre-Conquest period, coins were produced at numerous mints to facilitate the transactions carried out at such centres.

The privilege of holding a market or fair was extended down the social hierarchy as the Middle Ages progressed, and the royal records are full of references to grants of markets and fairs as the economy developed. How well these grants reflect the amount of exchange activity in the landscape is not clear, since some grants seem never to have been taken up and others clearly did not persist. Some markets, and many fairs, were important and regular activities without any apparent legal status. Only very detailed research will establish whether the legal definition of a particular market or fair reflected its economic importance in a region. It is an important aspect of local research to establish the identity and location of any markets and

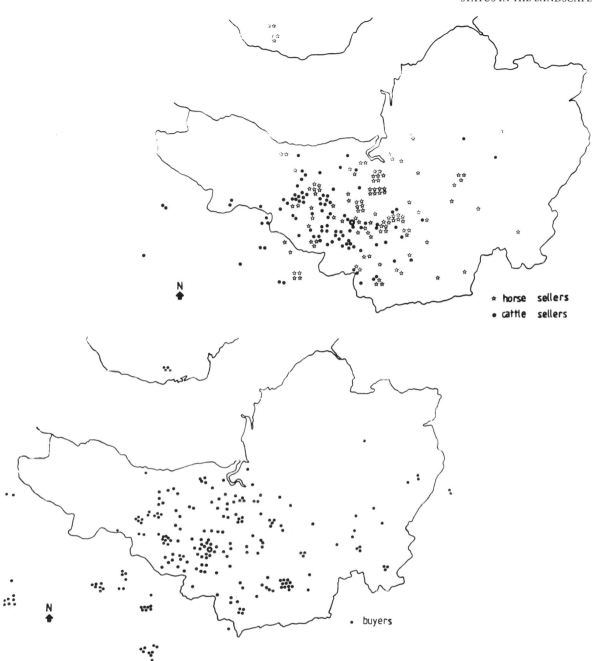

★ horse sellers
• cattle sellers

• buyers

19 *The influence of the Taunton fairs in the seventeenth century. These maps show the origins of the sellers of horses and cattle and the buyers at the fairs. The fairs served mainly western Somerset but their influence was felt all over the south-west peninsula and South Wales. (By permission of Christopher Gerrard)*

fairs, not only for the exchange of goods, but also as a background to the pattern of communications in an area.

We know very little of what went on in these places, from either archaeological or historical evidence, but

R. H. Britnell has suggested that most markets were 'closely related to the growth of local trade between food producers, craftsmen and tradesmen'. However, most luxury goods, such as gold, silver, wine and furs, were acquired either by recourse to the major cities of London, Bristol or York, or to one of the more ancient fairs, such as Stourbridge near Cambridge.

So little archaeological research has been conducted on the 'foreign' goods from excavations on town sites – goods like querns, hones, and pottery – that little can be said for activities at markets and fairs in the Middle

Ages beyond the relatively poor documentary evidence. It is only in the post-medieval period that movements of goods, crops, and animals to and from markets and fairs can be seen in any detail and some idea obtained of the importance of certain places in the distribution of items across the landscape. For seventeenth-century Somerset, J. H. Hamer has shown the influence of White Down fair near Crewkerne, and Christopher Gerrard has shown that two fairs at Taunton held only a few weeks apart had a major influence on the trading of cattle and horses in the West Country. For the more recent past, enormous amounts of information are available to show the changing economic importance of different localities in the landscape.

Ecclesiastical

Definition of the ecclesiastical hierarchy in the landscape and the status of particular sites at different dates is another difficult aspect, currently the subject of much research. The disposition of cathedrals from the earliest times onwards is well known, and early or important monastic sites can usually be identified, supported by estates in the ways already discussed. However, clarifying which churches were important at particular dates

is much more problematical. Many old established monasteries acted as minsters, or the major churches serving particular estates. There may have been other churches of lower status on such estates as well. By late Saxon times, however, there were many lesser minsters serving estates, with their canons visiting outlying 'daughter' and dependent churches and chapels. Many of the latter, while subsidiary in status, were also private or proprietary, belonging to a local landowner and situated next to the manor house.

There are few original documentary sources, but a number of churches are mentioned in *Domesday Book* (1086). While this is a very unsatisfactory source of information on early churches, as Peter Sawyer has shown, research in counties like Wiltshire and Somerset suggests that some, if not most, of those mentioned were minsters. This is particularly true if they had allocations of land and an estate attached. Many such minsters were on royal or major ancient ecclesiastical estates, often at the caputs of such estates.

At the local level, it is important to look at the interrelationships between churches, especially any that indicate status in the ecclesiastical hierarchy in the past. Mother churches tended to guard their privileges jealously and even in the nineteenth century some

20 *Bredon church in Worcestershire. This fine large Romanesque building indicates the former importance of the church at Bredon. It was a minster for the large episcopal estate with dependent*

Chapelries at Bredon's Norton, Mitton and Westmancote. (By permission of National Monuments Record, Royal Commission on Historic Monuments (England))

daughter churches and chapels were still dependent in some respects on the more ancient or more important mother church. Burial was the most cherished right, although baptism (and hence possession of a font) and marriage were also important.

Several examples can be seen in the Midlands of this early ecclesiastical organisation. Bredon church in Worcestershire had dependencies at Bredon's Norton, Mitton and Westmancote. The fine Romanesque work remaining at Bredon is an indication of its importance in the twelfth century. Fladbury in Worcestershire had dependencies at Wyre Piddle, Throckmorton, Bishampton and Abbot's Morton. There are also examples in Kent, where Maidstone, Newington and Milton each had a host of dependent churches and chapels. In Somerset, examples include St Andrew's near Ilchester, North Petherton, and Keynsham (now in Avon), while close relationships between mother and daughter churches existed on the royal estates at South Petherton, Crewkerne, and Chewton Mendip.

At Chew Magna, south of Bristol, eighteenth-century records show the minster's influence very clearly, even at such a late date, and although no Anglo-Saxon masonry remains, the earlier dependent status of surrounding churches can still be seen. In the vestry book for 1752 it is reported that Charles Wallis, Sexton, 'appeared at the vestry and being strictly examined touching the bounds of the churchyard do acknowledge and declare to the best of his memory that:

> the westgate with part of the wall as far as a particular upright stone in the said wall, between the said gates and the standing stile and steps belongs to Chew Stoke and is repaired by the parishioners thereof; the other part home to the poor house is repaired by the parish of Chew Magna; the east side is repaired and half of the wall and stile by the parish of Stowey; the other by the parish of Norton ... The north side is repaired by the parish of Dundry.'

It is interesting to note in this example how the dependent churches were responsible for the maintenance of sections of the churchyard wall of the mother church; similar examples exist elsewhere.

Some idea of status has to be obtained, therefore, if the local ecclesiastical hierarchy is to be understood. For example, there are many fine early fonts, particularly of Norman date, showing that by that date many places had acquired rights of baptism. However, the right of burial as the preserve of the more important churches remained stronger and persisted longer. Much evidence in the landscape points to this, including church paths (*Fig. 89*) and known routes by which coffins were carried. Outside Ablington in Gloucestershire, for example, is a *coffin stone*, locally reputed to be where coffins were laid while the bearers rested on their

way to the church at Bibury, where large late Saxon and Romanesque parts remain of the minster church.

Most churches, however, were of relatively low status. Our ideas of how these originated and fitted into the early Church hierarchy are only just developing, but already the pattern is becoming clearer. If all of the evidence for early church sites is put together, we can see that these were widespread before 1066. Richard Morris has suggested, in fact, that there were many thousands of small churches in England in the late Saxon period. Some were no doubt replacements for periodic meetings at pagan sites or in cemeteries with crosses. Not all, however, survived, and of those that did, not all became parish churches.

In the west, large numbers of chapels are known which never became parish churches, but which are clearly pre-twelfth century in origin and had burial and baptism rights by that time. Over the rest of the country, the large number of medieval chapels, most of which have not survived, may well be of pre-Conquest date, and they represent a fuller ecclesiastical landscape than has formerly been considered.

Along with earlier ideas of colonisation of the landscape, it was assumed that original churches had been supplemented with additional *chapels of ease* as needed. No doubt in some cases this was true, but as research has indicated a much denser pattern of settlement in earlier periods, and as continuity seems to be the norm, the role of churches has required re-examination.

It now seems probable that there were more churches in late Saxon and early medieval times than was formerly thought. As with settlements, changes of status have occurred in a poorly-documented period – the tenth to twelfth centuries. During this time, churches were frequently the private property of a local lord, they were part of the resources of an estate, and any revenue from them could be used by the owner. This is why *Domesday Book* does not refer to many churches which are known to have existed from other evidence.

Several churches have been excavated which were undocumented and previously unsuspected, such as at Raunds in Northamptonshire (*Fig. 32*). Elsewhere, churches seem to have lost their status and gone out of use. Examples include Odda's chapel at Deerhurst in Gloucestershire, the Saxon church of St Lawrence at Bradford on Avon, and the newly-discovered site, probably St Helen's, at Malmesbury in Wiltshire.

It is noticeable how early excavations of previously unsuspected churches were usually interpreted as the church having been moved, as at Eaton Socon in Bedfordshire and Potterne in Wiltshire. Recent ideas suggest that any late Saxon hamlet or earlier manorial centre might be expected to have its own church. What, then, happened to them all?

During the twelfth century, bishops began to excercise greater jurisdiction and, beginning with Archbishop Lanfranc, there was increasing pressure to get private churches out of the landowners' control and under episcopal control. This happened at the same time as parishes were being formed, and it seems to have resulted in the extinction of many churches, not only as private property but also as working churches. Others were selected, and it is not known how, as the parish church for an area, in which the sacraments of baptism, marriage and burial were allowed. Some seem to have been rebuilt on a larger scale, presumably to cater for a more centralised population; an example may be Wharram Percy in Yorkshire. The rest were either converted to dwellings, such as Raunds which became a manor house, or demolished, or downgraded in status to chapels of ease.

Thus the research so far on the origin of parish churches leads us to suspect that a lot of early churches disappeared in the reforms and rationalisations of the early Middle Ages. In some ways, this development may well have followed the development in settlements. As well as major settlements with minsters, hamlets and farms may well have had their own small churches. With agglomeration of settlements, some village churches were downgraded and abandoned; others became our parish churches.

Churches in the landscape

Apart from indicating status, each church represents perhaps the most important local focal place for any settlement, and we might spend a lot of time studying it in our local research. It has much to tell us of how the local landscape has developed, and we can read the clues, if we know how to examine the building and its surroundings. Dr Joe Bettey has drawn attention to the three main aspects we should examine – the site, structure, and fittings – all of which can provide valuable clues to the history of the local landscape.

Site

The site may offer important clues to the origin of the church: many reflect conversion to Christianity of former pagan sites. Early missionaries under Mellitus in AD 602 were exhorted by Pope Gregory to utilise earlier pagan sites when new churches were built, so that people could continue to use those places they were accustomed to frequent. This may explain the interesting siting of some churches close to or inside prehistoric monuments. Obvious examples are at Avebury in Wiltshire and Knowlton in Dorset, but Maxey church in Northamptonshire may be built on a barrow, at Berwick in Sussex there is a large mound, probably a barrow, in the churchyard, and at Rudston in Yorkshire there is a large prehistoric monolith next to the chancel of the church. Similarly, churches on

hilltops, dedicated to St Michael (the Archangel) or St Catherine, may be on previously pagan sites. Proximity to significant springs or wells may also indicate use of an early site.

Some churches are no doubt of Roman ancestry. Where villas have been found near to or beneath churches, as at Rivenhall in Essex or Cheddar in Somerset, there is at least good circumstantial evidence for continuity on the site. Elsewhere, villas have produced evidence of Christianity, with examples at Hinton St Mary in Dorset and Chedworth in Gloucestershire. At Woodchester in Gloucestershire the church sits over part of, and in the same alignment as, the vast Roman palace there. Wherever a medieval church is found in close proximity to a villa, it is now valid to question the origin of the church as a possible Christian structure in late/post-Roman times. Finds of Roman coins and pottery within the graveyard may indicate a similar relationship. Near Roman towns, it is highly likely that original churches were founded as mausolea or temples in graveyards outside the Roman settlement proper. St Alban's abbey is perhaps the best example, but others probably include St Andrew's at Northover, outside the Roman town of Ilchester in Somerset, and Fordington in Dorchester.

In the post-Roman period, new churches were built in Kent and the south-east after the activities of Augustine. Elsewhere, all over the north, the Midlands, and the south, various 'saints' established monasteries and cathedrals as Christianity spread. Most of these were at important royal or administrative centres, and many of the churches were in the form of minsters or missionary centres.

In the west and Wales, large numbers of churches were developed as a result of late/post-Roman Christianity by so-called 'Celtic Saints'. Many are indicated by dedications, but the circular churchyards, oratories, holy wells and inscribed memorial stones and crosses all indicate how widespread such Christian sites were by the time of the Norman Conquest.

Structure

Analysis of the structure of a church by reference to the architectural styles and fabric will give us some idea of how the building has developed. Detailed three-dimensional structural analysis of church buildings is helping to reveal great complexity in their development. It is no longer adequate just to produce a plan of a church: all walls and elevations need to be examined closely, since most churches are built, developed and extended over a long period.

It is important to remember that a standing structure such as a church can be read in the same way as an archaeological section: features cutting into or overlying others can be used to construct relative dating relationships. This can be clearly seen at St Oswald's in

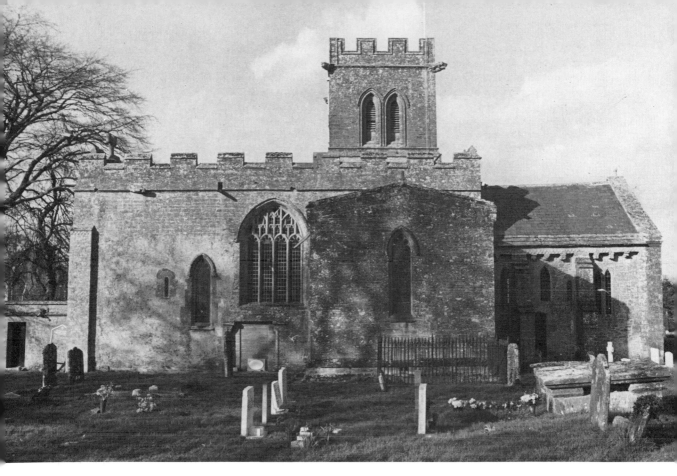

21 *East Stoke church, Stoke sub Hamdon in Somerset. A good example of a medieval parish church with many building periods and styles represented. A highly-decorated elaborate Romanesque building of nave and chancel has had thirteenth-century tower and transept added. In the fifteenth century the nave was raised and battlements added. A new perpendicular church was not provided in the fifteenth century, as most local investment went to the now demolished St Nicholas chapel at West Stoke. (Photograph by Alan Wilson)*

Gloucester, where the many phases of development are more clear in elevation than plan, and where, ironic-ally, the earliest masonry is up above arches put in at a later date. Other examples include Marston Magna in Somerset, where there are three undated phases of masonry before the Norman windows were inserted into the north wall of the chancel. This may have been a drastically altered Saxon church; there are Saxon windowheads elsewhere in the fabric, but the Norman windows clearly do *not* date the fabric of the north chancel wall. Other good examples are Bulmer in Yorkshire, Studley in Warwickshire, and Stoke sub Hamdon in Somerset. The fabric has to be read with care in order to understand the evolution of the building, which is clearly going to be impossible where churches have plastered interiors or stuccoed exteriors. Windows and doors of particular style are no means of dating whole sections of a church, as inserts and alterations are common.

Having examined the fabric of a church, what can this tell us of the local landscape? Firstly, building was always expensive and so periods of activity may well represent periods of prosperity. On the other hand, churches with poor workmanship, of small size, and altered rather than rebuilt, may well indicate poor localities, or a lack of interest in the church. Thus, a good example of an undisturbed Anglo-Saxon church might be an architectural masterpiece, but in landscape terms it shows no wealth or inclination to rebuild later. Medieval man was not appreciative of antiquity or great art – so lack of wealth rather than concern for conservation is the reason for survival; the same applies for any period. At the other end of the scale, rebuilding on a large scale in the fifteenth and sixteenth centuries in East Anglia, Somerset, Wiltshire and Gloucester-shire represents great prosperity at that time.

Within the church itself, different parts may rep-resent different degrees of interest. The chancel belong-ing to the rector may not be in the same style as the nave maintained by the parishioners, reflecting differ-ences in wealth or involvement. Even in those churches where the rector was a monastery, there may be a variety of interest displayed, from great ostentation where the monastery has been concerned to maintain its property, to neglect where the church is on a distant or poor estate, or where the monastery itself was poor.

Fittings

The fittings within and around the church can also be used in a similar fashion. We have already seen that possession of an early font is a significant indication; an early, large or well-used graveyard could be viewed in the same way. The graveyard is an important landscape feature, since in many cases it represents the burial place of most of the local population over a millennium or more, and is the logical successor to prehistoric barrow groups and Roman cemeteries. Its memorials tell of wealth and poverty, while its size and situation relate to the foundation of the church and its status. Sometimes, the churchyard wall was maintained by other people. We have seen this at Chew Magna, but also in Somerset, at both Creech St Michael and Locking, stones in the churchyard wall indicate obligations to of most of the local population over a millenium or parish. How common was this in the rest of the country?

Many churches have evidence of continuing interest in pagan themes. Fertility, for example, is well represented by *green men* and other themes by *sheela-na-gigs* and other grotesque figures on both the inside and outside of churches. Even after a thousand years or more, evidence of pagan beliefs is still widespread in churches.

Inside the church, the degree of elaboration and ostentation of both architecture and fittings indicates status and wealth in the community. Frequently the tombs, chapels, hatchments, private pews, and so on, indicate a local wealthy family. Elsewhere, the poverty of the fittings and lack of restoration point to a small or poor population.

Churches are full of such clues to their local importance and relative importance in their immediate region. If we take the four parishes of Coberley, Winstone, Elkstone, and Brimpsfield on the Cotswolds in Gloucestershire as examples, several points can be demonstrated.

At Brimpsfield, a very unusual church sits on its own away to the east of the present village. There was also a small priory at Brimpsfield, but it is not certain if the church was the priory church. However, pieces of Norman and medieval masonry can be seen in a nearby barn and in local field walls, and to the east of the church is a round mound, probably the motte of an abortive or adulterine castle. Next to the church is a large earthen ringwork, clearly a castle of some importance in the Norman period with substantial defences remaining today. This ringwork is the most impressive of a series of earthworks stretching away

west of the church towards the village. On the ground these are very confused, but they show on the air pictures as probable remains of structures connected with the priory and an earlier area of the village. Clearly, then, the church reflects the important early medieval status of Brimpsfield with its castle and priory, whilst also providing an indicator that the centre of gravity of the village has shifted westwards over the last 800 years.

Nearby at Coberley, the austere church is accompanied only by a farm, a deserted mansion site, and some garden earthworks. There were other medieval settlements in the area to the east of the church and at Upper Coberley, and this dispersed settlement pattern is reinforced by the possible site of a castle and other earthworks at Dowman's Farm, half a mile west of the church.

At both Elkstone and Winstone there are churches with substantial Saxo-Norman and Norman remains. Elkstone is now only a small settlement with a large farm to the south. Yet the church is a very elaborate structure with evidence of a Norman nave and elaborate stone-vaulted chancel. Between them is a third cell, represented inside by a stone-vaulted unit and outside by a strong buttress on the north side. These indicate the remains of a tower, and, together with the corbels and tympanum, suggest a very fine church in the twelfth century. Why was it never developed afterwards, except for the addition of an elaborate west tower?

In the adjacent parish of Winstone, however, there is also evidence of an early church, particularly obvious inside from the chancel arch and blocked north doorway and window, but the quality of the work here is not so fine. The church now stands relatively isolated with settlement earthworks to west and east. The main village is away to the west, with areas of shrinkage on its south side. At some date, presumably after the twelfth century, the village moved or was moved westwards and its gridplan suggests this may have been planned. The church was not much developed after that date, but its origins lie not only within an earlier area of settlement, but also in its position adjacent to a spring, one of the headwaters of the Duntis Bourne. It may possibly have begun as a baptistry or succeeded a cult centre at the spring head. Like Brimpsfield church on its hilltop, this church's site may predate any of the other local churches, even though the fabric is not as impressive at first glance.

These examples demonstrate how the church can be used as a source of information in the landscape. Not only can it serve as an indicator of status, but it can also throw some light on changing settlement developments, which will be examined in the following chapters.

5

Deserted villages and after

A great deal of our interest in the developing landscape is centred on the settlements within it. An enormous amount of research has gone on in the last few decades into how and when settlements originated and how they have changed over time. In the next three chapters we shall look at deserted villages, where recent studies began, and surviving villages, which are the subject of renewed and vigorous interest. We shall also look at the Cinderellas of settlement studies – hamlets and farmsteads, which have received little attention but are of immense importance because they are widespread and because they are clearly related to both the origins and the decline of villages.

THE STUDY OF DESERTED VILLAGES

We can trace the current state of our knowledge about village origins and changes back to the 1940s. At that time several scholars, notably William Hoskins and Maurice Beresford, were drawing attention to the large number of deserted medieval settlements which could be seen in the landscape. Despite the scepticism of many historians at the time, Beresford eventually drew together all his findings in *The Lost Villages of England*, published in 1954. It is difficult for us to imagine now, but at the time this was a revolutionary book, not only because it put a new type of archaeological field monument, the deserted medieval village (DMV), firmly on the map, but also because it heralded a new era in the study of rural settlements in this country. The Deserted Medieval Village Research Group (now the Medieval Villages Research Group), which was formed in 1952 as a multi-disciplinary research body, drawing in geographers, historians, and archaeologists as well as natural scientists, has revolutionised our concepts of rural settlement changes over the last 2000 years. The Group's long-standing excavations at Wharram Percy in the East Riding of Yorkshire have greatly contributed to this work (*Fig. 30*).

In 1954 Beresford listed 1353 sites of deserted villages; by 1968 the number had risen to 2263; in 1976

this was updated to 2813. Some counties like Worcestershire, Shropshire, Lancashire and Somerset, which in 1966 had few or no sites, can now be seen to have just as many sites as the 'classic' deserted village areas of Warwickshire, Oxfordshire, Northamptonshire and Yorkshire, where the sites were first located.

What do these sites tell us about settlement in the landscape? Firstly, they show that the pattern of villages and hamlets seen on the map today is incomplete and that, contrary to earlier ideas about medieval settlement, in some areas a large number of former sites has disappeared. This is an indication of how much change has taken place in the past. The fact that more sites have been identified as time passes shows that archaeological distribution maps only depict the activities of individual archaeologists or field societies up to any particular date, rather than the total picture of deserted medieval villages!

Following the identification of these sites, further work has suggested many reasons for their disappearance. The Black Death and subsequent outbreaks of the plague account for the smallest number of desertions, despite all the local traditions. Early research drew attention to the creation or extension of Royal Forests in the twelfth century, the establishment of Cistercian monasteries also in the twelfth century, and in particular the enclosure of arable land for pasture in the fourteenth, fifteenth and sixteenth centuries, all of which were often accompanied by well-documented evictions of peasants. The removal of whole communities for the creation of parks began in the fourteenth and fifteenth centuries, and hundreds, if not thousands, of instances can be cited from the eighteenth and nineteenth centuries.

Such apparently obvious explanations for the desertion of a settlement are, however, too simplistic. As with much else in the landscape, the reality is more complex. Frequently, the villages which were deserted were already very small and dependent on another larger and more stable settlement. They were, in fact, often the unimportant places in the local settlement hierarchy, founded late on poor land and marginal in

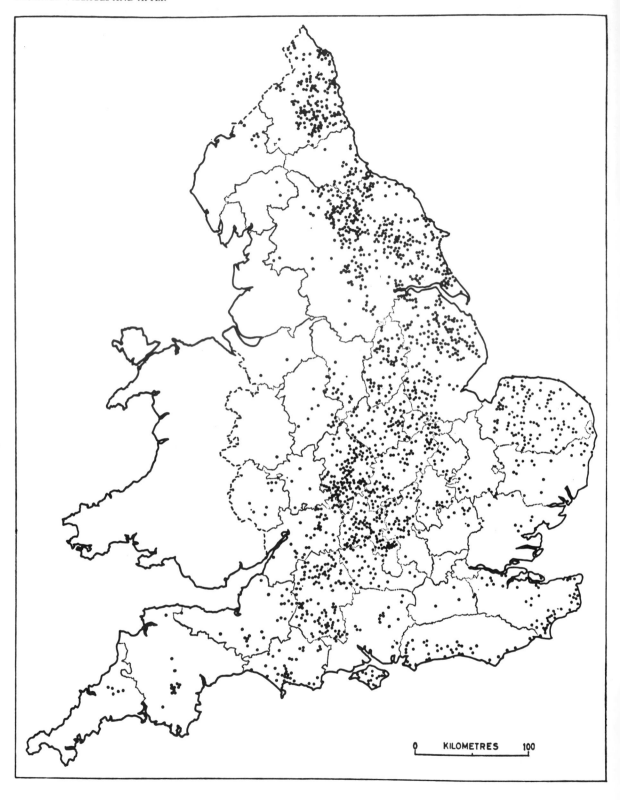

KILOMETRES

0   100

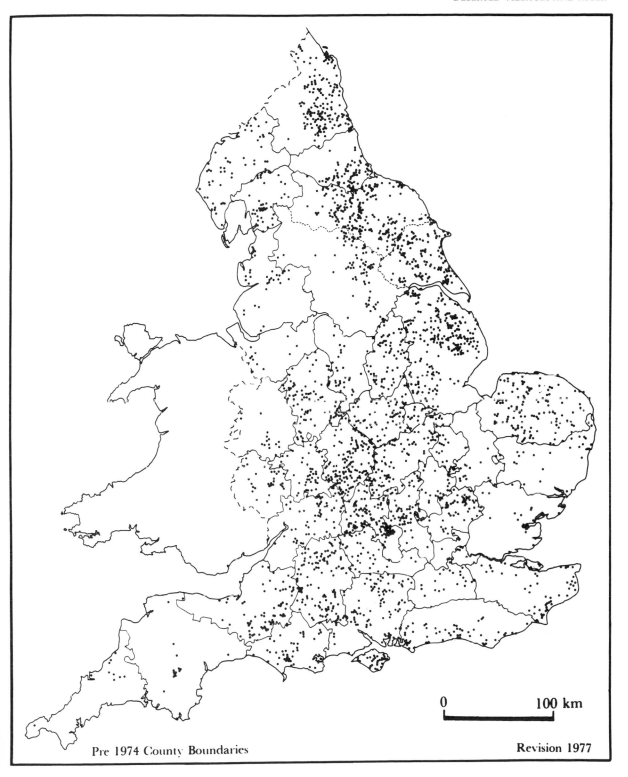

Pre 1974 County Boundaries

Revision 1977

0   100 km

22 *Deserted medieval villages in England in 1966 and 1977. In 1966 large numbers of deserted villages had been discovered in the Midlands and the north. Some counties appeared to have few or no sites. By 1977 many more sites had been discovered, especially in* *Cumbria, Lancashire and the Welsh borderland. Such maps are a reflection of the activity of archaeologists rather than the actual distribution of sites. (By permission of the Medieval Village Research Group)*

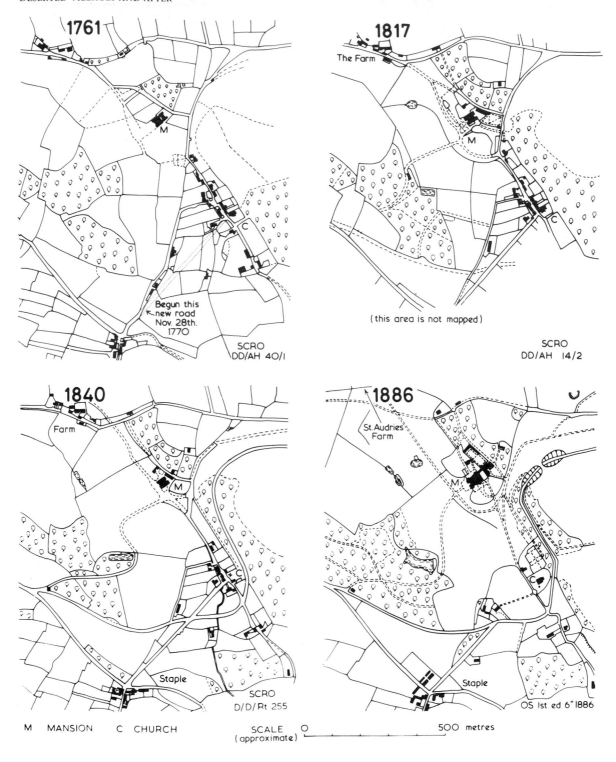

23 *West Quantoxhead or St Audrie's deserted village in Somerset. A good series of maps shows the gradual disappearance of this village as the parkland was extended and the road system diverted. This example could be paralleled by numerous others. It shows the gradual change in a village in post-medieval (rather than medieval) times resulting in the removal of the village to a new site (rather than total desertion). There are no tell-tale earthworks or foundations in the area where buildings are clearly shown in 1761–1840.*

24 *Shrunken villages in Leicestershire. Air photographs of Tugby (top) in Leicestershire (BLC 43 taken on 28th November 1972) and Cold Newton (bottom) in Leicestershire (BLC 64 taken on 28th November 1972). These pictures show the characteristic earthworks of partly deserted settlements between present farms, cottages, houses and gardens. (By permission of Cambridge University Aerial Photography Committee)*

terms of agricultural production. As with other aspects of the landscape, it was the slow, largely undocumented social and economic changes that spelt the death of such settlements, not at a single stroke but over a long period. For the Midlands, Christopher Dyer has assembled impressive evidence for the processes by which small ailing settlements shrank and disappeared. His evidence indicates sites of low status disappearing both before and after the Black Death, with relatively few being eliminated by the well-recorded activities of rapacious landlords.

The distribution maps of DMV sites also belie simplistic explanation. As work has progressed, it can be seen that every part of the definition of DMVs can be subjected to debate. Even in 1954, Beresford drew attention to the existence of shrunken villages, where, despite the continued presence of a church, shop, pub,

Post Office and many houses, there are also earthworks indicating that the village has formerly been larger or has moved. We know that shrunken village earthworks are very common, perhaps the most common of all archaeological field monuments, and that they must indicate shrinkage and movement of settlements at all times. We now have to think of a range of possibilities in settlements, from those which have completely survived to those which are completely deserted, with all shades in between.

Secondly, we must beware of the term 'medieval'. It is not difficult to show from documents that most of our villages were in existence in the Middle Ages, but many were certainly not deserted until after 1500. Most may have been there in the pre-Norman period, although whether as fully developed villages or not will be discussed below. Even where the name is recorded early on, however, we cannot be sure that we are dealing with the same site, bearing in mind the movement implied above. Desertion, shrinkage and movement can take place at any period.

Finally, the term 'villages' needs to be considered. Most settlements outside the Midlands are not large nucleated collections of farms and cottages. Many do not have churches, manor houses and mills; indeed most of the countryside today is worked from single farms isolated in the middle of their own holdings. Many areas in the Middle Ages did not have true villages. In Cornwall, parts of Devon, western Somerset, and the Welsh borderlands, in particular, medieval settlement was predominantly in the form of hamlets and farmsteads. In these areas we should not expect to find deserted, shrunken or moved villages, but the equivalent for hamlets and farms, and this is indeed the case with hundreds of such sites identified on Dartmoor and in west Somerset, for example; this will be discussed further in Chapter 7.

Thus, a consideration of earlier work on DMVs has led us to the conclusion that the settlement patterns we actually see on the maps and in the landscape consist of a range of settlements, at various stages of development at all periods; everything, in fact, from surviving medieval villages to totally abandoned farm sites. It would be impossible to depict accurately all the nuances of settlement development on any but the largest scale maps, such is the complexity and variety in the landscape.

FINDING DESERTED VILLAGES

What, then, should the researcher look for in the settlements in his area, and how should he set about analysing what he finds? Firstly, it should be possible to find out what is already known from the local Sites and Monuments Record or Royal Commission for Historical Monuments/Ordnance Survey records. The most important deserted villages and other abandoned medieval settlements will probably be listed already by the Medieval Village Research Group and there may well be surveys and air photographs available.

For most areas, and particularly for the smaller settlements, little work will have been done and here the local historian or archaeologist can easily add new sites and information to the record. Air photographs, particularly verticals, are likely to show village earthworks which can then be checked on the ground. Familiarity with the local history of the area is very important, as detailed local knowledge, both on the ground and with the available documents and old maps, will ensure that all remaining features of such deserted settlements will be found. In any locality a start can be made by checking any easily available documents which list settlements. If a place is missing on the map which is mentioned in *Domesday Book* (1086) or any of the lay subsidies or poll taxes, this is a possibility for a deserted settlement. In addition, those parishes covered by the Victoria County History, or even local histories, may well have other valuable details available. However, it is from fieldwork, old maps with field names, and the examination of air photographs that most progress will be made.

If we look at a typical Midland deserted village site with the aid of air photographs and maps, we can see that it is made up of certain features which occur again and again on such sites, the most distinctive being the sunken holloways marking the courses of old roads and paths. Parts of these may still be in use or have ponds or marlpits in them, but they are generally easy to recognise. Smaller paths and lanes frequently lead off the main holloway, but even this may be narrow and insignificant by modern standards. Occasionally such a road is cambered with ditches along each side. If you are very unlucky, such holloways will be the only recognisable features on your site.

The other obvious features are likely to be the *platforms* lying alongside the holloways, on which the farms and cottages formerly stood. These will be large embanked areas, only half to one metre (two or three feet) above the road in most cases, with rounded corners and perhaps slightly hollowed centres. Only on the best sites will any *house platforms* remain, that is where the buildings actually stood. Sometimes a few stones stick out of the grass to indicate this, but clumps of nettles give a general indication of former areas of occupation and of dung in houses and farmyards, because of the build up of phosphates in the soil. Ditches and lanes frequently divide up the platforms, so that a rough plan can be seen of the former crofts lying along the lanes.

All around such a site there would formerly have been fields and other areas of land use. If the area is pasture and has been little disturbed, it may be possible

25 *Deserted settlements in the Midlands. Air photographs of two typical deserted medieval settlements in the Midlands – (top) Moreton (Dinton parish) in Buckinghamshire (BKZ20 taken on 23rd November 1972) and (bottom) Cotes de Val (Gilmarton parish) in Leicestershire (AZU6 taken on 29th October 1969). Both show characteristic 'village' earthworks, were formerly hamlets, and have present-day farmsteads associated with them. (By permission of Cambridge University Aerial Photography Committee)*

to pick out areas of ridge and furrow, and the junction between the arable fields and the rear of the village closes may be detected. In many cases there is a hefty bank and ditch marking the village boundary, but in others this may be marked only by a slight change in level or by the continuous line of the rear of the platforms. Elsewhere, the platforms may run out into former meadowland near a stream or river. The definition of this village boundary is important, since it indicates the plan of the settlement, and some idea can then be gained of the size of the site in relation to its fields.

So far we have been looking at earthworks particular to deserted settlement sites. However, there may also be other features commonly found on other medieval sites, and there may occasionally be buildings. Moated sites indicating a former manor or grange are common, as are sites of fishponds, remaining as dry grassy hollows, or linear banks indicating the former dams. Occasionally a mill site may be recognised.

It is not generally appreciated that very many settlement sites exhibit earthworks of several periods. We know at Wharram Percy in Yorkshire, for example, that the medieval village was fitted into a prehistoric and Roman field system (*Fig. 30*), and at Hound Tor on Dartmoor the medieval hamlet was built around a Bronze Age settlement and its fields (*Fig. 47*). Many of the deserted and shrunken villages in Gloucestershire (including Hawling and Hullasey) lie across the ends of prehistoric fields which have been ploughed out beyond the village earthworks.

Christopher Taylor has recognised many cases of settlement remains intermixed with monastic and post-medieval earthworks. He cites Pipewell Abbey in Northamptonshire, where the earthworks of a deserted village mingle with the remains of the Cistercian monastic site. It is not uncommon to have the outworks of an earthen castle associated with settlement remains, as at Rockingham in Northamptonshire or Kilpeck in Herefordshire.

What is often not realised is that many deserted settlements have interesting and largely unappreciated post-medieval remains as well, such as mansion sites. Many earthwork complexes turn out in fact to have very little settlement evidence, i.e. village or hamlet remains, but rather more garden or landscaping remains (*Fig. 26*), or indications of activities such as rabbit farming. Settlements emparked in the eighteenth or nineteenth centuries tend not to survive too well as earthworks, but abandoned sixteenth- or seventeenth-century garden schemes often incorporate remains of village earthworks. Many such examples have been recognised in Northamptonshire, Oxfordshire, and elsewhere.

Sometimes, as at Chesterton in Warwickshire, obvious features remain. The house has disappeared there, although it is shown on an eighteenth-century map complete with avenues, ponds, and gardens, and today a fine eighteenth-century brick gateway, enclosed garden and levelled lawn remain. The stumps of the large trees of the avenue can also be seen, but the site of the large house is marked only by slightly hummocky ground, though there may well be cellars beneath. At Hardington in Somerset there are only a few traces of the village, which is said to have gone by 1584, but until recently there were very fine earthworks of a seventeenth-century garden landscape, with terraces, tree mounds, and park banks. The church and a gazebo or *feasting house* still remain. Elsewhere,

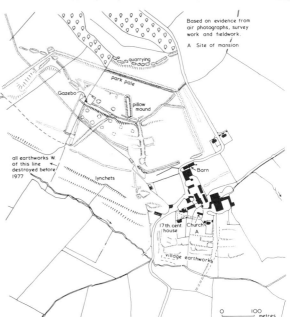

26 *Village and garden earthworks at Hardington in Somerset. The air photograph and earthwork plan show the remains of village earthworks south of the church and extensive garden and park remains (since destroyed) to the north-west. They are at slightly different scales.*

extensive *pillow mounds* show that the site was used as a rabbit warren later on.

At Wormleighton, studied in great detail by Professor Harry Thorpe, the fishponds must have been built after the village had been abandoned, as they overlie the village street. Other earthworks probably indicate an irrigation or leat system built in the sixteenth century to help the Spencer family's ranching activities. These later uses for deserted village sites need to be appreciated if the full landscape story is to be understood.

Apart from earlier and later earthwork features, there may also be buildings. Churches often remain, either complete, ruined, or only in part (e.g. tower or chancel), and, together with the extent of the grave-yard, they may give useful information about a site. There may also be one or more farms, cottages, or barns associated with the earthworks, as the majority of deserted villages are not entirely abandoned. These should be examined for early features, such as architectural fragments incorporated into them, and an assessment made of their original date, any changes through time, and former uses. The recognition of Romanesque or Gothic details in such buildings, however, should not automatically be associated with a former church or chapel, as small manor houses and other secular buildings often had windows and doorways in these styles. The interpretation of building details is a specialised aspect of studying the landscape, but careful recording by drawings or photographs may enable experts to give some guidance as to date or former use.

At High Meadow in the Forest of Dean a rather poor set of earthworks indicates a settlement shown on a map of 1608. The adjacent farmstead includes a building with a number of fine sixteenth- and seven-teenth-century doorways and windows, now used as a barn. This must be the former manor house of the settlement, which was downgraded in the eighteenth century and replaced by a larger house with its own gardens and park. These in their turn have now disappeared, leaving only earthworks of terraces and lawns. Almost any small feature in a building or even a field wall may say something of the structures that once stood on such sites. Elsewhere, particularly in the Midlands, there is widespread evidence for the overploughing of portions of deserted settlement sites, such as at Onley in Northamptonshire, where clear traces of ridge and furrow show a change of use from village to arable land.

So far, we have been looking at the rather more impressive remains of former villages. In most cases, however, such well-defined features do not remain and only vague areas of earthworks are visible. Some of these have been disturbed in the past, making analysis very difficult, especially where the site has been bulldozed and ploughed, leaving only slight changes of colour in the ploughsoil and scatters of potsherds. Such sites can be useful, however, as a collection of pottery may indicate earlier occupation on a site than could be discerned when it was pasture or a field of unploughed earthworks. At Ashington in Somerset, for example, a handful of Roman sherds was found when the deserted village site was ploughed, showing that there had been a Romano-British settlement on the same site as the medieval village.

Over much of the country, therefore, the local researcher should expect to find only slight traces of settlement remains, not as extensive or as impressive as those usually published. Many of these sites were not villages at all, but hamlets. In Somerset, the majority of the 500+ deserted settlements identified so far were formerly small hamlets of two or three farms and not large nucleated villages. Zany was such a settlement, located during the construction of the M5 motorway near Taunton, and now covered by the Taunton Dean Service Station. Another was Playstreet in Bickenhall, now a ploughed site littered with medieval and later potsherds and rooftiles, but with only slight earth-works.

The location of such deserted hamlets is an important task for the local fieldworker, since for many areas they were the most characteristic feature of the settlement pattern, although they are usually not as well documented as villages, churches and manor houses, nor are their remains as impressive or extensive.

SHRUNKEN VILLAGES

Much more common than deserted sites are the slight traces of former areas of habitation adjacent to present-day settlements (*Fig. 24*). Even villages and hamlets which are quite large today may have areas of earthworks adjacent to them, showing where build-ings formerly stood. The characteristic earthworks of holloways, platforms and house sites may be recognis-able, as well as areas of nettles and traces of stone or brick foundations. More often the remains will be very slight, but most villages would formerly have had farms or cottages occupying what today are often grassy paddocks in gaps along the streets. Local tradition may indicate where cottages stood until recently, but the fieldworker should be aware that much earlier structures may also have occupied the same sites.

Many villages and hamlets display, in the form of earthworks, evidence of a change of site or plan. This may range from small areas of earthworks within or at one end of a settlement, to large areas of earthworks with only a few farms and cottages in use today. South Bradon and Maperton in Somerset are typical of hundreds of examples. At the former there is now only a farm and two or three cottages. This looks today like a small hamlet in the parish of Puckington, where there is an important village, but South Bradon had a church of St Mary Magdalene until the sixteenth century at least and was a separate parish until the nineteenth century. The extent of the parish is shown on the tithe map of 1845 and the church site is known from burials dug up in a potato patch in 1953. There is also a mill site, though only the stone foundations and the sluice gate remain, together with the supply leat which now

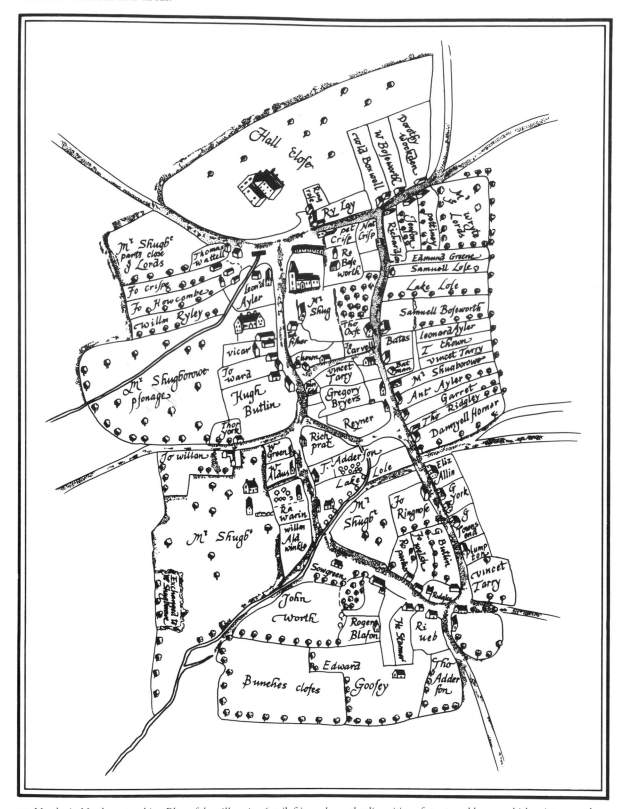

27 *Naseby in Northamptonshire. Plan of the village in 1630 (left) and earthworks in the present settlement (right). The early map* *shows the disposition of streets and houses which exist now only as earthworks. The plans are at slightly different scales.*

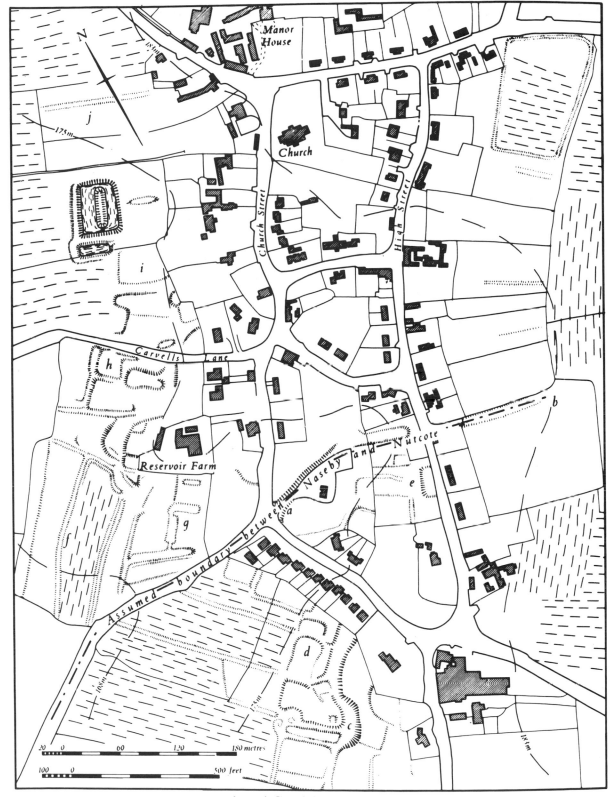

N

Manor House

Church

Church Street

High Street

Carvells Lane

Reservoir Farm

Naseby and Nutcote

Assumed boundary between

175m

180m

181m

j

i

h

g

f

e

d

c

b

a

| 20 | 0 | 60 | 120 | 180 metres |

| 100 | 0 | | 500 feet |

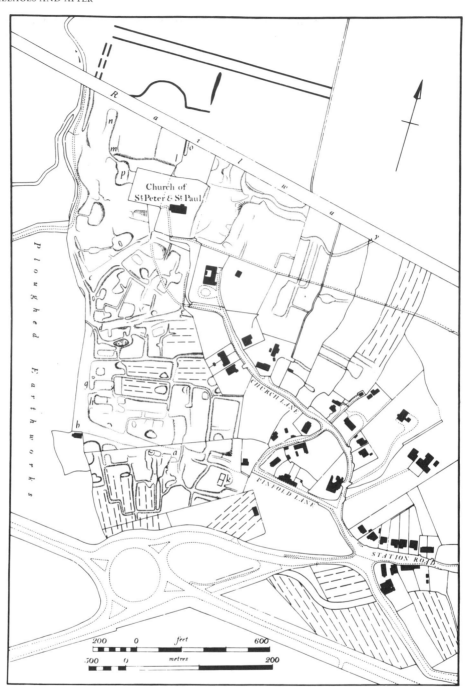

28 *Stallingborough in Lincolnshire. Plan of a severely shrunken settlement. Extensive earthworks show former settlement areas. Today there is only a scatter of cottages along the surviving road. (Crown copyright: reproduced by permission of Paul Everson and Royal Commission on Historical Monuments (England))*

carries most of the water of the River Ile. The clearest evidence of shrinkage, however, is in the form of platforms which surround the remaining buildings. One area has impressive stone footings and may well represent a manor site.

South Bradon is listed in *Domesday Book* and in most medieval tax lists. Its people were not killed off by the Black Death, nor was it enclosed for sheep in the fifteenth or sixteenth centuries; it just died gradually over a long period. Its history is largely unknown, but the story is there in the earthworks, church site and local landscape.

Maperton is still a civil parish with the church surviving and many cottages and farms. Yet on the east side of the village there is a field of earthworks indicating lanes and cottage sites, and elsewhere the remains of a village boundary bank and crofts. Maperton is still there, but it has lost large areas of settlement and has changed its plan to some extent. The shrinkage is so extensive that local archaeologists refer to the earthworks as a 'deserted village'.

In Northamptonshire, Christopher Taylor has mapped large numbers of shrunken settlements with extensive areas of earthworks. There, it can be shown that it is impossible to understand the plans of present-day villages without reference to the abandoned roads and former areas of farms and cottages which remain as earthworks. Examples are numerous, but Naseby has both extensive earthworks and an early map of 1630 showing the layout of the village at that date; as Christopher Taylor remarks in the RCHM Volume III for Northamptonshire, 'the extensive earthworks show clearly that the relatively simple layout of the present village is the result of complex changes which are by no means understood'.

At Stallingborough in Lincolnshire, Paul Everson has recorded vast areas of earthworks, including some from air photographs which are now destroyed. This survey shows that the present lanes and cottages are only the remnants of an extensive settlement occupying at least 28 hectares (70 acres).

There is a great need to study the context of such deserted or shrunken settlements, since it is only when a region is studied in its entirety that we can get some idea of the changes which have taken place in settlements and the settlement pattern in the area. In the modern parish of Mudford in Somerset there were formerly eight separate settlements. One of these, Stone, was probably never more than the farm it is today – it is mentioned as such in 1086. All of the others were hamlets, however, with the parish church at Mudford (or Mudford Monachorum), while Nether Adber and Hinton formerly had chapels. Of these seven places, two have completely disappeared – Nether Adber now has only two houses, built in the nineteenth and twentieth centuries, and Mudford Terry has none. West Mudford, Mudford Sock and Up Mudford are severely shrunken with extensive areas of earthworks. Only Mudford itself is reasonably intact.

Because of the clear survival of settlement earthworks and areas of ridge and furrow in this part of Somerset, together with the very good RAF air photographs of 1947, we can see the extent and plan of all these settlements. They vary in size from a single farm at Stone to the extensive sites at Up Mudford and Nether Adber, and in plan from the irregular Hinton to the regular Mudford Sock and Mudford. There are few indications in the documents as to when and why each of the settlements was affected, but at least in the sixteenth century we know that there was a shortage of land to provide food to feed everyone. The lands of the

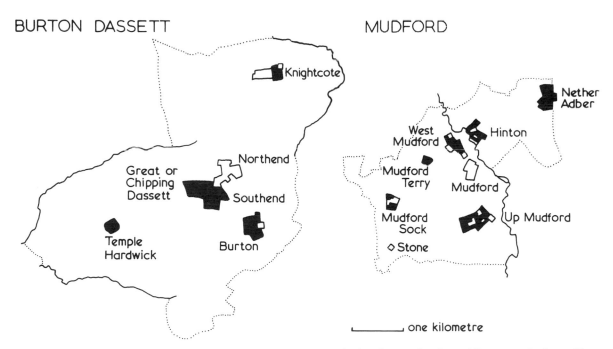

BURTON DASSETT

MUDFORD

Knightcote

Nether Adber

Northend

West Mudford

Hinton

Great or Chipping Dassett

Southend

Mudford Terry

Mudford

Temple Hardwick

Burton

Mudford Sock

Up Mudford

◇ Stone

one kilometre

29 *Burton Dassett in Warwickshire and Mudford in Somerset. These maps show both the number of settlements in each parish and the amount of desertion and shrinkage. Some sites have disappeared completely, others are shrunken, while some survive intact. (Burton Dassett after C. J. Bond)*

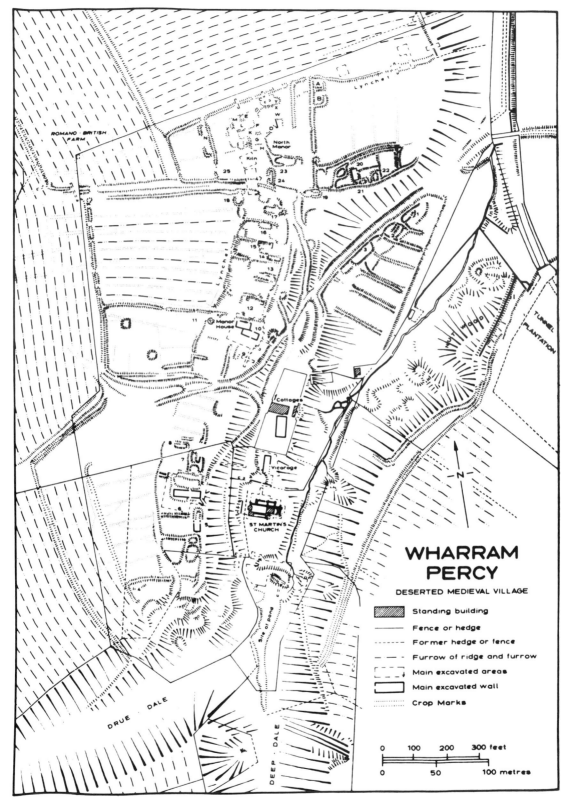

30 *Wharram Percy deserted village in Yorkshire. The complex earthworks of a deserted settlement which have been the subject of a long campaign of excavations. (By permission of the Medieval Village Research Group)*

lord of the manor at Hinton were reallocated to the peasants in the sixteenth century, and the manor house, now remaining as a moated site, was abandoned. Here, and at Mudford, the peasants decided in the sixteenth century to enclose the open fields and reallocate land, but there is no dramatic single or well-documented event to explain the picture we can see in the landscape today.

At Burton Dassett in Warwickshire a similar picture can be built up (*Fig. 29*). Of five former settlements, only Knightcote and Dassett Northend survive as villages. Burton, which has the large medieval church, is a very small hamlet; Temple Hardwick has been 'recolonised' by an army depot; Dassett Southend has a farm, a ruined medieval chapel of St James, and a priest's house, and is now threatened by the construction of the M42 motorway. There are extensive earthworks at Dassett Southend indicating an important market settlement in the fourteenth century, and further earthworks at Burton. In the fifteenth century there were some evictions in the parish ordered by Sir Edward Belknap, but the overall story, as worked out by James Bond, is very complex and no single reason can be found to explain what can be seen in the landscape.

These two examples show just how complex have been the changes affecting villages in the landscape in the past. In most cases, such changes are poorly documented, if they are recorded at all. Yet in order to understand the present pattern and appearance of settlements, allowance has to be made for varying degrees of change occurring in the past. Complexity and change are the predominant factors in the English landscape; the above examples are not exceptional and similar instances can be found in all the English counties.

WHARRAM PERCY

The work over the last 30 years at Wharram Percy in the East Riding of Yorkshire demonstrates how much can be learnt from consistent detailed research on one site about the development of the English landscape and of a site in its local setting. It is increasingly likely that many of the lessons learnt at Wharram Percy apply to settlements elsewhere in the country. It is important, therefore, that the implications of the work there are fully understood, though we must be careful not to assume as much for every settlement we study.

Wharram Percy lies in the Yorkshire Wolds in a dry valley near Malton. It was mentioned in *Domesday Book*, badly affected by the Black Death in 1350, and depopulated in the fifteenth century. The earthworks of the village have always been known: they were recorded by the Ordnance Survey surveyors in the nineteenth century and then re-discovered by Maurice

Beresford in the late 1940s. In the 1950s, he and John Hurst began excavations on the site and these have continued ever since. The work at Wharram Percy reflects the development of medieval rural settlement studies in England and our understanding of the implications of the development of the landscape over the last 30 years.

The aim initially was to examine medieval peasant houses and to obtain some archaeological information for the date of desertion. Later, the church was excavated and more recently the mill, fishpond, manor sites and boundaries have all been examined. Work is now proceeding on the fields and the prehistoric and Roman background. It was realised at an early stage that the earthwork plan belied a very complex situation and that there were clearly at least two phases of development. The church occupies an interesting site in relation to the rest of the village, and the manor sites can now also be seen to be very complex.

After more than 30 years' work at Wharram Percy, it is possible to give a general account of what happened on the site, and, in view of the detailed work there, this may have implications for studies elsewhere. The earliest excavation showed the typical plan of peasant dwellings – *longhouses* – with cattle in one end and people in the other. These are found generally over England in the Middle Ages, although surviving examples are now found only in Wales and the West Country. No doubt most settlements had longhouses in the early Middle Ages. At Wharram Percy they had been rebuilt of perishable materials – wood, wattle, turf – in almost every generation, only later having substantial foundations. Different alignments were adopted in a very irregular fashion. The plot boundaries defining the crofts on which these houses stood also changed, although the early impression of great change and lack of order has now been revised to one of combination and division of consistent units. The earliest area of crofts may have been situated on a bluff west of the church, while an extended area was later laid out to the north around a triangular green, with an earlier Norman manor house going out of use at the same time. It is likely that the whole village was deliberately planned, possibly with a revitalised field system, since *solskifte*, a regulated field system, has now been traced at Wharram Percy. The date when this would have occurred is not known, but it was probably in the late Saxon or early medieval period.

The northern manor house was formerly thought to be secondary to the Norman one, but it now seems that they were originally a pair. The church began in late Saxon times and developed over a long period, finally being made redundant in the 1960s, when part of it collapsed. Its site has not altered and the chancel arch (the division between the parishioners' area [the nave] and the rector's area [the chancel]) has remained in the

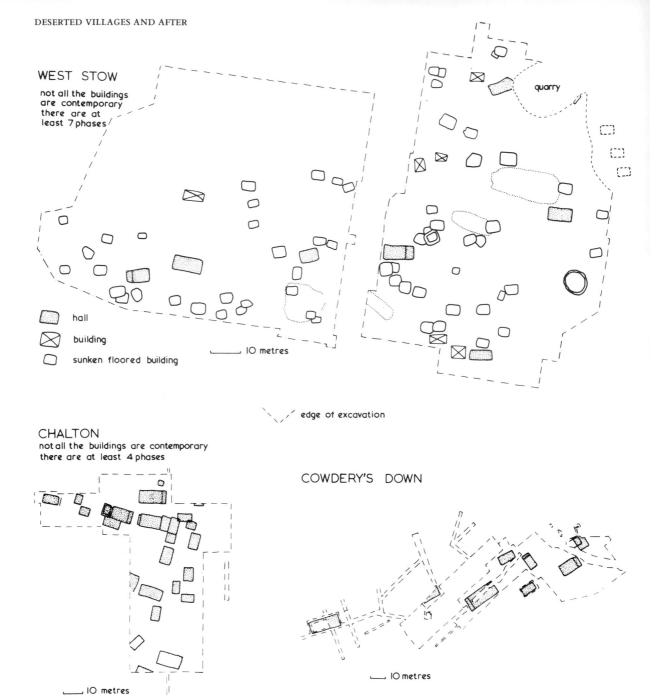

WEST STOW

not all the buildings
are contemporary
there are at
least 7 phases

quarry

☐ hall

⊠ building

▢ sunken floored building

⌐⌐⌐⌐ 10 metres

⌐ edge of excavation

CHALTON
not all the buildings are contemporary
there are at least 4 phases

COWDERY'S DOWN

⌐⌐⌐⌐ 10 metres

⌐⌐⌐⌐ 10 metres

31 Plans of Anglo-Saxon settlements: West Stow in Suffolk, Chalton and Cowdery's Down in Hampshire. These plans show recent excavations of Anglo-Saxon settlements abandoned before the medieval period. Not all the structures are contemporary, so that at each phase there would have been only a small group of buildings – more like farmsteads or hamlets than villages (By permission of Stanley West, Tim Champion and Martin Millett)

same position for 1000 years or more, notwithstanding additions, alterations, and demolitions.

Many of the boundaries surrounding the village earthworks have been sectioned, and surprisingly some have turned out to be of prehistoric and Roman date. It is thus apparent, as has been indicated elsewhere, that not all of the earthworks are contemporary with one another; indeed, the basic outline of the settlement seems to have been determined by land divisions laid down several thousand years previously. How much more of the landscape possesses this ancient framework? We have already seen how persistent early

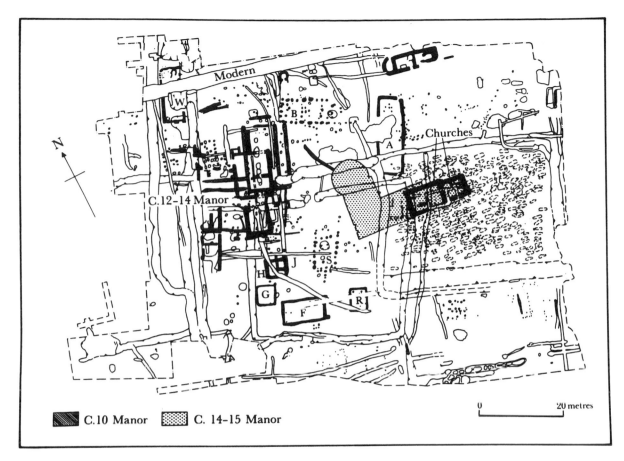

C.10 Manor   C. 14-15 Manor

C.12-14 Manor

Modern

Churches

N

0   20 metres

32 *Furnells, Raunds in Northamptonshire. This composite plan shows all the features revealed in the recent campaign of excavations. These date from the sixth to the fifteenth centuries; there are also prehistoric and Roman features. There is no evidence that this settlement was ever a village – it is really a complex of manor houses with ancillary buildings. The churches, one on top of another, with* *their cemeteries, date from the tenth to twelfth century. They were attached to manors, which are labelled, and were succeeded by another in the fourteenth and fifteenth centuries. (By permission of Alan Hannan and Northamptonshire County Council Archaeology Unit)*

boundary features can be, but perhaps we have underestimated the extent of these earlier divisions. Cropmarks and pottery scatters of the prehistoric and Romano-British settlements contemporary with these early land divisions have been located at several points within the later village complex at Wharram Percy: each appears to represent a farmstead site.

This latter point is an important consideration, because the earliest 'village' of Wharram Percy has proved very elusive. Not only can no prehistoric or Roman nucleated settlement be found, but Saxon settlement in the area seems to have consisted of a scatter of farms (vills or manors) with an isolated church between them. This may have been the situation at the time of *Domesday Book*, and it may be that a nucleated village was not established until late Saxon times or the twelfth century. This nucleated settlement, the crofts west of the church and the

northern extension, seems to have been deliberately planned, since the widths and lengths of the crofts are very consistent, with continuous front and rear property lines. This arrangement continued until the desertion of the village in the fifteenth century, when the settlement pattern reverted to its former arrangement of isolated individual farms.

It can be seen, therefore, that there has been a nucleated village at Wharram Percy for only 400 years or so out of at least 2000 years, and that, in effect, the village as a form of settlement was an aberration, the single farm being the normal settlement from which the land was worked. It is also likely that the common open field system in use in the Middle Ages was only in use during the lifetime of the nucleated village; this will be discussed elsewhere.

The implications of the work at Wharram Percy are of enormous interest for our understanding of how settlements and the landscape developed. Is such evidence available anywhere else and is it possible to suggest a general model of settlement development which may apply to local studies elsewhere in the country? There have been excavations on other sites, but these have added further complications. One surprise has been the lack of Saxon settlements beneath the medieval villages which have been excavated. Indeed, although many settlements of the pagan Saxon period and a few of the middle and late Saxon periods have been excavated, they are in general not directly associated with 'modern' villages. Neither do they have the sort of plans and features which accord with our earlier ideas of what a Saxon village should look like.

At West Stow, for example, the settlement was established in the early Saxon period and abandoned in the seventh or eighth century. It consisted of a line of timber post-built 'halls' and numerous sunken-floored buildings; there is no formal plan and little can be seen of streets or boundaries. At contemporary Mucking, two Saxon cemeteries were found to accompany a widely dispersed scatter of sunken-floored buildings – the same situation occurred at Eynsham in Oxford-shire. At Chalton in Hampshire and Cowdery's Down near Basingstoke, the buildings were more regularly laid out but not extensive enough to be called villages, while at Catholme in Staffordshire and Thirlings in Northumberland, the earlier settlements had not only been abandoned, but probably forgotten when areas of ridge and furrow were laid out over the top.

None of these sites had the classic village green and plan which we expected, and all were found by accident in open country, away from medieval settle-ments. In many parts of the country there has clearly been a shift of settlement in Saxon times and the implication of this is that a number of Saxon settle-ments remain to be found, away from the medieval villages, in what are former open field areas. The local fieldworker needs to give serious consideration to this if he attempts to explain the pre-medieval settlements in his area. Sometimes field names can help, particu-larly where they have habitative elements within them, such as -tun endings. William Ford cites examples of field names with the elements -worth, -thorp, -cote and -tun in Warwickshire. He suggests that Cley-hemsugworth in Farnborough, Weresworth in Tan-worth and Bosseworth in Warwick were all former settlements. Elsewhere in Warwickshire excavation of fields named Norton and Ditchingworth (in Brailes) and Baldicote (in Tredington) revealed evidence of early occupation. This method would probably pro-vide a fruitful line of enquiry elsewhere.

The example of Raunds in Northamptonshire demonstrates other difficulties. This is a large village with earthworks on the periphery which were ex-cavated initially by David Hall in advance of re-development for houses. The first trench revealed a late Saxon grave slab in the cemetery of an undocumented Saxon church. Later excavations have shown a long sequence of development from a late Saxon farm or manorial complex with two phases of churches, to a medieval manor house. What appeared to be merely an area of shrinkage on the edge of the village has, therefore, turned out to be very important in the history of settlement in the area – a small independent hamlet with its own church which was eventually abandoned. Another small manor lies nearby and there is still a church in the village. It is not known whether these were contemporary and whether the settlement of this area was in the form of hamlets before the village was created. The implications of these develop-ments will be discussed in the next two chapters.

6

Surviving villages

Now that we have looked at Wharram Percy deserted village and seen something of the 30-year long excavations there, we should look at other studies and excavations on village sites which seem to suggest the same developments implied at Wharram Percy. In this chapter we shall look at such topics as village planning and regulation, the origins of villages, polyfocal villages, and whether pre-village elements can be distinguished.

PLANNED VILLAGES

The idea that villages might have been planned, or at least regulated in their growth, is a relatively new one. Towns, which have been more intensively studied and for which there is generally more documentary and cartographic information, were thought to be organic or haphazard creations until recently. Exceptions were

known, of course, like Salisbury, Winchelsea and Ludlow, where deliberately created towns were well documented and where the regular gridiron street pattern suggested town planning. In 1967 Maurice Beresford published *New Towns of the Middle Ages* and established beyond reasonable doubt that large numbers, certainly hundreds, of towns had been created *de novo* in the early Middle Ages on green field sites or next to existing villages.

Professor Conzen has shown us how to analyse town plans to reconstruct their phases of development and discrete planned units. From this work the idea that the physical arrangement of an urban settlement reflects planning has now been accepted. It is but a short step to relate the same topographical analysis to village plans and to suggest, from their regularity and consistency, that they may also have been planned. In many cases, the plans of known planned towns are no different in

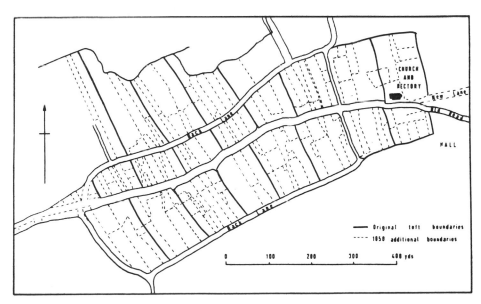

33 *Wheldrake in Yorkshire. Plan of the 16 original units making up the early medieval planned village. (By permission of June Sheppard)*

extent, size or arrangement from those of the most regular villages. The difference between towns and villages was one of status, with the town having particular privileges, but 'There is no extant documentary record that explicitly describes the establishment of even one regular village plan ...' (Sheppard 1976). Some villages are, however, failed planned medieval towns, as is evident in their layout, areas of earthworks and documentary references.

June Sheppard was probably the first to draw attention to a planned village. In 1966, in her study of Wheldrake, outside York, she drew attention to the regular nature of the village. She showed that the plan must be earlier than 1300, when a new road was added to it. Looking in detail at the fiscal assessment of the settlement around 1200, she came to the conclusion that the village was originally planned between 1066 and 1086, when it consisted of 16 crofts, eight on each side of the village street.

field system of three fields also replaced the infield/outfield system.

Pamela Allerston came to the conclusion that there was good evidence in Yorkshire for village planning, and suggested the period from 1070 to the end of the thirteenth century for the origin of many villages. In some cases she suggested that there had been coalescence of settlements, with the abandonment of the earlier pattern of hamlets and combining of lands and holdings. From this she deduced that the earlier arrangements had been of hamlets with infields, but, following growth in population, settlements had been replanned on new sites with the coalescence of population and lands.

In Durham, Brian Roberts has been studying village plans and has now extended his research to other northern counties, as well as looking at England's village plans generally. For the north, he finds evidence of village planning by c.1200 on well-documented

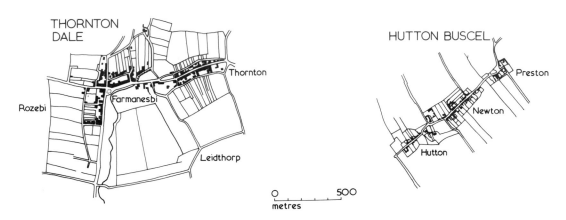

34 *Thornton Dale and Hutton Buscel in Yorkshire. Two villages made up of individual hamlets, each separately named. Pamela Allerston's research suggests many villages developing from hamlets in the twelfth century. The hamlets are recorded in Domesday Book in 1086. (After Pamela Allerston, with permission)*

The idea of planned Norman villages was found difficult to accept by scholars at that time, but since then further evidence has been found, particularly in the north of England. In 1970, Pamela Allerston, for example, looked at villages in the Vale of Pickering and was able to show that some with very regular plans had come into existence in the early Middle Ages and replaced an earlier arrangement of scattered hamlets. Thus, at Appleton le Moors the very regular two rows of the village were there by the fourteenth century, replacing the two earlier settlements of Appleton and Baschebi. At Spaunton the regular two-row village had originated by the thirteenth century, replacing a hamlet 450 metres (490 yards) away which was remembered in the field names 'old field' and 'tofts'. A new

estates like those of the Bishop of Durham. Often these villages have two rows with square or rectangular village greens, and the regular plan of the crofts is related to early fiscal arrangements in the townships.

When and why were so many northern villages planned? Again, the research of June Sheppard in Yorkshire suggests something of the timing and the occasion of village planning in that area. She looked at 100 village plans and assessed them as regular or partly regular. One opportunity for village planning in the north of England followed William the Conqueror's 'harrying of the North' in the 1060s. Large numbers of vills which are now still in existence are described as 'waste' in *Domesday Book* (1086). June Sheppard did not make a direct correlation between waste vills and regular plans on the basis of the limited evidence available. Rather, there is the strong suggestion that the replanning took place on the sites with higher status owners, such as abbots and the Archbishop of York.

The next likely period for the initiation of planned villages would be the eleventh to mid twelfth cen-

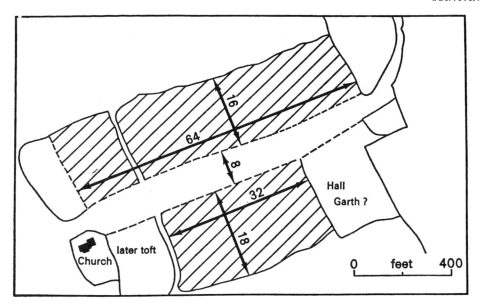

Hall

Garth ?

later toft

Church

0   feet   400

35 *Thornton le Beans in Yorkshire. June Sheppard's plan indicating the early measurement used, probably the 18-ft (5.5-m) perch, to lay out the crofts in the village. The number of perches used is indicated. This planning probably took place in the late eleventh or twelfth century. (By permission of June Sheppard)*

turies, as demonstrated by June Sheppard when she looked at village plans in relation to early fiscal arrangements. Discussing the use of the 18-foot (5.5-metre) perch for measuring plots, the fiscal assessment in *Domesday Book* and the 1284 Kirby's Quest knights' fees, she examined in detail the plans of Hemingborough, Thornton le Beans and Upper Poppleton, and showed that the plans of these and other villages seem to be related to early feudal arrangements. Brian Roberts argues a similar case for village planning in Durham. There, 66 per cent of villages have regular plans, with their crofts aligned in rows. Most seem to have developed between 1130 and 1200, but on some estates the process must have been complete by 1183 when the *Bolden Book* was compiled. Only one regular planned village has been excavated (Thrislington in County Durham, by David Austin) and this showed archaeologically that the plan was earlier than 1200.

The evidence, then, indicates village planning in the north from the early Middle Ages. Although Maurice Beresford suggests a late thirteenth-/early fourteenth-century date for East Whitton, in Yorkshire, and excavations generally have shown regular plans replacing less regular layouts in the thirteenth and fourteenth centuries (see, for example, Wawne in Yorkshire and Holworth in Dorset), the favoured period is the eleventh to thirteenth centuries. Other possible reasons for this will be discussed below, but in 1976 June Sheppard suggested that we need to pay more attention to the correlation between land tenure and social

structure in the feudal system of these settlements, since there seems to be some relationship between ownership, devastation in 1069–70, and new planning in the north. 'It seems feasible therefore that subinfeudated and honorial vills may have differed in village planning policies ... suggesting that it was under honorial administration that they [regular village plans] were most likely to be established.' In other words, not for the first time, it was the estate policies pursued by a particular landowner which produced the northern village plans.

What about village plans in the Midlands and south of England? There are very many villages with regular rectilinear plans, and we should perhaps now regard these as planned villages, even if we are ignorant of when the planning took place. Large numbers of villages, however, have very complex plans which at first sight defy description and explanation, both on the ground and on the maps. We can see two major aspects in them – firstly, their complexity. Brian Roberts, in his analysis of village plans, has drawn attention to the range of village types and attempted to classify them according to their plan units. Thus, we have basic shapes of agglomerations and rows, the degree of regularity, presence or absence of greens, and composite or polyfocal plans. Many villages have several of these elements.

These different units and elements have led Christopher Taylor to suggest that many of our villages are polyfocal, that is, they have a number of discrete centres within them which are joined (or separated) by other properties, open spaces, or abandoned crofts. Thus, a settlement might have a church, a manor house, a village green, road junction, and/or pond as foci. Classic examples can be found at Wollaston in Northamptonshire and Fenny Compton

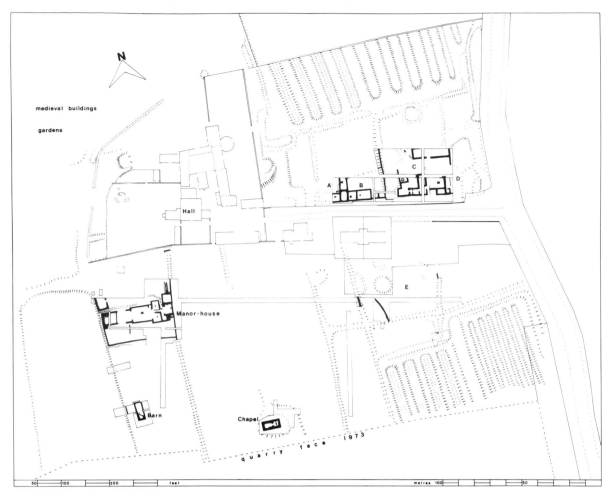

36 *Thrislington village in County Durham. This example of a planned northern village, which later became deserted, has been partially excavated by Dave Austin. His work revealed the manor house and chapel and some of the farmsteads. These and the* earthworks *show regular plots along the street with village boundary bank and ridge and furrow beyond. (By permission of David Austin)*

in Warwickshire. In fact, very large numbers of villages have this sort of plan, and the idea of polyfocal centres in villages has proved a useful concept in village plan analysis.

Marston Magna in Somerset provides a useful example of some of the ideas which can be generated by this method. The plan and air photograph show that the village consists of two main units. These can be seen on the modern OS maps and the tithe map, and they can be picked out on the ground from changes in level and property boundaries. The first unit is centred on St Mary's church and consists of a large rectangle, aligned north-south, east-west. Except in the south-east corner, the properties in this unit are at right angles to the north-south road, and the overall rectilinear arrangement of the plan is clear. A stream flows westwards across the centre of the unit, and this is

followed rather irregularly on its north side by the road from Corton Denham to Little Marston. The southern part of this unit is occupied by the fine earthworks of a moated manor site in a field called Court Garden, seventeenth-century houses, one of which is a former manor house, and Marston House, the nineteenth-century successor. This unit is separated from the fields of ridge and furrow all around the village by a break of slope or change of level of 1 metre (39 in) or more in height. On the south side is a prominent boundary bank, next to the moat.

The second unit encroaches on the southeast corner of the first and consists of a slightly raised rectilinear platform with rounded corners, aligned on the east-west road but at a different angle to the first unit. Marston water mill occupies the north-west corner of this second unit, and its leat flows along the western

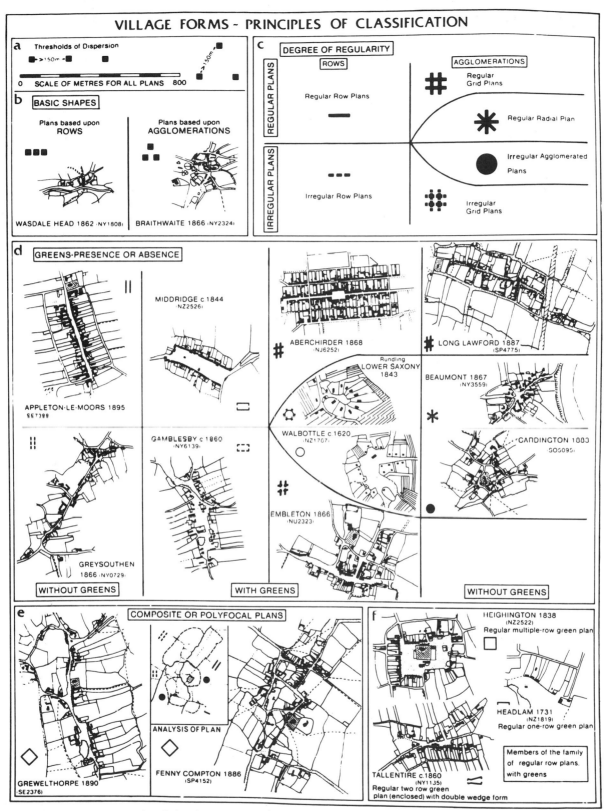

37 *Village forms – principles of classification. Brian Roberts' scheme for village plan classification is based on basic shapes, degree of regularity, and presence or absence of a green. Polyfocal plans are* *shown to consist of several basic forms. (By permission of Brian Roberts)*

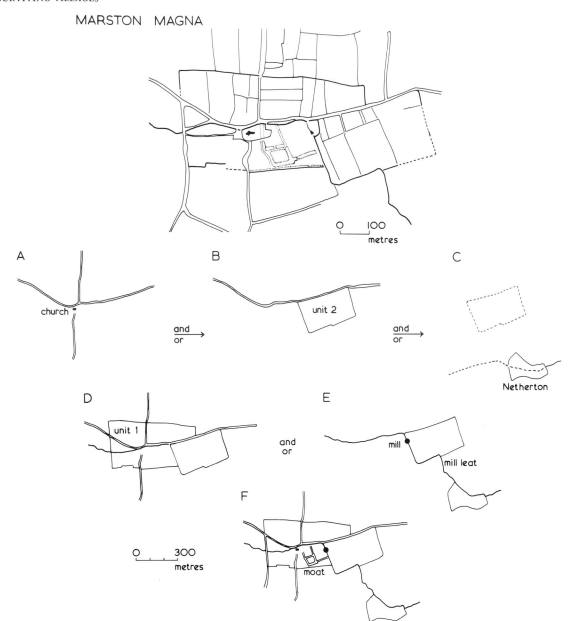

MARSTON MAGNA

church

A

B

unit 2

and
or

C

Netherton

and
or

D

unit 1

E

mill

mill leat

and
or

F

moat

O   100
metres

O   300
metres

38 *Marston Magna in Somerset: village plan analysis. This preliminary analysis of the plan of the village suggests that it may have originated as a series of enclosures. Such examination owes a lot to town plan analysis as developed by Professor Conzen, and indicates all sorts of possibilities to be examined in future research.*

half of the south side and the west side. Properties within this unit are long and rectangular and there are traces of ridge and furrow in them.

Marston Magna lies in a flat lias clay area of south Somerset, and its name suggests marshy surroundings. The stream crossing the village enters the parish from Rimpton to the east and is immediately diverted from its meandering course into an embanked channel

which runs across country to the mill mentioned above. The area to the west of this stream diversion is poorly drained, embanked today, but contains the earthworks of the deserted settlement of Netherton.

What can we make of this pattern and can we suggest dates for the elements within it? The church of St Mary contains good evidence for a Saxo-Norman building, including two Saxon windowheads (not *in situ*) and herring-bone masonry punctured by Norman windows. It was clearly there by the eleventh century, and stands aligned on the stream and road and the alignments of the first unit. We can guess at the relative dating of the units, but unit one makes most sense as a secondary feature, since it seems to be butted on to unit

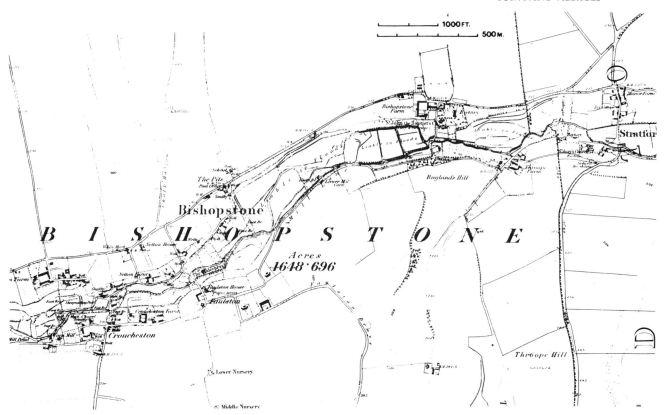

39 *The settlements in Bishopstone, near Salisbury in Wiltshire. This early 6 inch to 1 mile map by the Ordnance Survey shows the six settlements in Bishopstone parish. Each was formerly a separate hamlet with its own fields and some had their own church or chapel.* *They are* (left to right, top to bottom) *Flamston, Netton, Bishopstone, Croucheston, Faulston and Throope. Bishopstone and Faulston have extensive areas of shrunken village earthworks. (Reproduced from the 1886–88 Ordnance Survey Maps)*

two, with banks overlaid south of the mill. If unit one is earlier, we would need to postulate the complete removal of any earthworks in the north-west corner of unit two, although this could have happened.

The mill site and its supply leat must surely have been constructed on the outline of unit two – the course of the leat would be strange if it was earlier and had conditioned the shape of unit two. It would have been difficult to develop Netherton as a settlement before the building of the mill leat enabled the draining of the stream from its marshy site. It would thus seem that unit two pre-dates unit one and that the mill was laid out after unit two. Netherton was probably developed later (it is first recorded in 1327). The date of unit one might be eleventh-century at least, so how much earlier is unit two?

The moated site and its fishponds also offer interesting problems. Although the complex is situated in unit one, its alignment relates to unit two, and thus the earthworks in their present form (but not necessarily the house they enclose) should date from the same period as unit two. The digging of the moats on this alignment caused problems, since the earthworks on the south-west corner became tangled with the bound-ary bank of unit one. This type of analysis and the problems revealed provide useful lines of enquiry towards unravelling the complexity of how village plans have developed and at what periods.

The second important feature about surviving villages and their plans is the factor of change. The English landscape is constantly developing and altering, and villages are no exception. It is clearly important to establish what the earliest plan of a village was, since there have often been many post-medieval changes. Old maps help, especially if they go back to the sixteenth or seventeenth centuries, and surveys of earthworks can also show early elements. In Cambridgeshire, Jack Ravensdale has been able to show from documentary references how the village plans of Cottenham, Landbeach and Waterbeach have changed and developed over the centuries. Some roads have been lost, whilst others have been created or moved, and features previously thought stable, like village greens, can be shown to be recent additions to some plans. A similar analysis has been made for Kibworth Harcourt in Leicestershire.

Change is also implicit in the idea of polyfocal villages, since the suggestion is that such plans are

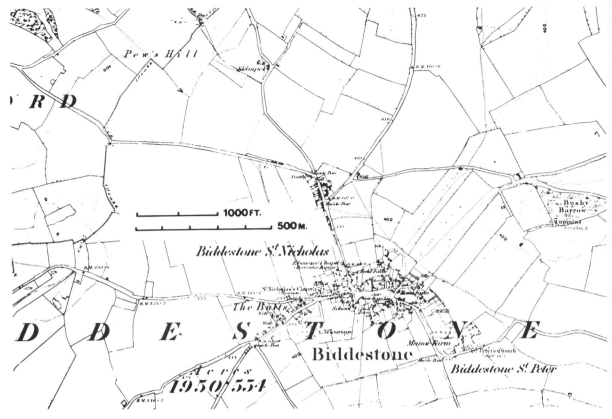

40 *Biddestone village in Wiltshire. This settlement appears to be the 'classic' English village with green, duck pond, manor house and church. It is built of Cotswold stone. Closer examination, however, suggests that it originally consisted of two hamlets, each with a manor house and a church, with an open common between.*

Biddestone St Peter retains its manor but has lost its church – part of it was taken to nearby Castle Combe. Biddestone St Nicholas has become the village church. (Reproduced from the 1889 Ordnance Survey Map)

produced by filling in properties between existing or earlier centres. The idea again emerges of dispersed farms or hamlets around which villages grow. Some of these centres clearly had separate names at one time and some must have had their own churches. In Yorkshire, for example, Thornton Dale is composed of the hamlets of Formanby, Rozeby, Thornton, and the lost Leidthorp; and Hutton Buscel consists of Hutton, Newton, and Preston (*Fig. 34*). In Northamptonshire and Warwickshire, the separate hamlet names are often not evident, but the suffix -end may be added to different parts of the village. Elsewhere, the suffix -tun indicates in the place name the former existence of a farm or hamlet.

Some of the most spectacular examples can be found in Wiltshire, where not only do the names of separate elements remain or can be relatively easily traced, but frequently the individual churches attached to each hamlet are still in existence, or were until recently. In the Ebble valley near Salisbury, for example, the parish of Bishopstone has two main centres. One, around the parish church, was Bishopstone proper (with

Throope), but the agglomeration of buildings 1 kilometre ($\frac{1}{2}$ mile) away to the west consisted of four separate settlements. Only Croucheston and Faulston are now named (the others were Flamston and Netton), but at least two of them had their own medieval chapels. There were thus originally six separate hamlets in this stretch of the valley. Nearby, Bower Chalke is similar, and so is Broad Chalke, with hamlets called Gurston, Knapp, possibly Middleton, and several unnamed elements.

Some Wiltshire villages have several surviving or known church sites attached to former hamlets. The attractive village of Biddestone, for example, which at first sight consists of a village green, church and sixteenth- to seventeenth-century buildings – almost the classic village – can be shown on analysis to consist of two elements, each with a manor and church, between which the green developed. The western hamlet has survived with the present parish church of St Nicholas. A manor house remains of the eastern hamlet, but the church of St Peter has been demolished; part of it remains in the grounds of Castle Combe

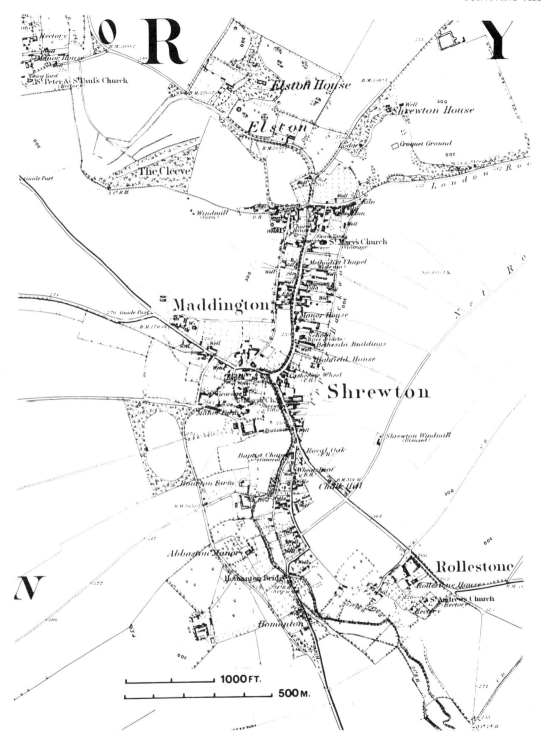

41 *Map of the Shrewton settlements in Wiltshire. Shrewton, between Devizes and Salisbury, is now thought of as one large village. Originally, however, it consisted of eight hamlets which have had varying fortunes. Elston is deserted and has lost its church; Shrewton and Maddington survive with regular, probably planned, layouts and churches; Bourton and Abbaston have gone; Homanton and Rollestone (with a redundant church) are severely shrunken, and Netton (unlabelled, west of Chalk Hill) has been resettled with modern housing. This is a very good example of a polyfocal village and shows how a collection of hamlets can agglomerate into a large complex village. (Reproduced from the 1889 Ordnance Survey Map)*

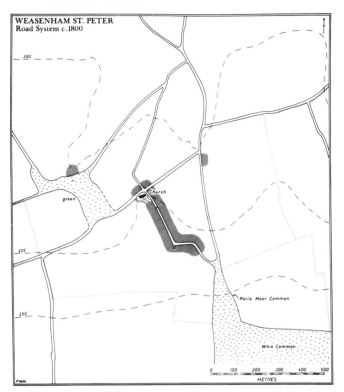

42 *Maps of Weasenham St Peter in Norfolk. Dr Peter Wade-Martins' fieldwork and research into early maps has demonstrated that the settlement area in Saxon times was nucleated around the church. It was only in late medieval and later times that the settlement around a former common developed, giving the misleading impression of an original nucleated 'green' village. (After Peter Wade-Martins, with permission, from* East Anglian Archaeology 10, 1980)

manor house nearby. Several other villages in the county have or had one or more churches. Chitterne formerly had both All Saints and St Mary's, and Alton had St Mary's at Alton Barnes (an Anglo-Saxon church) and All Saints at Alton Priors. There are other examples elsewhere, such as Swaffham Priors and Burwell in Cambridgeshire.

Perhaps the most spectacular example of a polyfocal village anywhere in England is Shrewton in Wiltshire, where the individual hamlets can be seen with their churches, both extant and lost. What appears to be one village (and is marked as such on modern maps and on the road signs) can in fact be seen to consist of no less than eight separate hamlets – Elston (largely deserted, with a former chapel), Shrewton (from which the village has taken its name), Maddington, Netton, Rollestone (largely deserted with a redundant church), Homanton (deserted), Addestone (deserted) and Bourton (deserted). These hamlets were mostly called Winterbourne in 1086, and distinguished by their separate owners – they were on the probable former royal estate of Winterbourne, possibly centred on Winterbourne Stoke (*Fig. 15*). The -tun element of their place names suggests they were hamlets once, while many of the place names indicate their former

owners: Maddington belonged to the 'maidens', the nuns of Amesbury Abbey; Shrewton to the Sherrif; Addestone to the Abbot of St Peter's, Winchester. Interestingly, some names are of a relatively late date: Elston is 'Elias' (Giffard's) tun' and Rollestone is 'Rolf's tun', both twelfth-century names. Churches remain at Maddington, Shrewton, and Rollestone, while Elston formerly had a chapel which may once have been a church. We can no longer be certain, however, that there were never churches at the other hamlets, especially with the example of Raunds in Northamptonshire before us.

Change and complexity in village plans and settlement development can also be seen in Norfolk from the research of Peter Wade-Martins. Despite the present bleak, prairie-like appearance of much of East Anglia, it has two major advantages for the field archaeologist. There was a well developed and long-lived post-Roman pottery industry in the area (based on St Neots, Stamford and Ipswich) and this means that, because the area is intensively ploughed, scatters of potsherds are revealed on former settlement sites. Using early maps, Peter Wade-Martins has been able to show that the present scattered settlements and small fragmentary villages are merely the remnants of former late Saxon settlements and medieval nucleated villages. The sites and forms of these have constantly been changing, so that often what appears as a nucleated village around a green can be shown to be the last, and a relatively late, development in the landscape. Good examples include Horningtoft and Longham, but Weasenham St Peter shows the same process.

From both deserted village sites and surviving nucleated settlements, a very complex picture of change and development is beginning to emerge. If we ignore the majority of buildings in villages which invariably date to the sixteenth century and later, we are left with settlement plans of bewildering complexity. We must, however, now accept that these plans are developments from the original forms and that great changes may have taken place before we get to the earliest arrangement we can distinguish. Some element of planning and/or deliberate regulation is evident in many settlements, and so we must pay attention to regular croft and property arrangements and consistent front and rear property alignments. Earlier elements in many cases seem to consist of much smaller settlements, either in the form of farmsteads or hamlets. Sometimes, these remain in the landscape or are incorporated into complex village plans; else-

where, they were abandoned in what seems to have been wholescale replanning and resiting of villages. In many cases, these hamlets had churches which had survived to become parish churches, or were demolished, or forgotten, as at Raunds.

In the north we have seen that this village planning may have taken place in the eleventh and twelfth centuries. However, where there are very regular field systems it may have occurred earlier, perhaps in the Scandinavian period. In the rest of the country we cannot be sure of the date, although the evidence begins to suggest some time in the late Saxon period, the centuries before the Norman Conquest. It is thus likely that many (perhaps most) villages are relative latecomers to the English landscape. They are certainly not early Saxon, as was previously thought, but many were in existence by the thirteenth and fourteenth centuries; we can see this from the abundant documentation. It begins to look as if villages, like fields and land units and much else in the landscape, were largely defined in the hazy centuries before the Norman Conquest, developing from complex and distant origins in earlier times. It is to the primeval forms of such settlements, together with concepts of their development, that we must now turn.

7

Farms and hamlets

In the last two chapters we have been looking at deserted and surviving villages. From this has emerged the suggestion that villages were an aberration in the landscape and that, in many cases, hamlets and farmsteads predated the villages and in some way represent a more normal form of settlement. Travelling through England it is at once apparent that a great deal of the settlement in the landscape is today not in the form of villages, nor was it for much of the past. Numerous small groups of farms, isolated farmsteads on their own land, cottages and roadside settlements predominate.

Almost any substantial group of buildings with perhaps a shop, or village hall is today called a village and this leads to great confusion, both for researchers looking at earlier arrangements, and for the inhabitants for whom finer definitions are not needed. For our analysis, however, we need to be able to differentiate between what we call a village and those places which are hamlets. We must recognise that villages in the past were nucleations of farms and cottages, generally in a discrete unit of land, with a separate field system, managed communally so that all farmers and land-holders were interdependent on each other. An important factor also was the village's ecclesiastical independence, with its own church, generally medieval.

A definition as strict as this, as we have already seen, means that many deserted medieval 'villages' were never really villages at all. Similarly, most villages today do not qualify by these standards – most are suburban or retirement centres, not more than half a dozen practise communal agriculture, and most do not even have working farms in them. Yet the definition is useful in drawing our attention to those agglomerations of more recent origin, those which have become important in post-medieval times, acquiring a church and a separate status, and the large numbers of hamlets which have never had any particular distinguishing features about them. We must now look at these hamlets: when they originated, how they developed and how they managed the landscape.

THE ORIGINS OF HAMLETS

The earlier model for settlement development was based on the idea of a lot of villages established by Anglo-Saxon settlers clearing the land and creating open, common fields. To a large extent this was based on an assumed chronology of place-name development with the earliest names generally ending in -ton. Large numbers of these settlements were listed in 1086 in *Domesday Book* and it was assumed, therefore, that they represented the primary Saxon settlement over much of England. Hamlets and farmsteads within the parishes of these villages were generally not documented before the twelfth or thirteenth centuries and were therefore assumed to be secondary or daughter settlements created as the population expanded, more land was cleared and farmed, and new settlements were needed.

We have already seen how this model can be seriously questioned on many points. The chronology of place-name developments was rejected by place-name scholars after seminal research by John McNeal Dodgson in 1966 and, to the extent that it has been replaced at all, place names are now seen to represent the hierarchical status of places in the landscape with no particular significance attached to when they are first recorded. The chronology of settlement development based on documents is wide open to misinterpretation, since it relies entirely on the vagaries of documents surviving and the place under discussion being important enough to be mentioned. We have already seen that many of the most important and significant developments in settlements took place before documents were generally available.

Archaeological and landscape studies have also shown the antiquity of many of the assumed secondary hamlets. In Yorkshire, Pamela Allerston showed that some villages were replacements of earlier hamlets and others were agglomerations of pre-existing centres (*Fig. 34*). In the south, Christopher Taylor, David Hall

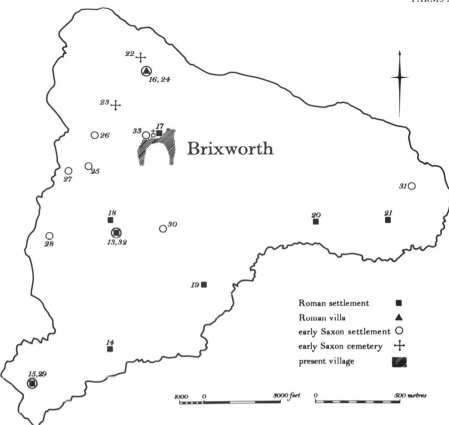

43 *Brixworth in Northamptonshire. The present nucleated village was preceeded by dispersed farmsteads in Roman and early Saxon times. These sites are indicated by scatters of pottery in ploughed fields. (Crown copyright: reproduced by permission of Royal Commission on Historical Monuments (England))*

and others have shown that in pre-Roman, Roman and Anglo-Saxon times, the landscape was densely packed with dispersed settlements. These may have been farmsteads or hamlets, but they were certainly not large or extensive enough to be villages, whatever their status or internal arrangements. Villages developed later, either as deliberate creations or as agglomerations of hamlets.

We have seen how many of the excavations of medieval settlements have revealed no Saxon settlements beneath, and that most of the Anglo-Saxon settlements, despite the title used in excavation reports, are not villages but rather more like hamlets (*Fig. 31*). Excavations elsewhere have demonstrated that in pre-Norman times small hamlets and farmsteads were widespread, occupying even the most inhospitable upland sites. Examples include Mawgan Porth in Cornwall, Ribblehead in Yorkshire, and Simy Folds in Durham. In many parts of the country, but particularly in the west, hamlets and farmsteads are the normal settlement pattern today, with the few villages

mostly of post-medieval development. Often churches are isolated, serving widely scattered farmsteads. In early ethnic models of settlement origin it was assumed that this was a Celtic pattern of settlement, but could it be that this pattern in fact represents the oldest arrangements in the landscape?

Some years ago, W. G. Hoskins argued that the *Domesday Book* entries for Devon referred to hamlets and farmsteads rather than villages, and that any particular vill comprised a whole series of villein farms. In Somerset, Roger Leech has shown that there was a Romano-British settlement about every 1 kilometre ($\frac{1}{2}$ mile) across the landscape. This is particularly evident around Somerton, but can also be seen in the Bath area. Over much of medieval Somerset, to judge from the documents, the pattern was similar, leading Roger Leech to suggest that much of the settlement pattern in the county is a survival from Roman times. Indeed, using archaeological and documentary evidence, it can be postulated that, in parts of west Somerset in particular, present-day settlements are the successors to prehistoric and Romano-British predecessors, even if not actually on the same site. North of Dunkery Beacon, for example, the well-preserved ringwork of Sweetworthy is next to the abandoned medieval farm site – and possibly the Saxon predecessor which gives us the -worth element in Sweetworthy. As a result of a

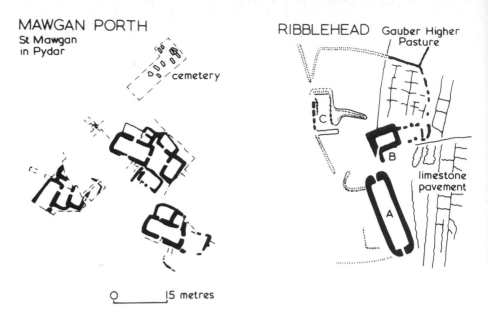

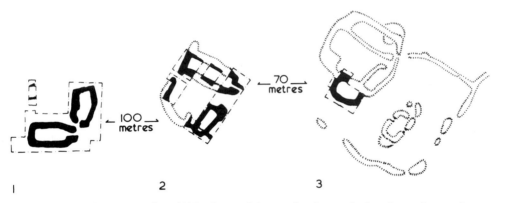

44 *Mawgan Porth in Cornwall, Ribblehead in Yorkshire, and Simy Folds in Durham. The excavation of these sites has shown that farmsteads and hamlets, often in inhospitable upland situations, were in existence by the eighth, ninth and tenth centuries. (By permission of Rupert Bruce-Mitford, A. King, Denis Coggins and others)*

superb air photograph by John White, the nearby deserted Domesday site of Bagley can now be seen to have a ringwork adjacent to it. Here, and elsewhere in the south-west, the pattern of farmsteads today reflects the earlier pattern of dispersed settlement.

In both Devon and Somerset it is possible to show that some of the surviving medieval farmsteads represent former hamlets. Harold Fox has shown this in the vast upland parish of Hartland, where many farms are the remains of former hamlets, while other hamlets have disappeared completely. In Brompton Regis in Somerset an interesting seventeenth-century document shows us that what are now farmsteads were

formerly hamlets of several separate farmsteads with tenements and cottages.

Are there any examples which clearly show these hamlets to be an early form of settlement? In Devon we can see at least three clear cases. Lettaford in North Bovey parish, consisting of three longhouses with later farm buildings, represents perhaps the best surviving example. One longhouse has survived almost intact and can be leased for holidays from the Landmark Trust; another is disguised, although the former arrangements with cattle at one end and people at the other can still be distinguished; the third has been rebuilt. They stand in a cluster next to a stream around an open space, for which the term 'village green' would be too grand. A later non-conformist chapel is the only relatively recent addition to the hamlet, otherwise it demonstrates Brian Robert's original 'rural nucleated cluster' almost exactly (*Fig. 50*). We do not know, however, how old Lettaford is (the oldest longhouse dates only to the sixteenth century) or what its earlier arrangements were.

45 *Bagley and Sweetworthy, Luccombe in Somerset. Air photograph of two late prehistoric ringworks associated with deserted farmsteads of at least medieval date. Beyond Sweetworthy to the left are further ringworks and earthwork enclosures. Such examples suggest direct continuity of land use, if not actual settlement site, from prehistoric to medieval times in the west. (Copyright West Air Photography, Weston Super Mare, No. 27534)*

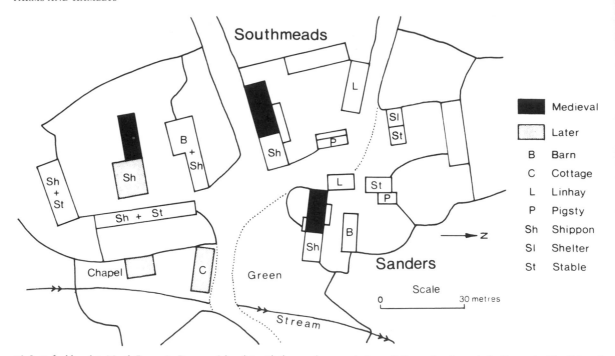

46 *Lettaford hamlet, North Bovey in Devon. A hamlet with three farmsteads, two of which have surviving longhouses. The buildings cluster around an open space (the 'green') by a stream. (Reproduced by permission of Peter Beacham (ed) Devon's Traditional buildings 1978)*

Babeny, near Dartmeet, is a partially deserted example. There were originally three tenements, each with its own longhouse, yard and outbuildings. One has disappeared, but its *ash house* remains; another has been rebuilt and is now the main farm. The third is partly ruined, with the cattle end used as a barn, while at the upper, living end a substantial fireplace, stack and bread oven remain. These farmsteads were on different levels around an open space. There are the remains of a medieval stone-built water mill on the stream below.

Hound Tor is a deserted settlement in Manaton parish, high on the east side of Dartmoor, which was excavated some years ago and has been left open so that visitors can see it. Although called a village, an examination of its plan on the ground shows that it consists in fact of three or four farmsteads, almost identical in their units, among their garden plots. Each unit consists of a large longhouse, a smaller cottage or longhouse, and a barn with a kiln. Excavations suggested that the site was abandoned in the fourteenth century, possibly for climatic reasons, but that it originated in middle Saxon times. It may have begun as a seasonal steading, only later being permanently occupied. Its original turf and timber buildings were eventually replaced by stone ones.

To a very large extent, Hound Tor represents the archetypal hamlet described by Harald Uhlig as representing the original west European type of settlement – what would be called a *drübbel* in Germany or a *clachan* on the Celtic fringes – a hamlet inhabited by relatives, working the land together. We shall see later the suggestion that such hamlets were operating infield/outfield systems before the well-developed common field system of the high Middle Ages was introduced. Hound Tor shows this very clearly, with its infield demarcated by *corn ditches* and endless pasture on the moor beyond.

COLONISATION

If many of the hamlets in the countryside are at least pre-Norman in origin, rather than the homesteads of early medieval peasants colonising the landscape, can we see any evidence for this colonisation, clearance, and the opening up of new areas to cultivation? There was clearly an increase in population from probably the ninth and tenth centuries right through to the troubled fourteenth century, but there are several ways in which extra people can be fed and accommodated on the land. An improvement in technology leading to increased efficiency in food production would have helped, but as yet there seems little evidence for this, unless intensification of field systems to open common fields is a manifestation of this. Increase in individual settlement size, together with greater intensification of land use, would also accommodate more people; perhaps this is why many hamlets grew into villages or why polyfocal villages developed. Thirdly, new land

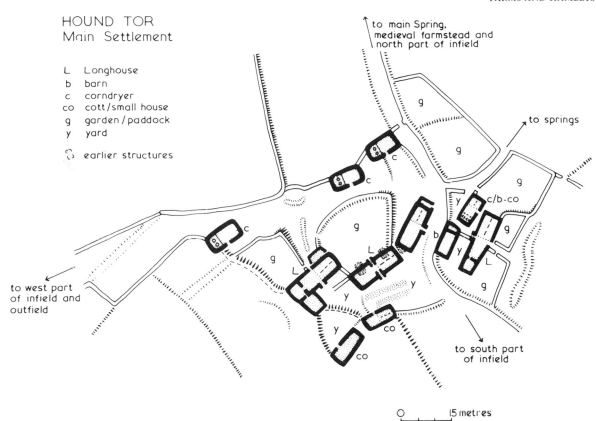

HOUND TOR
Main Settlement

L Longhouse
b barn
c corndryer
co cott/small house
g garden/paddock
y yard

⌒ earlier structures

to main Spring,
medieval farmstead and
north part of infield

to springs

to west part
of infield and
outfield

to south part
of infield

0 _____ 5 metres

47 *Hound Tor, Dartmoor in Devon. A hamlet settlement of three or four farmsteads, each consisting of a longhouse, small house or cott, and 'corn dryer' surrounded by yards, gardens and paddocks.* *Such a settlement may be thought of as the model for early hamlets all over western Europe. (By permission of Guy Beresford and the Medieval Village Research Group)*

can be taken in, cleared and farmed, and new settlements created.

Much of the evidence for settlement colonisation is based on the first reference to a place in documents, but this cannot now be accepted as a date for origin. It is also based on the first appearance of identifiable pottery types, but this ignores the possibility of aceramic phases when pottery was not made or used. Nevertheless, we can distinguish areas where new land was being taken in and new settlements created. We are probably wrong, however, to see this as happening on a large scale or as a particularly significant development in many areas. England was already an old country by late Saxon times, and the new evidence suggests a relatively large population utilising much of the landscape to a greater or lesser degree. Any major phases or colonisation are as likely to have taken place in the seventh, eighth or ninth centuries, as Peter Sawyer has suggested, and therefore to be undocumented, as they are to have happened in the thirteenth century, when we hear of them for the first time from surviving records.

Domesday Book makes it clear that large areas were wooded and that waste and underused land was widespread in 1086. We cannot assume that such areas were unsettled, however, since areas of woodland often belonged to other places which are better documented. These places are mentioned in the eleventh century, while the dependent settlements in the woods may not be first mentioned until the twelfth or thirteenth centuries. This may well be true for the Weald, as Peter Sawyer shows. Nevertheless, some wooded areas were more intensively settled and used as time went on. Brian Roberts has been able to show how the Forest of Arden in north Warwickshire was systematically settled in the twelfth and thirteenth centuries, with hundreds of new moated farmsteads being created. At Gannow Green in Frankley in Worcestershire the woods were cleared, trees burnt, and the area levelled with clay before a moated farmhouse was built.

Colonisation also occurred in the north, in Yorkshire and in the Pennine Valleys. Again, these areas were not empty. Simy Folds (*Fig. 44*) was there by the seventh century, high up in Durham, and many places already existed in the uplands of Yorkshire when the new monastic 'colonisers' arrived. Indeed, the activities of the Cistercian monasteries in the twelfth century demonstrate how full the landscape

49 *Chalton in Hampshire. Diagram to illustrate changing settlement patterns and forms over the last 2000 years. The blocks show nucleated settlements with desertions and shifts of site; the circles show farmsteads, agglomerating into villages and being colonised from villages. The end result of farms and hamlets has a complex ancestry. (Reproduced by permission of Barry Cunliffe)*

the first Carthusian house in England was founded in the late twelfth century in the apparently empty Selwood Forest. At Pipewell in Northamptonshire, earthworks remain of the pre-existing hamlet, mixed up with earthworks of the Cistercian abbey buildings. If the uplands and woodlands were apparently settled by the twelfth century, other colonisation probably merely filled in the gaps.

Elsewhere, new land was reclaimed and new settlements eventually founded. Around the coast, in low-lying and fen areas, embanking, drainage and improvement resulted in much new land being opened up in Lincolnshire, the Fens, the south-east, and the Somerset Levels. Again, the assumption has been that this took place in the twelfth and thirteenth centuries, because that is when documents mention the activities of lords and peasants in these areas. In the clay belt of Somerset along the coast, however, the land was already drained and productive by the eleventh century. This can be seen in *Domesday Book* and reflects much activity by the tenants of the Abbots of Glastonbury and the Bishops of Wells. The process must be post-Roman, because the Roman land surface over much of the area is buried by approximately 1 metre (3–4 foot) of marine clay. The process of drainage and enclosure was probably occurring in a piecemeal fashion all through the late Saxon period. Indeed, it is tempting to see it as a tenth- and eleventh-century activity, after the reorganisation of the abbey at Glastonbury by St Dunstan. The farmsteads and hamlets thus created may have been used initially as temporary steadings, but eventually a number were permanently occupied. They were never very significant, few are well-documented, and many are now abandoned, but they represent, in the old and densely occupied county of Somerset, one of the few cases where an area was colonised and settled.

We need to look carefully and critically, therefore, at areas where colonisation *de novo* into an empty landscape is assumed. We now know that there was a

48 *Drainage at Brean in Somerset. This air photograph shows a landscape drained and reclaimed from late Saxon to early medieval times. The Roman landscape is buried, so the present pattern of drainage ditches and abandoned stream courses must have been created in more recent times. The abandoned moated settlement in the centre may have begun as a seasonally-used steading.*

was by that date, when they had to create artificially the wild, inhospitable landscape they preferred. In north Warwickshire, Stoneleigh Abbey had to move Cryfield hamlet, and Combe Abbey destroyed two hamlets called Smite; further examples are documented by Robin Donkin. Elsewhere, depopulation can only be inferred. The hamlets of Bordesley and Osmerley in Worcestershire ceased to exist when Bordesley Abbey was established. A settlement at Witham in Somerset may have been disturbed when

50 *Processes of change in rural settlement. Brian Roberts' diagram attempts to show how nucleated rural settlements may have developed from a variety of simple early types. Only by such analysis can the bewildering variety of village and hamlet forms begin to be understood. This diagram should be compared with Fig. 37. (Reproduced by permission of Brian Roberts)*

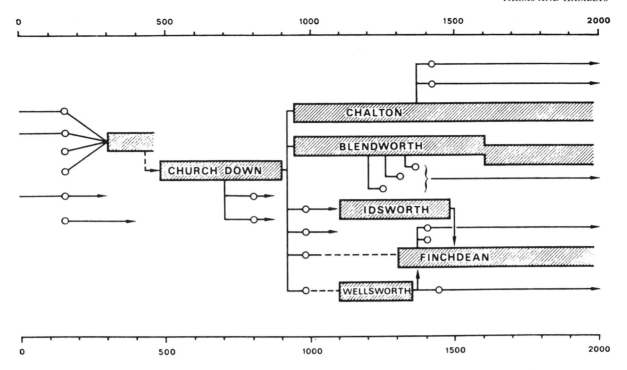

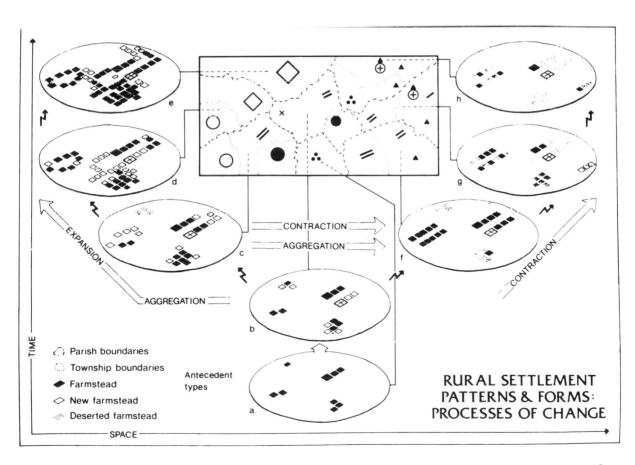

RURAL SETTLEMENT
PATTERNS & FORMS:
PROCESSES OF CHANGE

larger population, more sites in earlier periods, and greater continuity of land use, if not actual settlement sites, into later periods, and therefore there was less opportunity for colonisation and the creation of new settlements. The situation can be seen either as successive waves of colonists from old established centres filling in the landscape with daughter settlements, or as a scatter of settlements, some of which develop while others remain unaltered. The former idea represents the older model, the latter the newly emerging picture. The truth, however, is likely to lie somewhere in between.

Perhaps there were some early villages around the caputs in the oldest, or most continuously settled places. All around, the general pattern was probably one of hamlets, some larger, some small, in varying densities. Some of these developed into villages, others remained the same, yet others disappeared or shrank to farmsteads or even smaller hamlets. In some areas woodland, waste or upland pasture was cleared and developed and new settlements established. Any area, in fact, may display a wide variety of settlements at all stages of development at any one time. There have been few attempts to show this, but Barry Cunliffe's diagram of Chalton settlements and the series of changes shown for Bullock Down in Sussex are interesting analyses which deserve to be emulated.

The picture of settlement development in the landscape, then, is a dynamic picture of great complexity, great age and constant change, but we only see it at one time. Unless we study villages, hamlets and farmsteads as dynamic, changing, developing entities, we will miss the significance of the form and function of them when we see them at a particular date. In this sense, Brian Roberts' complex diagrams attempt to clarify the difficulties of interpretation.

8

Sites and patterns

Having looked at the development and decline of settlements, let us now look at why the settlements are where they are and the patterns they make in the landscape. People are always asking why a particular village or farm is sited where it is and so, sooner or later, the landscape historian will have to give this question some consideration. In this chapter, we shall look at the actual physical position of settlements, their sites in relation to the geography and topography of an area, and in relation to other settlements in the vicinity. We must also be aware that very important cultural factors will also be involved in choice of site for a settlement and that this is related to the overall settlement *pattern* in an area. In the past much ink has been spilt on this problem, but little progress made. This was formerly the preserve of geographers, who related the sites of villages and hamlets very closely to areas of drift geology, or the outpourings of abundant springs. They are not now so physically deterministic, but others, some place-name scholars and archaeologists for example, are now in danger of the same simplistic reasoning.

Most of the work of geographers on settlement location, that of Von Thunen, Christaller and Weber for example, has concentrated on settlements as part of a hierarchy of places linked to trading patterns. Any discussion of siting has, therefore, concentrated on such factors as communication links, defensive positions and local bridging points. All of this is very relevant and important when considering why some places became *towns* and perhaps why a castle was built in a particular place, but it is not so relevant to people in an agricultural community whose main consideration would be disposition of the local resources. Some geographers have considered this aspect and we will look at their work in a moment, but our basic concern, when considering settlement sites, is more likely to be the relationship to local land uses and access to resources. I emphasise this point because popular topographical books still tend to suggest that any particular place is sited where it is for defence reasons, or because it is near a source of water.

We do not know and we will probably never know why any particular settlement is placed exactly where it is. We are not told directly in documents why one site was chosen rather than another, and, as yet, no one has developed the insight of the prehistoric, Anglo-Saxon or medieval colonist to understand fully the reasons why he used a particular bit of the landscape as he did. However, there are ideas, hypotheses and techniques of analysis which can help us make an intelligent guess. We need to consider the site from at least two points of view: firstly, its context in the local region, particularly in relation to contemporary sites, and secondly, the actual physical site.

Michael Chisholm has considered the problem of the site of a settlement in relation to surrounding resources which are exploited for subsistence. He proposed a model which attempted to 'weight' various commodities used by settlers to a greater or lesser degree, including land use, which will be considered further below. Water was considered most important and given a weighting of 10. Certainly, water is used a great deal in settlements, not only for drinking by people and animals, but also for various crafts and simple industrial processes, and as a source of power. It is heavy and a constant supply is useful, so positioning a settlement near a constant source is desirable. However, there are large numbers of settlements, particularly in earlier periods, which are not near water, and so it is obviously not an essential consideration (*Fig. 57*).

Societies with the technology to dig wells enlarge their number of potential settlement sites. In Britain, in particular, there can be few areas where water is not available at a shallow depth. Modern man must remember that in earlier times people washed less frequently and that, however chauvinistic we may find it today, women were usually available to fetch water whenever it was needed, even over a distance of several miles. Different levels of technology (which also implies economic surpluses available to implement them), together with different social values in earlier times, might mean that water was less important than we think. Nevertheless, for many late Saxon and

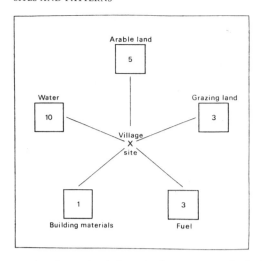

51 *A settlement in relation to local resources. Michael Chisholm's model shows a village with the surrounding resources it uses. These are 'weighted' in a way likely to reflect the importance attached to them by the villagers. Logically the village should be sited to reflect the higher weightings. (With acknowledgement to Professor Michael Chisholm* Rural Settlement and Land Use, *3rd edition 1979, Hutchinson)*

be evaluated in any consideration of settlement siting. Rather than any physically deterministic or geological reasons, we need to consider the social and religious organisation of the original settlers, their technological capability (i.e. what tools and techniques they had knowledge of) and whether, like us, they saw their economy in terms of least effort/cost-benefit or whether some aesthetic or non-practical consideration was equally important. In other words, there is a choice in settlement sites which depends on value-judgements and what people want to do. The considerations and factors thought important will vary at different times in different places.

We can best illustrate this with two absurd examples. The first concerns growing strawberries on Snowdon! We do not do this, but we could – and the reasons we could, but do not, tell us a lot about the factors involved in decisions about activities in the landscape, including settlement siting. We live in a society which greatly enjoys strawberries – our aesthetic appreciation of them is high and we will go to great lengths to acquire them. We have the technology to grow them anywhere. We can move glasshouses, power, light, heat and soil anywhere to produce them. We could even grow them on Snowdon. But because economically, in terms of effort and expense in and profit or return out, it would not be sensible, we grow them where it is cheapest to do so. However, if we worshipped a goddess who lived on Snowdon and adored strawberries, then non-practical, non-economic ideas might dictate that we did grow them on the mountain top.

The second example concerns the availability of resources such as coal and iron. The geological availability of these is used by geographers and historians as a

medieval settlements, if not earlier ones, it is clearly a factor which influenced the choice of where to settle. Thus, streams, rivers, and particularly springs and wells have been important considerations in settlement siting.

Mention of 'different levels of technology', 'different social values' and 'economic surpluses available' serves to demonstrate some of the aspects which must

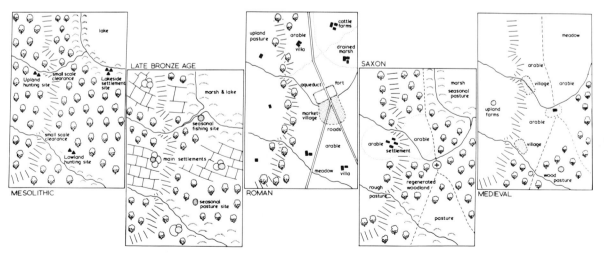

52 *Diagram to show changing settlement sites. These maps attempt to show settlements in relation to changing land uses and topography. Different factors are considered important at different periods and settlements are sited accordingly to minimise effort and maximise return.*

strong argument for why settlements are sited near them when engaged in mining them, or when a particular industry which uses them as a raw material has to be nearby. It is usually conveniently overlooked that there was settlement in the area beforehand and that for most of man's life on earth neither iron nor coal has been particularly important. This is not to say that man can mine coal where it does not occur geologically, or that some settlements do not originate because of the existence of some material which the inhabitants extract; what it does mean is that people themselves determine what is exploited and how they deal with the extraction. No doubt Palaeolithic man lived on coal deposits and Bronze Age man lived on iron deposits, but, until people appreciate the use of such materials, they are of no interest to them. We can use as an example the mining of xyzkqu, which is used in zyxuqk machines. This has not yet been discovered and we do not know what the machines are for – rather as nineteenth-century people did not know about plutonium and nuclear reactors – so we do not know what such developments will lead to in terms of aesthetic and economic considerations, and eventually the effects on the landscape and the settlements in it. What we can say is that the landscape and the resources are already there as background noise and it will be *people* who decide on the importance of the new material and how, or even if, it is used. It will be their aesthetic appreciation, economic system and technological abilities which will be the real determinants on any settlement changes that take place as a result of exploiting the new material.

SUBSISTENCE

The same sort of criteria would have been applied, perhaps unconsciously, in the past. In general, groups of people apply the 'least effort' principle to achieve a livelihood, using the technology they have available to overcome difficulties. In a mainly subsistence economy, the site of a particular place will be largely related to the uses of the land around to maintain the crops and animals which produce the food to sustain life. In our climate, at this latitude, the choice is relatively limited and a complex system of arable crops and domesticated animals has developed, needing different types of land – broadly classed as arable, pasture, meadow, waste and woodland. Each of these will be considered in more detail in the next chapter.

The siting of a settlement is very closely connected with the decision to use the land around for subsistence agriculture. There will inevitably be a number of actual physical sites that could be chosen and, while we can never know what criteria were applied, a good spring or a good view, or a particular happening which was never recorded may all have influenced the choice of site. The technique of 'site catchment analysis'

attempts to see settlements in their economic regions like this.

In addition to such economic considerations, there would be other physical factors: people have usually avoided living on slopes that are very steep, difficult to build on and traverse; they have also avoided marshy or floodable areas (*Fig. 52*).

What is really needed, though, are some rules of thumb that represent a summation of reasoning about settlement sites, and B. J. Garner of the Geography Department of Bristol University has provided these in 'some underlying regularities' in models about settlements. He considers, for example, that:

1 The spatial distribution of human activity reflects an ordered adjustment to the factor of distance. Without concentrations of activity at a given place at a given time there would be no patterns, no spatial or areal differentiation. How far away resources, other settlements or influencing factors occur is therefore fundamental to settlement siting. Following on from this:

2 Locational decisions are taken in general so as to minimise the frictional effects of distance. Put another way, people are usually trying to gain the maximum return for the minimum effort, in settlement siting as in much else.

3 All locations are endowed with a degree of accessibility, but some locations are more accessible than others. Accessibility is difficult to define, but a place is clearly located in relation to systems of land usage, relationship to other places and methods of transport. There are thus, as in other concepts here, variables which need to be considered.

Geographers have traditionally been concerned with the relationship between settlements and the physical and/or natural background. Where they have considered human reasons these have tended to be simplistic explanations of defence or relationships to field systems and land uses. Any settlement is sited, however, in its region and in some relationship to the other settlements in the hierarchy. It may also have different siting relationships to some of these than the purely exploitative patterns indicated above. Again, B. J. Garner has considered these and suggested three premises:

1 There is a tendency for human activities to *agglomerate* to take advantage of scale economies, meaning the savings in costs by concentrating activities at common locations. This happens even in the farm in relation to its fields, but it is more obvious with the village in relation to its territory or the town in relation to its region. Prehistorians have rationalised this recently in the absence of documentary evidence by looking for different 'activity areas' within settlements and such

concepts as food processing, craft areas, food storage areas, etc. could usefully be developed for sites in the historical period.

2 The organisation of human activity is essentially *hierarchical* in character. There are always centres or *head places* and subsidiary centres. Not all places are equal, and their siting must be considered in relation to other places to which they look for social, economic, religious or administrative relationships. Such factors can be discussed in relation to communications and local central places, but they are important in siting as well. Following on from this:

3 Human occupance is *focal* in character; the nodes about which human activity is organised are agglomerations of various sizes. Each of these premises can be seen acting to a greater or lesser degree in the siting of any particular settlement. Equally, the human considerations of where a settlement is placed in a region are as important as the physical characteristics of the landscape which must be allowed for.

DEFENCE

A defensive position is often suggested as the reason for a settlement's site, especially where the site is impressive. Clearly some places, especially a number of fortified towns, were sited to take advantage of easily-defended positions. It is doubtful, however, if defence was ever the only reason, or even the dominant reason, for the siting of mainly subsistence settlements. It may be, though, that after all the locations best related to local land uses had been considered, the most defensible site was selected if local considerations dictated that a better-defended site might be a good idea. One can only see such decisions, though, against the social and political conditions of the time when such a choice was made, and in the light of contemporary warfare and weaponry. Such a site, once selected, may remain by inertia, occupied in the landscape on the old site, although changing defence and siege technology and political climates might mean that it is never again truly defensible.

INDUSTRY AND MINING

So far, we have considered settlement siting in relation to water, economy-subsistence, and defence. Each of these relates to a community producing food from its lands in the most convenient way, having regard to economies of effort and the expertise available. As has already been said, if mining or industrial activity is involved rather than agriculture, we can expect settlements nearby to minimise the access time and cost of transporting materials. Mining can only take place where the commodity is available, although transport of and returns on the exploited material will always

dictate if resources are mined or not, together with whether people think the resources important or not. Industrial location depends not only on a good water supply or plentiful, cheap, raw materials, but also on capital, surplus wealth, and, perhaps above all, someone to start the activity – entrepreneurial spirit. Would there have been an Industrial Revolution without Darby and others, even with the coal and iron?

Other considerations of siting relate rather more to towns, and they are not considered in this book. Focal places have already been considered, but much of the discussion in the past on settlement sites has concentrated on places which were in some way in competition with others for trade, communication or exchange activity. This is not the same as the problems experienced by a group of peasants and farmers minimising their efforts to gain a livelihood from the land around.

Finally, there is the factor of inertia. We have already looked at the movement of settlements, changes in plan and form etc. in the landscape, but nevertheless for most of today's settlements the criteria which applied when the settlement originated are no longer relevant. There is a lot of inertia in the landscape with places persisting even after their former economic base has disappeared. It is possible to regard villages like this, particularly in functional terms. Whenever they were founded and however they were organised, these reasons have now disappeared. In many parts of the country, villages are dormitory and retirement centres; the farms that now work the land are for the most part out in their fields away from the villages. Inertia has kept the sites occupied, but functionally many of them are not related to their countryside surroundings.

CHANGES IN THE POST-ROMAN LANDSCAPE AND SETTLEMENT SITING

There is increasing evidence that both the Romans and medieval man were capable of large-scale engineering schemes resulting in great changes in the landscape. Almost every river and stream valley demonstrates the ability of early medieval people to move rivers, divert streams (*Fig. 48*), and construct elaborate embankments for mills and ponds. This aspect will be examined below, since it is of great interest and importance in any local landscape.

What we are concerned with, however, are the changes which have occurred in the local site conditions of many settlements. It is impossible to envisage the original siting of a settlement, and the reasons behind that siting, without some consideration of whether conditions have altered since the place was founded. We are all aware that streams dry up, valleys fill with silt (*Fig. 3*), and that changes can occur along the coast, but we perhaps underestimate how great these changes may have been in the last 1000 years. In some cases, the collapse of Roman technology, and the economic structure which supported it, marks a clear break between what went before and the developments through to the present day. Attention has been drawn to this in particular by Claudio Vita Finzi.

The fate of Dunwich, a cathedral city which has been eroded by the sea in Suffolk over the last 1000 years, is generally well known. Other areas can also be quoted, like Winchelsea in Sussex, which was destroyed by storms and the French to be refounded in 1288 by Edward I on a hill nearby. Selsey in Sussex has also disappeared in the post-Roman period. More local changes can be seen in the examination of the towns of Sussex by Fred Aldsworth and David Freke. They show that the sites of Shoreham, Seaford, Pevensey, Hastings, Rye and Winchelsea can only be understood in the context of considerable, and in some cases drastic, coastal changes in the last 1000 years.

At Hastings and Shoreham great erosion of projecting headlands has removed most of the castle of the former and half of the town of New Shoreham at the latter. At the other places, retreat of the sea and silting of shallow valleys and estuaries has left them almost literally high and dry, with their present situation completely divorced from their original siting. At Hastings, one inlet is now infilled; Rye, formerly on a peninsula, is now 3 kilometres (2 miles) inland. The inlets behind the spit at Seaford are now infilled; at Shoreham, the early harbour is now silted up, and at Winchelsea, the sea which destroyed the earlier site has now abandoned the second. Elsewhere in this region places like Arundel, Burpham and Pevensey, which were originally surrounded by tidal marshes, are now left stranded in areas of rich meadow pasture.

All of these are part of coastline changes which have been carefully studied around Romney Marsh and Walland March by Barry Cunliffe and others. They have charted complex changes since 1000 BC, showing that even in the last 1500 years the area has evolved from a series of tidal inlets, through the development of spits and dunes, to the triangular area that it is today, with the vast recent pebble dumps of Dungeness. Such changes can be seen off the Kent coast with the cementing of the Isle of Thanet to the mainland and the silting up of the Wantsum Channel in post-Roman times. Since then, the Saxon shore forts of Richborough and Reculver have been left inland in changed contexts, the former surrounded by dry land, the latter half-eroded by the sea.

It is clear, then, from these examples and others in Yorkshire and Norfolk, where numerous towns and villages have disappeared, that, following coastal erosion by the sea and extensive silting of estuaries and shallow coastal areas, the context of many sites is now very different. Two other aspects are relevant to this theme: the formation of sand dunes and the drying out of low-lying marsh areas.

All along the north coast of Cornwall and the south coast of Wales there are extensive sand dunes. These areas look wild and unaffected by man, until they are closely examined. We can then see that such areas have developed fairly recently, and very largely at the expense of man-made landscapes. In the west, for example, there is a scatter of abandoned farmsteads and church sites stretching from St Ives Bay in Cornwall to North Devon. Sites at Gwithian in Cornwall include a medieval and possibly earlier chapel, a medieval farm, and pre-Norman fields, as well as many prehistoric sites. Mawgan Porth, also in Cornwall, was found buried in sand (*Fig. 44*). Chapels have also been lost all along the coast, the most spectacular being at Perranporth in Cornwall where not only the early (how early?) St Pirans Oratory, but also the later medieval church have been abandoned to the rising sand. In South Wales the medieval town of Kenfig has disappeared, leaving only slight traces of castle and buildings. In North Wales, sand dunes have affected the new medieval town of Newborough and the old royal estate of Aberffrau in Anglesey.

All around the coast the story is similar. Eroded cliffs and headlands have taken away towns, villages, castles and churches; sand dunes have buried villages and churches; silted up estuaries and shallow seas have deprived sites of their former importance and even livelihood. Failures like Newton in Poole harbour and Alnmouth in Northumberland owe their misfortunes to natural, even if man-induced, changes.

We have already mentioned the marshes of Sussex and Kent as examples of areas drying out. This has usually resulted in richer grassland and a different land use, frequently to the benefit of local settlements, but it has also deprived local centres of former defensive or navigable areas of water or marsh. The story of the Fens in post-Roman times is one of sea retreat, drying out and reclamation (*Fig. 62*), and, in studying the settlements of the area as Christopher Taylor and David Hall have done, it is important to know the position of the sea, sea defences and main drainage at any particular period.

In the Somerset Levels there have been great changes since the Roman period (*Fig. 48*). Throughout post-Roman times, areas have been drained and reclaimed, a story unravelled by Michael Williams, and considerable large-scale physical changes have taken place. Much of the Roman landscape is now buried by up to 1 metre (1 yard) of alluvial silt, on to which later settlements have been built and into which have been dug thousands of miles of drainage leats. Along the coast is a wide belt of sand dunes with a man-made sea defence incorporated into them. Roger Leech has drawn attention, however, to a lost river, the Siger, to

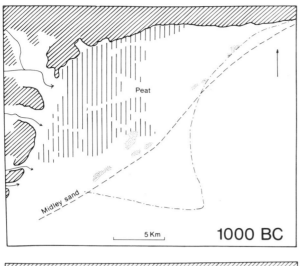

1000 BC

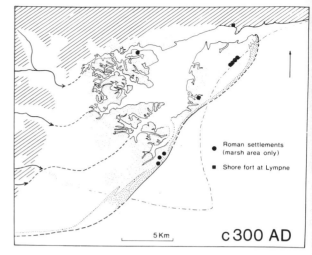

- Roman settlements (marsh area only)
- Shore fort at Lympne

c 300 AD

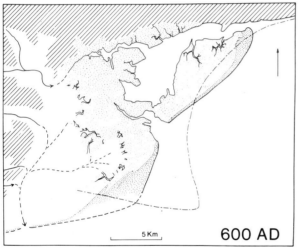

600 AD

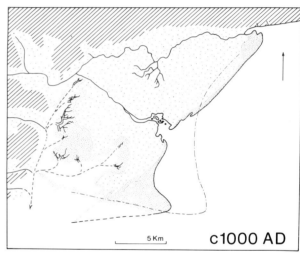

c 1000 AD

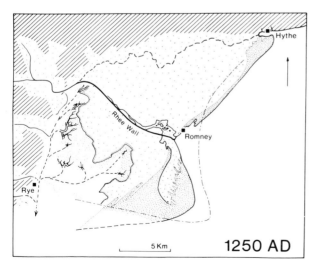

1250 AD

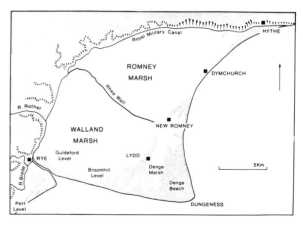

53 *Changes in the disposition of Romney and Walland Marshes. These maps show Romney and Walland Marshes developed from 1000 BC to AD 1250. Although the changes here have been dramatic, they are merely an extreme example of natural changes generally around the coast. The final map shows the area now. (By permission of Barry Cunliffe)*

54 *Air photograph of the lost River Siger in Somerset. The course of the former river is revealed after heavy rain as a 0.3 m (1 ft) deep channel near to Burnham on Sea in October 1960. This river is mentioned in an Anglo-Saxon charter in the seventh century, but it is not known when it disappeared. It may have lost water through changes in the peat levels inland and been blocked off from the sea by sand dunes. (By permission of Douglas Allen Photography, Bridgwater)*

the south of Brent Knoll, and air photographs reveal extensive abandoned river meanders and stream courses in the lower River Parrett area. As yet the picture of modifications to the drainage, build-up of sand dunes and coastal change is very difficult to understand in this area. It is clearly related to man's activities inland in draining the wetlands, cutting peat and altering the courses of the rivers Brue, Axe and Parrett. As elsewhere, the changes which seem natural can be shown to have been initiated or exacerbated by man, even on such a large scale.

Inland changes to sites over the last 1000 years do not seem to have been so drastic. Forest clearance in earlier times clearly initiated great changes which have been discussed already (*Fig. 3*). Even in the medieval period, hillwash, increased sediment in rivers, and obstructions in them such as fish weirs and mills have all had an effect. It is unlikely that any river improved in the seventeenth, eighteenth and nineteenth centuries bears much relationship to its earlier regime. Medieval water

engineering is now known for many sites, shown particularly well at Rhuddlan in North Wales, Rievaulx Abbey in North Yorkshire and Kenilworth Castle in Warwickshire, but smaller schemes too have resulted in great changes.

Landslips, earthquakes and faulting are not everyday occurrences in this country and do not usually have to be allowed for in settlement siting. However, some natural change has gone on and is still going on in the country, and physical changes need to be anticipated in any local study. This, together with an appreciation of the steeper slopes, soil erosion and the local changes in level and aspect, make for a finer assessment of the subtler aspects which may have been of great significance to the original selector's choice of site for the particular settlement under study.

SETTLEMENT PATTERNS

Like the siting of settlements, attempts to examine and

understand the patterns, and the distribution of settlements across the landscape, have traditionally been the preserve of geographers. Most of this work has concentrated on the historical period, using readily available sources of information, and looking in detail at particular localities. As has already been noted, however, most of this research has been on villages, rather than the more difficult scattered settlements; the atypical patterns, such as the strings of villages in chalkland valleys, have received a disproportionate amount of attention (*Fig. 15*).

With the large numbers of early sites that have now been recognised in the landscape, particularly those cropmarks and pottery scatters of prehistoric and Romano-British date, archaeologists have also become interested in patterns of early settlement. The recognition of Saxon settlements, not under medieval villages but in open sites which were later abandoned, has also indicated that settlement patterns themselves have altered and the desertion of individual settlements within the pattern, even in quite recent times, means that settlement patterns are as dynamic and changing as the settlements themselves. What we are clearly seeing in some areas is roughly the same group of people exploiting the same local landscape for their subsistence requirements over a long period, but with successive generations living on different sites at different times. Changing preferences will be shown in siting, and occupation will tend to move about within an area. The settlement pattern will change correspondingly over time (*Fig. 52*).

Such an observation is important because it can be assumed, as has already been discussed, that there are only certain sites which can be occupied in an area and therefore the settlement pattern should be predictable. To some extent this is true, since Michael Chisholm's research has shown that subsistence land use results in settlements being not more than 1 kilometre ($\frac{1}{2}$ mile) or so from most of their land (*Fig. 59*) and hence settlements should perhaps be expected to be 1–2 kilometres ($\frac{1}{2}$–1 mile) apart. However, many more variables are involved in settlement siting and patterns. In particular, habitats which appear inhospitable at one period may be quite acceptable and considered normal at another.

Let us look, then, at some examples of settlement patterns in different areas. In a very stimulating book, *Spatial Analysis in Archaeology*, Ian Hodder and Clive Orton have assembled many of the ideas and techniques for examining settlement patterns. There are four main points we need to consider, particularly for the earlier, undocumented settlements.

Firstly, before documents are available which give a general comparison and assessment at one date across an area (like *Domesday Book* or a medieval Lay Subsidy) it is very difficult to know whether all the sites we are comparing as part of our settlement pattern are *contemporary*. Examination of pottery scatters might help in this, and in some ways we can consider pieces of pottery as documentary references. They show us that something is there at that time, although they tell us nothing of origins, date of abandonment, use of the site, or its importance. Researchers of medieval settlements would do well, perhaps, to regard their scanty documentary references – often only the name and owner of a site at a particular date – in the same way that the Romanist looks at his sherds and the prehistorian his flint scatters.

Secondly, as already mentioned, some consideration must be given to the *status* of the sites being compared in the pattern. Just as today there are towns, villages, hamlets and farmsteads, so there were in the past. Some idea of relative size and hierarchical organisation is important, although without earthworks or clearly defined areas of finds this is often difficult to assess. Thirdly, permanence and *seasonality* of occupation are important. Some of the sites under consideration may be of the same date and status, but they may be occupied for part of the year, or for a few years only.

Finally, and most importantly, we need to be sure of the *reliability* of the information. Are we, in fact, comparing like with like, even allowing for the above factors? Christopher Taylor has given perhaps the best example of this in a study of settlements in the Nene Valley. His distribution map of sites suggests a strange pattern, with some sites along the main river and others around the confluences of several streams some miles away. Attempts to explain this pattern would be fraught with difficulties. A second map, however, shows the controlling factors which include areas where no fieldwork or air survey was possible – in other words, areas where at present it is impossible to assess whether sites exist or not. Areas of woodland and permanent pasture are mapped together with built-up areas as inaccessible to archaeologists. In all areas where evidence of sites can be found, the pattern is clear and dense, suggesting, in fact, that this is probably the case over the whole area. Any attempts to explain the first map without the controls indicated on the second would be nonsensical. More such studies and indications of the limits of the information are clearly necessary before settlement patterns can be fully understood.

Having discussed the above ideas for the sites in an area, various analyses can then be tried out to examine the relationships between settlements which could have interesting and important implications. Ian Hodder and Clive Orton discuss analyses of randomness in settlement patterns, as well as various uniform and clustered patterns, much of which rests on 'nearest neighbour' analysis. Many of the theories and models proposed can be shown to have application to observ-

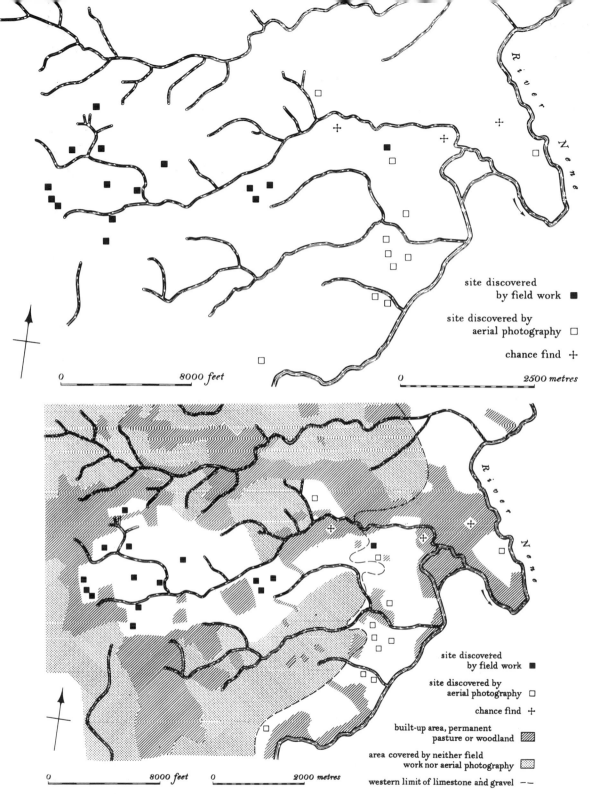

site discovered by field work ■

site discovered by aerial photography □

chance find +

site discovered by field work ■

site discovered by aerial photography □

chance find +

built-up area, permanent pasture or woodland

area covered by neither field work nor aerial photography

western limit of limestone and gravel --

0   8000 feet   0   2000 metres

0   8000 feet   2500 metres

55 *Roman settlements near Oundle in Northamptonshire. The first map shows the position of sites discovered by fieldwork and aerial photography in recent years. It would be easy to assume certain reasons for the pattern and density of these settlements in certain areas – along the River Nene and around the headwaters of a side stream – were it not for the factors depicted on the second map. These show that everywhere that the landscape has been examined, evidence of sites has been found, though there is reason to believe that there may be sites in the areas that are inaccessible to archaeologists. (By permission of Christopher Taylor)*

99

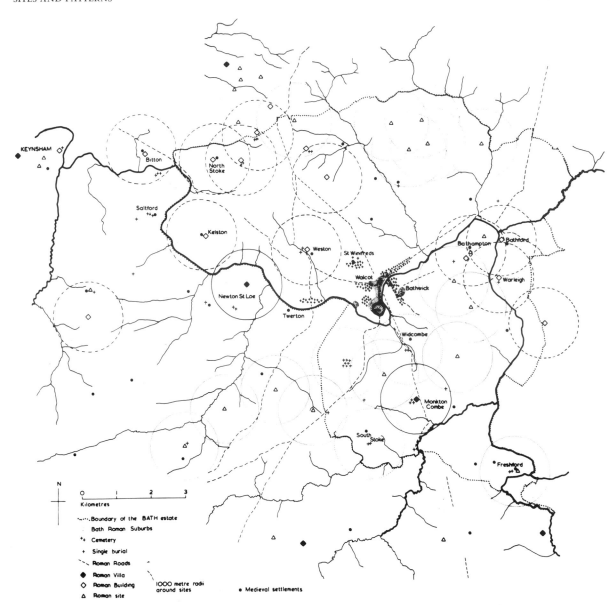

56 *Roman settlements around Bath in Avon. Large numbers of sites have been located in the last 200 years showing a settlement pattern evenly spread across the uplands around Bath at a density of one site* *for every 1 km ($\frac{5}{8}$ mile) or so. Gaps probably represent sites not yet discovered rather than a lack of Romano-British settlements.*

able patterns of settlement on the ground. We can take an example to demonstrate some of the implications of these ideas and the additional information which can emerge.

It is difficult to gauge accurately what the densities and patterns of prehistoric settlement might have been. Usually we do not know all the sites, and we do not know if they were all contemporary or only used seasonally. However, in well-studied areas such as western Cornwall, the Wessex chalklands, and the major river valleys, settlement is dense and even, fully exploiting the local resources.

For the Roman period, settlement patterns are perhaps a little more precise. The large amount of fieldwork in the past and the early attention to classical matters mean that, in some areas, perhaps all of the Romano-British sites that formerly existed have been recognised – especially as fine pottery, metalwork and stone foundations were more easily noted by early antiquaries. Around Somerton in Somerset, for example, Roger Leech suggests that all the settlements that existed in late Roman times have been located over the last several centuries, and so the pattern we see is probably a true reflection of the state of affairs in the

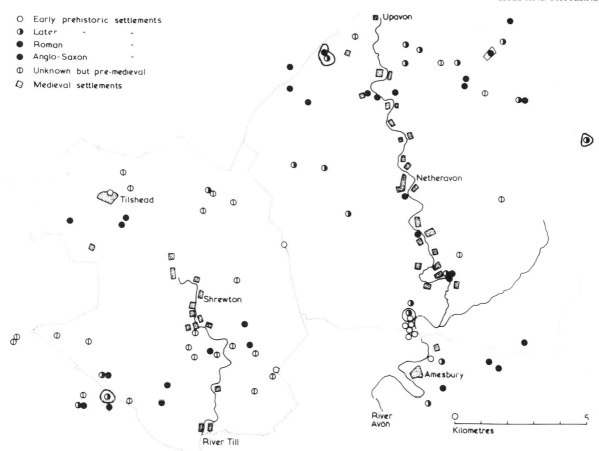

Legend:
- ○ Early prehistoric settlements
- ◑ Later " "
- ● Roman " "
- ● Anglo-Saxon "
- ◑ Unknown but pre-medieval
- ▱ Medieval settlements

Upavon

Tilshead

Netheravon

Shrewton

Amesbury

River Till

River Avon

0   Kilometres   5

57 *Early settlements on Salisbury Plain in Wiltshire. Modern settlement in this area is confined to villages in the Avon and Til valleys. It is generally assumed that this is the 'natural' place for settlements in such dry chalkland environments. Yet sites of all periods exist on the uplands away from running water; no doubt more remain to be identified. The valley settlements are probably only the surviving part of an early settlement pattern which was once more widespread (The areas outlined with dots are shown in Fig. 15.)*

Roman era, showing farmsteads and hamlets 1–2 kilometres (½–1 mile) apart, scattered evenly across the landscape. A similar pattern can be seen around Bath, where, over the last 200 years and more, changes in the landscape have been noted by local antiquaries with all discoveries being carefully recorded. The high status of the visitors to Bath, their classical education, complemented by the Grand Tour, again indicates that all that can be recovered probably has been. The only major gaps in an otherwise even pattern of settlements are the present villages, and it is likely that many if not most of these are on earlier sites.

For the medieval period there is more information. Not only do documents name sites, but often settlement earthworks remain and areas of ridge and furrow, meadow, and so on demonstrate where it is unlikely that there has been settlement. Also, we can usually say whether it is a farmstead or a village which is under examination. In river valleys like the Avon, Til (*Figs. 15, 39 and 41*), Ebble, Piddle, Gussage and Tarrant in Wiltshire and Dorset, dense settlement was almost continuous down each side of the valleys, and a similar pattern can be seen in south-east Somerset. In such areas the gaps are of great interest – were there settlements there, and, if not, why not? We must be careful not to assume that this 'beads on a string' pattern is the norm, because in such areas there is frequently abundant prehistoric and Romano-British settlement on the dry and now abandoned chalk uplands. This may not just be a change in location and hence in pattern, since there may be contemporary settlements beneath the present villages, an aspect Bob Smith is examining in the Wiltshire valleys. In areas where farmsteads are the normal form of settlement, the pattern is very dense on good land, such as at Hanbury in Worcestershire, and less dense in upland areas such as Exmoor and Dartmoor. Even in these areas, though, the farmsteads or small hamlets are rarely more than 1–2 kilometers (½–1 mile) apart.

The consistency of this distance, and the pattern

HANBURY in Worcestershire

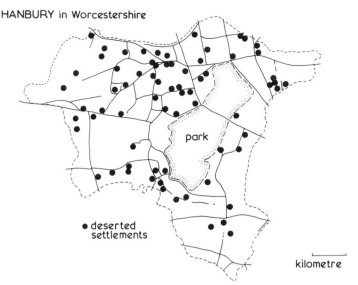

58 *Deserted settlements in Hanbury in Worcestershire. This map shows an unfamiliar settlement pattern in great contrast to areas of villages. As a result of detailed fieldwork, large numbers of abandoned farmsteads have been found in this single Midland parish, formerly in the Forest of Feckenham. The pattern is dense along a close mesh of small roads and tracks. (By permission of Christopher Dyer and Stephen Bassett)*

implied by it, is remarkable, as Michael Chisholm remarks:

> A point which emerges ... is the frequency with which the same orders of magnitude keep on recurring among people of widely different technical achievements and inhabiting areas with markedly different physical characteristics. Any distance up to about a kilometre from the dwelling is of such little moment for any specialised systems of irrigation and garden farming that little adjustment is called for in either the pattern of settlement or of land use. Beyond about 1km the costs of movement become sufficiently great to warrant some kind of response ...

Generally, then, we should perhaps think of settlements being 1–2 kilometres ($\frac{1}{2}$–1 mile) apart as the norm. Where farmsteads are grouped together, and in poorer land perhaps, the distances may be greater. In certain topographical regions, linear patterns may develop if water is at a premium, as in the chalk valleys, or if factors other than subsistence are important, such as roads or water routes. The relationships between settlement patterns, local land use and communication networks will be discussed in the next chapters.

9

Land uses

The majority of the English landscape is occupied by crops growing in fields. These crops still provide the sustenance for animals and people, and hence, after settlements, the land use of the countryside is of most importance to the landscape historian: effective use of the land has always formed the basis of survival. Several problems immediately present themselves when we look at the land around any settlement. Firstly, how old is the pattern of fields which we see both in the landscape and depicted on the maps? Secondly, is this the earliest pattern in this area and, if not, can we detect anything of the previous arrangement? Thirdly, if no early arrangements can be seen in the form of earthworks, cropmarks or soilmarks, can we still ascertain something of how the land was used in the past?

Let us take the last point first, because land use itself, irrespective of how the fields are arranged or under what system they are worked, has interesting implications. In our temperate climate, land use can be divided into four main categories: **arable** areas, where crops such as cereals and legumes can be grown, generally well drained and fertile with relatively easily worked soils; at most times in the past rotation was employed, alternating one crop with another, and crops with **pasture** where cattle, sheep, goats, horses and so on grazed; **meadowland** where hay was grown for winter fodder; and **woodland** to provide the wood and timber. Arable will be discussed in the next chapter.

In some regions there was permanent lowland pasture, particularly in fenland and level areas which were liable to be under water for some of the year, or where the risk of flooding was endemic. Such areas were not often used for arable, until later drainage operations ensured that water could be kept off the fields for most of the year. These were in contrast to upland permanent pasture, where arable farming could only be undertaken infrequently, in special circumstances. These upland areas may have been in the form of downland, with good quality grassland, or rough

upland pastures, such as the commons and wastes of the higher mountainous regions. The term *wastes*, as used in early documents, is in modern parlance a misuse of the word, as they also existed at lower levels where arable and pasture might be expected. In the past, waste was not useless, but provided fuel, building materials and industrial materials, as well as rough grazing.

Most settlements set aside special areas for use as meadowland. This meadowland or *mead land* was usually low-lying and damp for much of the year, but it produced an abundance of grass which was cut for hay. This provided valuable winter fodder for animals taken indoors or kept in pens or *crew yards* over the winter, when the grass in the pasture had stopped growing. Meadow areas were also used as pasturage when the hay crop had been removed.

These basic land uses of arable, pasture and meadow were, of course, supplemented at different times. Not only were there extensive wastes or commons in some areas, but also rough woodland, unreclaimed land and undeveloped land to a greater or lesser extent wooded, which is the natural vegetation for cool temperate areas like Britain. These areas provided extra (sometimes distant) resources and also reserves of land for colonisation as population increased, and new, more highly developed farming methods were employed. It has been said that the history of the landscape of Britain is 'one long assart' (clearance). This is an oversimplification, but the relative areas of and the relationship between the main land uses outlined above and the wildwood is always an important consideration for any period for the landscape historian.

There is another aspect which must also be carefully considered. To the urban dweller, all woods look the same, but in landscape terms we must be careful to distinguish between the wildwood (the remnant or successor of the natural or semi-natural woodland of Britain – which certainly does not exist anywhere today and probably has not since the Roman period) and woods which have been to a greater or lesser degree managed for the production of timber and

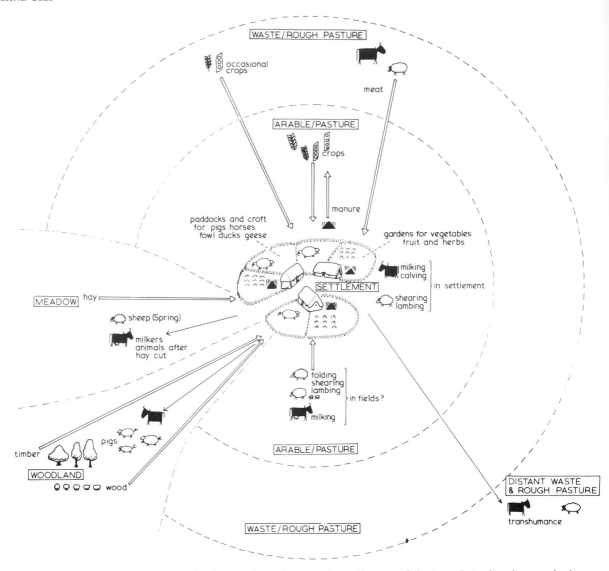

WASTE/ROUGH PASTURE

occasional crops

meat

ARABLE/PASTURE

crops

manure

paddocks and croft
for pigs horses
fowl ducks geese

gardens for vegetables
fruit and herbs

milking
calving

in settlement

MEADOW   hay

SETTLEMENT

shearing
lambing

sheep (Spring)

milkers
animals after
hay cut

folding
shearing
lambing

in fields?

milking

timber

pigs

ARABLE/PASTURE

WOODLAND

wood

DISTANT WASTE
& ROUGH PASTURE

transhumance

WASTE/ROUGH PASTURE

59 *Land uses surrounding a settlement. This diagram shows the types of land and their probable disposition around a settlement, together with some of the interrelationships between land use, animals and crops.*

wood(*Fig. 63*). These latter would also have had a role as pasture, particularly for pigs or for cattle and horses in more open areas of woodland.

There are interesting relationships between these land uses. Areas of upland pasture and areas of waste can be used for both arable and more intensive pasture as circumstances dictate, though some acidic upland wastes require draining and liming first. Without adequate drainage, lowland pasture can be used for little else. However, when flooded, these areas provide a wealth of fish and wildfowl for food and sport, as well as rushes and reeds for building and furnishing. Similarly, areas of meadow can be used for little else without massive investment in drainage, and hay crops and rich pasture seem to have been too valuable to

consider using this land in any other way. In other areas, however, land could be used for arable, arable and pasture, pasture, or wood, and how it was used depended to a large extent on the proximity of settlements and in what sort of economy the local farmers were engaged.

The relationship between these different land uses depends on a number of factors. The local topography, soil types, relative areas of upland and lowland will all be important considerations, but ultimately the ability of a community to feed itself will be the deciding factor; in a subsistence economy, at any period, land will be used to the best advantage. We have looked at the different types of land and seen roughly what could be done with them. If we now look at the different animals and crops that have been available over several thousand years, we will begin to see how basic systems of land exploitation worked in the landscape.

Animal resources

The main animals kept were cattle, sheep and goats, pigs, fowl and, to a lesser extent, horses. Cattle required good quality pasture and plentiful hay if they were to be kept over the winter, which they generally were. They could also be taken on to rough pasture, to distant resources, or even kept in woodland (their natural habitat), though milkers would not be taken too far from the settlement. They provided traction (pulling carts, ploughs, harrows etc.), meat, leather, and a host of other resources like bone (for glue), grease, sinews, together with milk (for butter and cheese to store) and manure – either deposited on or taken out to arable fields.

Sheep could be kept on poorer land and also taken to wastes, commons and distant resources. They provided meat, wool, milk and cheese, and also manure – very important in some areas where they were folded overnight on arable land. Pigs had to be kept near to the farmstead, probably in nearby closes, but they could be taken to wastes and pasture and, of course, woodland, where traditionally they ate acorns and beechmast. They were important for meat (though not milk – which has never been adequately explained) and manure.

Fowl, including ducks, geese, chickens and also pigeons, were kept near to the settlement in closes and open spaces. They provided meat, eggs, probably feathers and, when available in large enough quantities, manure. Horses have to be considered initially as status symbols and later as draught and transport animals as well. However, they required good pasture and plentiful hay and would probably always have been kept in closes near to the farmsteads. Apart from their strength and status, their manure would have been useful; but was their meat eaten?

Other animal resources were very important. Fish, for example, were widely used. Sea fish would be caught all around the coast and estuaries, perhaps for most of the year, and traded some distance inland. Near to large rivers and lakes, fishing would always have been a major activity, particularly for salmon and the ubiquitous eels. Elsewhere, fishponds were constructed for breeding fish or as stock ponds or *stews* for holding fish caught in rivers and pools until they were needed.

Wild animals have always formed part of the diet, depending on the existence of any natural habitat in the locality of the settlement. Wildfowl, such as ducks and geese, were caught, and deer, boar and hares were hunted. Rabbits were bred specially and do not seem to have been common until relatively recently. To what extent bears, wolves, beavers, otters, hedgehogs, badgers and so on were important as food resources at different dates is not yet known.

Plant resources

In addition to the cultivated crops, we need to allow for a wide range of wild plant resources. More attention is now being paid to the sort of plants available for food and other uses as a by-product of the way people used the land. Woodland harboured herbs for medicines and food and also several edible varieties of mushroom. Hedgerows produced berries, fruits, and herbs: the *lore* concerning these products would have been common knowledge in former times when they were more widely used.

The cereals grown would have formed the staple of the diet, with wheat, barley, oats and rye all being represented in the archaeological and historical records. They were grown in many combinations, so that we frequently get references to *drage* (barley and oats) and *maslin* (wheat and rye). In economic terms, arable farming was a very labour-intensive activity with a lot of field work involving preparation of the land, sowing, weeding, harvesting and processing. Labour was the greatest input, but we must also remember manure, especially if the area was cropped annually. The latter would not only include animal manure but also marl, sand, seaweed where available, ash, and a host of other materials, not all of which were beneficial. Other field crops included peas and beans before the sixteenth to seventeenth centuries and, later on, numerous new introductions, some of which would have been grown earlier as garden produce but which were grown on a larger scale from the seventeenth and particularly eighteenth centuries. These crops were sometimes rotated with grass, depending on the type of field system employed.

Meadowland was used primarily for the growing of grass for hay production but would also produce reeds (for floor-covering, roofing and containers) and osiers (for building work and containers as well as hurdles for fencing). Closes in and adjacent to the settlements have already been mentioned. These would have contained garden-like areas for growing vegetables, herbs for flavouring, dyes and medicines, fruit trees and space for hives – honey being an important commodity and mentioned as goods rendered from some estates.

A diagram can be used to depict the links between settlements and the various land uses which have been discussed, together with the possibility of distant resources, in a predominantly subsistence economy (*Fig. 59*). Not only might such a diagram act as a checklist of the types of land use to look for in a study of any area, but it may also serve to prompt questions about the working of the basic agricultural economic units which make up the English landscape. As we shall see

60 *Land use at Deerhurst in Gloucestershire. Most of the land above the 10-m (35-ft) contour line has at some time been used for arable cultivation; over much of the area this is marked by ridge and furrow, visible as earthworks and soil marks on air photographs. Extensive areas of meadow exist alongside the River Severn and in the south of the parish. The arable would have provided pasture areas under rotation but there is also a series of drove ways linking the settlements with the floodable land.*

The early estate of the Deerhurst Saxon monastery was centred partly on the Severn valley and partly on the Cotswolds, where there were extensive sheep runs and probably woodland. In the Severn valley the area to the west of the river contained much rough land for pasture and woodland. To the east there was extensive arable.

later, such a diagram can be related very closely to other aspects of the landscape (*Fig. 93*).

For a settlement which is more involved with commercial activities, different factors will come into play. Provision of particular products for a local market will change the balance of land uses, and other factors may also alter over time. This latter point raises a whole range of issues related to economics and avail-

able technology. Under normal conditions, people will usually do what requires least effort for the maximum return. However, conditions are rarely standard, and such factors as population increase, soil fertility, slope, drainage and proximity to markets will all help to determine how land is used. A preference for a particular crop, and other aesthetic considerations, as well as an innate conservatism, may be much more relevant than our intensely practical approaches allow. Similarly, how much capital and what technology is available, together with the decision on whether to use them or not, will also determine whether a particular course of action is taken.

We must always be aware of the ability of people to change the environment, either deliberately or by accident, and of the likelihood that the appearance of the landscape today may not be the same as it was half a millennium ago, when different land uses may have been appropriate. Thus, any attempt to analyse the former land use around a settlement needs to take into account more than just the present physical nature of the land: changes may have taken place in any period under the influence of the technical abilities, and social and economic conditions prevailing at any time.

TWO CASE STUDIES OF LAND USE

The case of Deerhurst in Gloucestershire may serve as a useful example to show what can be learned about early land use and also to indicate some of the pitfalls. During the research project into the architectural and archaeological development of the Saxon church of St Mary at Deerhurst, a survey was undertaken of the local parishes and the former Saxon estate of the monastery centred on St Mary's. It was hoped that such a survey would throw some light on the contemporary landscape in the late Saxon period and perhaps locate earthworks associated with the early monastery. Although large areas of ridge and furrow and numerous previously unrecorded field monuments were discovered, little of definite pre-Norman date could be indicated.

Yet the topography of Deerhurst parish and the early estate suggests particular land uses for certain areas. For example, there is a wide flood plain alongside the River Severn and a great embayment of flat land covered by drainage ditches south of Apperley in Deerhurst. It is most unlikely that either of these areas has been used for arable in the last 1500 years, and this is confirmed to some extent by field names recorded on the earliest maps (of the early nineteenth century) and in medieval documents. The flat area to the south was drained at some time in the eighteenth century and a canal was built across it.

Much of Deerhurst parish consists of islands or near islands, rising above this floodable land. The distribution of ridge and furrow shows the extent of former arable land within the area, and, where it is absent in the field or on the air photographs, it can sometimes be shown to have existed. We can thus see that the whole of the rest of the parish could be used for arable. No doubt it was also used for pasture, either in rotation with arable or when areas were abandoned from arable cultivation. Much of the ridge and furrow has survived because the areas are now semi-permanent pasture. It is not possible to indicate with confidence areas of former woodland, although some of the steep wooded bluffs along the river may have been so used, and there are no upland areas of permanent rough pasture.

Despite these reservations, we can say something of the landscape of the Saxon Deerhurst estate, because, even without the fine detail, we can see vast areas of arable and pasture in the Severn Valley, areas of woodland and waste to the west over the river, and upland pasture on the Cotswolds to the east in a detached part of the estate. The work of Martin Bell elsewhere, however, indicates that the landscape and its use can change, and we need to be aware of this for earlier periods. From AD 1000 over much of England this type of simple land use evaluation exercise can be usefully employed to provide a functional background to any settlement under study.

The other example, at Ashington in Somerset, indicates further lessons. This small parish, east of the Roman, Saxon and medieval town of Ilchester, has no obvious archaeological monuments to attract the fieldworker (*Fig. 90*). However, it does have distinct areas of relief and there are very good air photographs of the area, taken by the RAF in 1947, which show that there was formerly an extensive deserted village near the present church and manor house and that most of the parish was covered with ridge and furrow earthworks. Most of the village site has now been ploughed, and medieval potsherds can be picked up in abundance; almost all the ridge and furrow has been levelled. The air photographs, however, enable us to map the former extent of these features.

To the north and east of the village there is extensive meadowland along the river Yeo, with no earthworks except drainage ditches. In the south of the parish is Ashington Wood, and field examination of this shows that there are no ridge and furrow earthworks inside, so it was never part of the open arable fields, and it has a large bank and ditch surrounding it, characteristic of medieval woodland boundaries. The ground flora, and to some extent the coppice and standard trees remaining, suggest that this is an area of ancient woodland.

For Ashington, therefore, we can suggest the basic land uses of the medieval parish, with meadowland, arable, pasture and woodland all represented. During the survey a medieval water mill site was also located, traced from the now dry but substantial mill leat, with the stonework of sluices and mill buildings surviving in undergrowth at the end of a track from the village.

We can, however, understand something of the way this land was used in more detail. Michael Chisholm, in discussing the siting of settlements, has shown a general consistency in the use of land around settlements, with paddocks close at hand, arable immediately adjacent, and resources such as pasture and woodland at some distance. This relationship of land usage to settlement is conditioned primarily by the intensity of effort put into different land uses and their distance from the settlement. Thus it is important to have paddocks and gardens close to farmsteads, for overnight penning of animals, and garden crops for use in cooking; but both the latter and the arable need a lot of manure from the farmstead and are also intensively worked in terms of man hours. Economy of effort in walking dictates that such land should not be too far away. Woodlands, however, can be at some distance, as people will only need to fetch firewood, poles, and so on for tools and fencing, or timber for construction, periodically. Similarly, extensive pastures can be at some distance, since

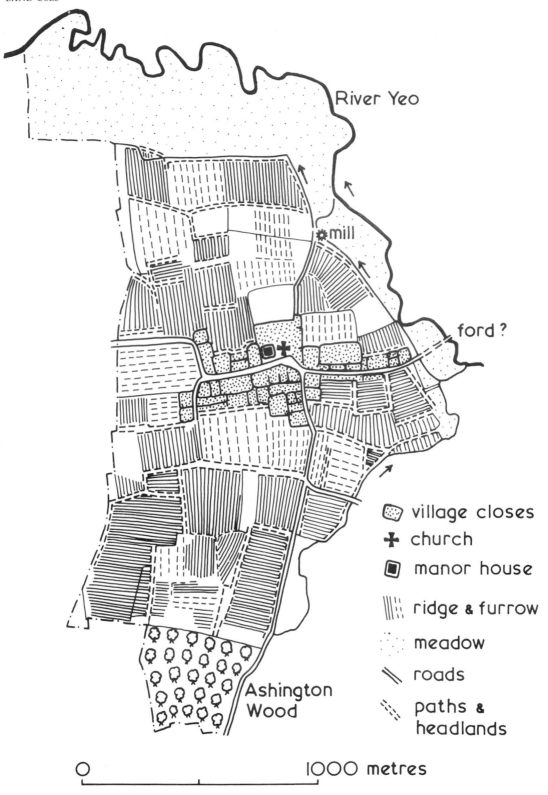

River Yeo

mill

ford ?

village closes

church

manor house

ridge & furrow

meadow

roads

paths & headlands

Ashington Wood

O   1000 metres

61 *Land use at Ashington in Somerset. This example shows very simply the disposition of arable/pasture, meadow and woodland in a typical English parish.*

animals can be walked there and kept there for some time by herdsmen. Meadowland should not be too far away, though it need not be adjacent to the settlement. However, the proximity of many settlements to streams and rivers means that the meadowland is frequently close by.

Ashington can be seen to fit very neatly into Michael Chisholm's model of *ideal* land use around a settlement; indeed, most of the villages in south-east Somerset do (*Fig. 90*), as do many thousands across England. The often quoted examples of the linear parishes in Lincolnshire and Wiltshire (*Fig. 15*) are so arranged that each of the land uses, and access to them, is equal for all settlements.

Through such models, some understanding can be gained of the way in which many settlements formerly operated in their local landscape. Even without details of field systems and earthwork remains some attempt can be made to see how early farmers were exploiting the resources available to their settlement. At Ashington we can see the areas of ridge and furrow, part of which would be ploughed and planted with cereals and legumes in open fields, while the rest would be fallow and down to grass – this would have been fenced off and grazed by cattle and sheep. Along the riverside, hay would have been cropped several times through the summer, and then, at the end of the summer, the animals who had been on the fallow would be turned on to both the meadowland and the stubble of the arable before coming into the paddocks by the village over the winter, to be stall-fed on the hay cut from the meadow.

The cereals grown would have been taken down the long lane to the water mill to be ground for flour, whilst vegetables, poultry and perhaps pigs would have been raised in the crofts behind each farmstead in the village street. Pigs may have spent some time with the swineherd in the distant woodland, but part of the wood would have been cropped for fuel, poles, wood for repairs to buildings, fences, implements and so on, while a few trees may have been cut down for constructional work on the bridge over the Yeo or to build a new house. Incidentally, this picture of the working of Ashington suggests all sorts of local routes to and fro across the parish in performing these various activities. Such visual pictures, and thinking oneself into the functioning of landscapes, is essential if any true understanding is to be achieved.

DISTANT RESOURCES

In the documented medieval period, we know that communities often used distant resources, such as extensive pasture or woodland, on a communal or seasonal basis, sometimes involving travel over quite long distances. This transhumance to distant resources is often thought of only in connection with more primitive and foreign communities, but it was certainly common in Anglo-Saxon and medieval times and must have been in earlier periods as well (*Figs. 11, 59 and 93*). David Clarke suggested use of resources over a very wide area by the lake village at Glastonbury in the Iron Age, and John Coles suggests that the pattern of land use in the Levels shown by Michael Williams for the medieval period probably has a prehistoric ancestry.

Transhumance needs to be acknowledged as a factor when attempting to understand the functioning of any settlement or parish under study. It is often reflected in parishes or estates with detached portions elsewhere, or areas shared in common with neighbouring parishes. Elsewhere, there are clear documentary references to long-distance links between various places. Such distant resources usually comprised woodland, commons and wastes and sometimes meadowland.

Woodland

We have already seen that not only was forest the natural primeval vegetation of Britain, but also that enormous areas had been felled to create arable land by the Bronze Age and that woodland management probably existed by the Neolithic period. The preservation qualities of the Somerset Levels have demonstrated to us a wide range of prehistoric woodworking skills and the uses to which wood was put, not only for use in trackways (*Fig. 5*), hurdles, and so on, but also for making artefacts. The apparent management of woodland to produce trees and wood of specific sizes and to meet demand is demonstrated in the structures dating from around 3500 BC which have been excavated in the Levels. Even at this early date, therefore, we have to allow for managed areas of woodland, as well as wildwood, in the landscape. Peter Reynolds has shown how much woodland was needed to provide fuel and building materials continually for an Iron Age farmstead of c.300 BC in southern England – some 8 hectares (20 acres) (out of 52 hectares [130 acres]). Such evidence at least suggests that, after the initial vast prehistoric clearances, conservation of woodland was necessary and woodland management would have been widespread. Regeneration of forest clearly occurred in the post-Roman period – but it was *regeneration* over areas which had either been managed woodland or arable (*Fig. 92*).

Woodland has, therefore, been managed for a very long time and we shall examine this further in a moment. However, it must be pointed out that the traditional explanation for the destruction of woodland from the late prehistoric period onwards to provide fuel for ironworking (and salt boiling in the Midlands) fails to take into account the fact that such activity is more likely to have engendered conservation

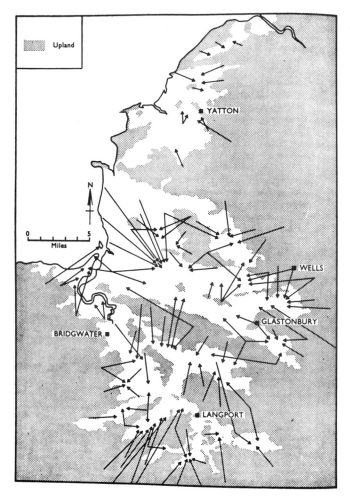

62 *Distant resources shared by numerous parishes: the Somerset Levels and the Fenland. In both the Somerset Levels (left) and the Fenland (right) of eastern England many places had rights to the low-lying seasonally flooded grasslands. This valuable resource was shared communally before recent enclosure and drainage: com-* *munities were prepared to travel considerable distances with their herds to get to the rich pasturage. (Reproduced by permission of Cambridge University Press, Dr Michael Williams and Professor H. C. Darby from M. Williams* The Draining of the Somerset Levels, *1970; H. C. Darby* The Changing Fenland, *1983)*

and careful management of woodland resources rather than wholesale clearance. The resulting open landscapes are more likely to be the result of overcropping and failure to allow sufficient time for regeneration to take place.

Oliver Rackham has shown how complex traditional woodland management was, in contrast to modern forestry, in that a self-generating system was employed so that the resources of wood and timber were infinitely renewable and two types of 'crop' were taken. The first crop, taken out at intervals of 30 years or more, was that of standard trees for timber production. These trees included oak, ash and maple and the timber was needed for construction – of buildings, boats, carts, defences, and so on.

The second crop was of underwood and coppice, with felling taking place at intervals of seven years or

so. A system of rotation was used for this crop, with coppices being taken from a different part of the wood each year. A wide variety of species was used, but hazel (which coppices naturally) was particularly important. These shrubs were cut off at ground level so that stools developed from which new shoots emerged – the stools can therefore be of very great age, having been through many cycles of cutting. In order for the shoots to grow and mature they have to be protected from browsing animals, and hence woodbanks are common features of woodland archaeology. These would originally have been topped with a fence of dead wood or a live hedge to keep the animals out. The line of such a woodbank may be marked by pollarded trees, which have, in effect, been coppiced at a higher level, above the reach of cattle. The coppicing produced wooden poles and rails for firewood, fencing, implement

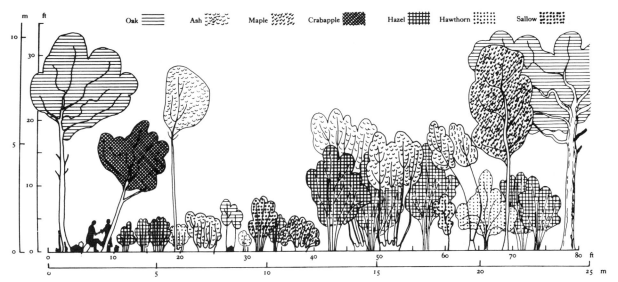

Oak · Ash · Maple · Crabapple · Hazel · Hawthorn · Sallow

63 *Reconstruction of woodland structure under classical coppice management as used in the Middle Ages. As well as the standards (oak, crab apple, ash, and maple) there are two areas of coppice. The left-hand area was felled last winter and is now sprouting from coppice stools. The right-hand area has five seasons' growth and is ready for felling, although it may be left for several more seasons. (After Oliver Rackham with permission)*

making, constructional work such as wattles, and small-size material for a host of uses around the farmstead and house. It also produced wood for charcoal burning – the only fuel used extensively for industrial activities before coal became more intensively mined and more widely available.

We have already mentioned that woodland could be located at a distance from the settlement, as only infrequent visits needed to be made. Timber for construction needs to be acquired only from time to time, and enough firewood can be collected in one journey to last several months. Nevertheless, these apparently simple arrangements belie more complex interrelationships (*Fig. 85*): not all places had access to sufficient wood stocks, and owners of well-wooded land would not only supply their own estates but also sell wood to less-wooded estates. This is demonstrated by Oliver Rackham in his study of Hayley Wood.

In the last decade a new branch of field archaeology has developed – woodland archaeology. In addition to the palaeo-environmental research in woods and forests, and the current interest of nature conservancy agencies in maintaining the plant and animal communities within them, there is the recognition that there are many field 'monuments' to be recorded and understood within ancient woodland. Most woods have a multitude of banks, ditches and enclosures relating to their former management, which can be shown to have developed at different times. There may be charcoal pans where charcoal burners camped periodically to use the wood from the area around to produce charcoal. Saw pits have been recognised in some woods – a late medieval one was excavated in

Wetmoor, part of the former Horwood in Gloucestershire. All sorts of other strange and inexplicable man-made features have been recognised, the most exciting of which are pre-woodland settlement, field and burial sites which have been engulfed by the trees. Several examples were found in woods on the line of the M3 motorway in Hampshire.

The former management of woodland has resulted in many complex patterns and administrative arrangements, and great complexity may be expected from the documentary and topographical records. The use and appearance of the land depend in so many cases on the period under discussion and the intensity of management, and many more detailed studies are needed of present and former woodland areas.

Royal forests and parks

The term 'royal forest' always conjures up the wrong picture. Many forests, like Dartmoor, Exmoor and the Peak District, were not wooded, and many encompassed vast areas of fields and settlements. The term refers to the law applied to these areas, which was designed to maintain and encourage wild animals, principally deer, and the greenery on which they depended. Since most royal forests were subject to common rights held by surrounding settlements, there was a tendency for the woodland to degrade to wood pasture, and eventually common, unless it was specifically managed in the ways already described. Many areas did indeed degrade in this way, which can be seen particularly from later maps. Around many forests and other parts of the country, parks were created to maintain areas of wood pasture for grazing animals and deer. Elaborate banks

THE FOREST OF NEROCHE
THE LATE MEDIEVAL LANDSCAPE

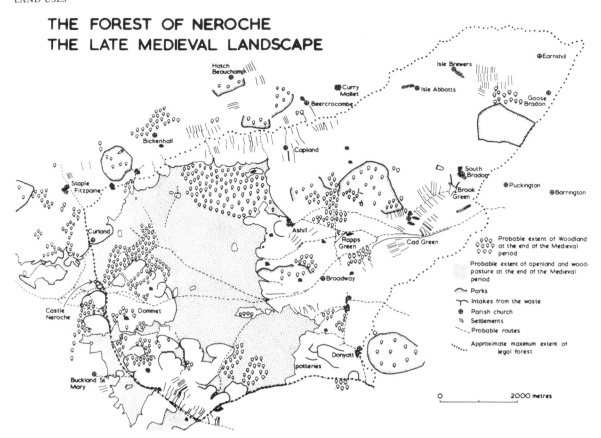

64 *The Forest of Neroche in Somerset. This map shows the probable appearance of the royal forest before enclosure in the seventeenth and nineteenth centuries. The central area was an extensive open common of wood pasture. Around this are the* *'funnel' access ways from enclosed land, evident as intakes from surrounding settlements. All around are parks. Notice the potteries at Donyatt.*

and ditches were often constructed, with timber pales on top and deer leaps to encourage deer to enter (but not escape). In addition to earthworks, field names often indicate parks, and sometimes curvilinear field boundaries can be seen on maps and air pictures.

Within the forests themselves a number of features should be looked for. There may be lodges or park keepers' houses (often with moats and fishponds), rides or open access ways through separate coppices or fells (felled in rotation and often embanked) and areas of open land or common. Frequently, the latter have funnel-shaped access ways on to them and former forest from the enclosed areas around. Good examples can be seen at Hatfield Forest in Essex and Neroche Forest in Somerset (*Figs. 64 and 83*). Even after all the forest and common has been enclosed, this often leaves characteristic triangular field boundary arrangements.

Commons and wastes

Far more settlements had access to areas of common and waste than is generally acknowledged in books about the English landscape (*Fig. 82*). Huge areas of open land were evident until enclosure from the seventeenth century onwards; large areas of common, former royal forests and openly grazed rough wood pasture areas disappeared in early nineteenth-century acts. In general, those areas have not been studied to see either how they evolved to their final pre-enclosure state or how they were utilised by surrounding settlements.

Perhaps the most commonly used distant resources were upland rough pasture and common in use at summertime by settlements surrounding the upland. Dartmoor in Devon and Exmoor and Mendip in Somerset were all used like this. Dartmoor was used by the inhabitants of both Devon and Cornwall until AD 850, after which date common rights began to develop for the Moor, protecting the rights of all but the people of Barnstaple and Totnes (who were excluded after AD 900), while allowing the area to be hunted by the Wessex kings. It became a royal forest in Norman times, but, after its disafforestation in 1239, some settlement took place. In the parishes of Dartmoor various farms held *venville* rights (from *fines*

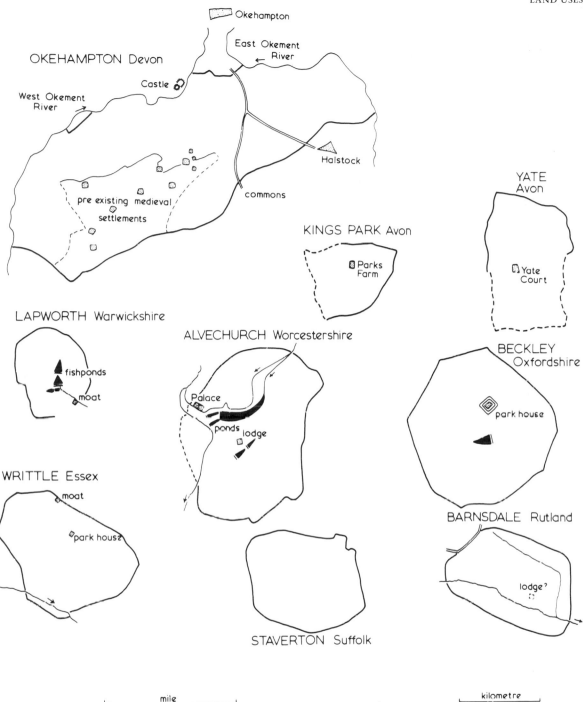

65 *Plans of medieval parks. This selection shows typical medieval parks with their characteristic curvilinear boundaries and typical features within them, such as lodges, moats and fishponds.*

villarum). Venville tenants paid a certain, very small, fixed rent to the king or duchy, and were allowed free pasture on the commons and forest by day, but had to pay extra if they remained in the forest by night. The numbers of animals were supposed to be limited to the number their farms could support in winter. They could also take from the forest all they needed for fuel, building, hedging, and so on. Other rights were held by the householders of the rest of Devon, who were classed as 'strangers' or 'foreigners' and were allowed to depasture beasts on the commons of Devon surrounding the forest, without payment, and on the forest only on payment of certain small fees. This system was recorded in 1269, but was already well established.

On Exmoor, a similar legal distinction was made between the royal forest and surrounding commons, clearly seen on 'The Map of Exmore' of 1675. As on Dartmoor, there were ancient tenements, in Withypoole and Hawkridge, and complex arrangements for the number of cattle which could be agisted on the commons. There is a similar early map of Mendip showing the upland pasture surrounded by the villages and hamlets which had rights of common over the area. On Mendip, lead mining was also important and, like Dartmoor's tin industry, this was closely regulated.

Other upland pasture with such regulations includes the Clee Hills, where Trevor Rowley has been able to explain the many routeways as a reflection of the *straker routes* of commoners herding animals from lowland settlements to upland pastures. As we shall see, such pasturage was increasingly valuable (and hence subject to regulation) and this was part of a general concern from the Middle Ages onwards with providing sufficient grass and fodder for animals all through the year.

Commons nearer to settlements were used for a variety of purposes. Pasture for horses, cattle, sheep, pigs, geese and ducks was very important, and any ponds would probably have held fish. However, as implied for Mendip, digging took place for stone, sand, gravel and clay, for building and other purposes, and minerals like iron and coal were extracted if they were available. Several important medieval and later

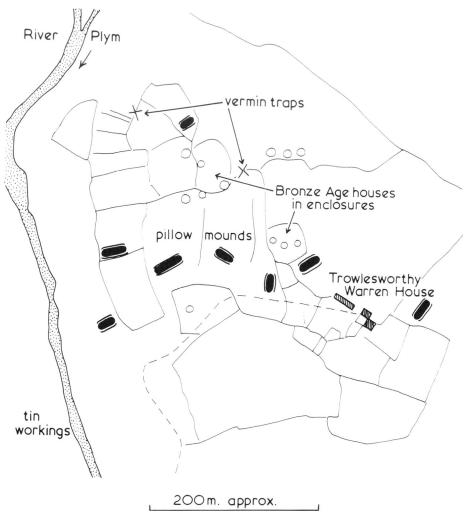

66 *Trowlesworthy Warren on Dartmoor in Devon. The vertical air photograph shows at least three superimposed landscapes: round houses, pounds and enclosures of the Bronze Age; a farmstead, fields, enclosures and tin streaming of the medieval period (if not earlier); and a warren of the Middle Ages and later. The main features of the warren are shown on the map and consist of the warren house, pillow mounds and vermin traps, some of which are more evident on the ground. (Air photograph by permission of Royal Commission on Historical Monuments (England) SX 5664/1/15)*

pottery industries were located in such areas – Leafield and Nettlebed in Oxfordshire, Minety in Wiltshire, and Donyatt in Somerset, for example. Turf and peat could be cut and dried for fuel and building materials, rough wood was used for firewood and construction, and reeds, rushes and bracken were gathered for bedding, roofing, flooring and building. The term 'waste' applied to such areas gives the wrong impression, and the tidy enclosed appearance of many of these former landscapes today makes it difficult to appreciate their importance to earlier people. Like woodland, such areas have their own archaeology and their own characteristic field monuments. Two will be described here: pillow mounds and former rabbit warrens, and decoys for taking wildfowl.

Rabbit breeding
All over England there are enigmatic earthworks called *pillow mounds* by archaeologists, although they are more cigar- or bolster-shaped. They can occur associated with ridge and furrow and village earthworks, but they are more widespread on upland areas like Dartmoor, where hundreds of them are scattered across the upland pasture. After much debate it seems that these were built for rabbits to live and breed in so that they could be caught for meat and fur. This may have been done in the Middle Ages, but many warrens seem to date from the sixteenth century onwards. Their construction and use indicates permanent pasture, thus they presumably represent abandoned areas when occurring on village and field sites.

While the pillow mounds, either isolated or in groups, are the most obvious field monuments, other features should be looked for. There was often a warrener's house with sheds where feed, nets, and other equipment would have been kept, and sometimes a boundary, rather like a park pale, can be distinguished around the warren area. Much more difficult to find, although probably widespread, are the cross-shaped vermin traps, built to intercept predators like rats and weasels. They are fully described in operation by Hansford Worth on Dartmoor, where

67 *Vermin trap at Trowlesworthy Warren on Dartmoor in Devon. The low granite walls of the cross-shaped vermin trap are difficult to distinguish in the boulder-strewn landscape. The figure stands at the trap site: behind is a pillow mound. The trap is built into the wall of a Bronze Age enclosure.*

they remain as stone-built structures. Others exist in the hillfort which became Dolebury Warren outside Bristol, and a fine earthwork example, all of 15 centimetres (6 inches) high, remains on Minchinhampton Common near Stroud in Gloucestershire. There must be more of these warrens and their associated structures in the landscape and they represent interesting early aspects of pasture land use. Only one seems to be securely dated: that at Bryncysegrfan, Llanfair Clydogan in Dyfed, which was excavated and found to have stone tunnels within it; radiocarbon dating suggests a date around AD 1375 ± 60.

68 *Pillow mound at Bryncysegrfan, Llanfair Clydogan in Dyfed. The excavation of this pillow mound revealed a network of artificial burrows and nests dug into the underlying subsoil. Radiocarbon dating suggests a fourteenth-century date for construction. (By permission of David Austin)*

69 *A duck decoy in operation in the nineteenth century. A 'pipe' running off the main pool is covered with a net on metal hoops and is lined with screens. The decoyman is supervising a small dog which* *is enticing the ducks up the pipe to the traps at the end. (From Payne-Gallwey* The Book of Duck Decoys, *1886)*

Duck decoys

Lowland areas were not only important for pasture; seasonal flooding of such areas attracted large numbers of wildfowl which were an important source of food in such localities for a very long time. When these areas were drained and enclosed, less water accumulated on them and there was less natural habitat suitable for visiting ducks and other water fowl. From the seventeenth century onwards, attempts were made to create artificial pools with trapping systems, but it was not until the eighteenth and nineteenth centuries that ideas became at all sophisticated. The result was the duck decoy, consisting of an artificial pool with pipes leading off which were covered with nets and lined with screens. Small dogs were used to decoy the ducks, and large numbers were taken each winter. In some parts of the country, such as eastern England and the Somerset Levels, the dry grassy hollows left by such decoys are widespread. Together with circular and rectilinear stock watering ponds, they form distinctive elements of lowland landscapes.

Meadows

From the sixteenth century onwards, various improvements were made to increase the amount of grass and hay that could be produced from low-lying meadowland. These developments are best known from the chalkland valleys of Wessex, but they certainly exist elsewhere, although they are poorly recorded, if at all. Water was conducted into the meadow via artificially constructed channels and elaborate sluice gates and allowed to flow across the grass. It was not allowed to stand, merely to percolate through the roots, and channels were dug to conduct the water away into another meadow or back into the stream or river. Such *floated meadows* produced early grass for sheep, especially young lambs, and were frost-free in early spring, as the running water was not as cold as the grass itself.

This system was well developed by the eighteenth and nineteenth centuries, with complex regulations to control the use of the water. The elaborate earthworks of the meadows, which look like ridge and furrow, still

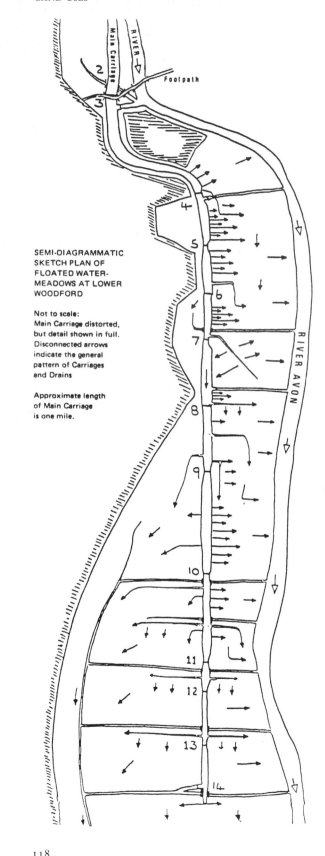

SEMI-DIAGRAMMATIC
SKETCH PLAN OF
FLOATED WATER-
MEADOWS AT LOWER
WOODFORD

Not to scale:
Main Carriage distorted,
but detail shown in full.
Disconnected arrows
indicate the general
pattern of Carriages
and Drains

Approximate length
of Main Carriage
is one mile.

exist over vast areas, but few are now used. It was part of a wider agricultural system with sheep pastured on the rich meadow grass then walked to be folded on fallow arable areas overnight, where their dung helped to maintain fertility on the thin chalkland soils.

A similar system was also used in the West Country on steep hillsides from the seventeenth century onwards. There, springs would be tapped at their source and conducted along a horizontal leat on the hillside. No outlet was provided and, once the leat was full, the water was allowed to overflow down the hillside via sluice gates or boards, raising the temperature of the frosted land to that of the spring water and encouraging the grass to grow early – again to help feed sheep and lambs in the early spring. At Holnicote in Selworthy parish in Somerset, a modified plough was kept to clean out the gutters of the water leats, while the Knight family, who reclaimed Exmoor forest in the nineteenth century, kept records of water temperatures, showing clearly the effect of slightly warmer spring water on the growth of the grass. Such water leats are widespread and, again, are generally poorly recorded. The slight channels have been interpreted as mill leats, paths and sheep walks; the association with a spring (or springs) is critical, as is the fact that there is no outlet.

Each of these developments represents another aspect of the wide variety of new techniques and ideas being employed in land use management from the sixteenth century onwards. Frequently, local researchers come across such features, but there is little published to help explain them.

70 *Floated watermeadows at Lower Woodford in Wiltshire. This sketch map shows a watermeadow system probably of seventeenth-century date and still operative. 'The system becomes live at point 4, with the first of a series of hatches on the main carriage which enable the intervening sections to be isolated. In the early part of the year there is usually enough water coming down the river to enable most of the system to be drowned at once. At other times water may have to be used more sparingly and only one part flooded at a time. In the past the needs of others up and down stream have also had to be considered ... By lowering the paddles at the next lower hatch a section of the main carriage can be filled so that the water spills into the carriers. These are trenches cut along the top of the ridges from which the water spills down the sides, or panes, to create the moving film required.' (By permission of M. Cowan from* Floated Water Meadows in the Salisbury Area, *South Wiltshire Industrial Archaeology Society, Historical Monograph 9, 1981)*

71 *Waterleats at Tolland in Somerset. These channels along the hillside were used in the same way as watermeadows. Water from the springs, which can be seen marked by boggy patches, was conducted along the waterleats which have no outlet. It overflowed the banks, watered the hillsides (encouraging early growth of grass) and was conducted away in the stream in the valley bottom.*

10

Field systems

Having looked at different land uses, it remains to discuss how these were arranged into particular field systems. There was an enormous range of possibilities in the way animals could be managed and arable areas could be organised in the past. It is worth emphasising this, because the literature on fields and field systems is dominated by the common field system of the Midlands, much like settlement studies have been dominated by considerations of the village. This chapter will not attempt to describe all the variations, as almost every parish and township was different, but we shall be concerned with origins, main types and how these altered into the modern or present landscape. Let us begin with the common open fields of the Midlands.

The Midland system

Gonner's map of the enclosure of common fields in the eighteenth and nineteenth centuries demonstrates the location and demise of the common field systems. These were based on two or three large open fields which were unenclosed and unhedged. They were divided into furlongs and these were sub-divided into strips owned by individual tenant farmers. Later, more and more fields were developed by sub-dividing larger ones or re-arranging the furlongs. These fields were farmed in common, with all the farmers jointly agreeing on cropping, rotation, use for pasture, and so on.

This system is particularly associated with nucleated settlements, and characteristically with the village. The places that worked this system often ended up with little or no woodland, pasture or waste within their territories, although they usually had meadow or upland grass for sheep runs. In order to accommodate animals, a system of rotation had to be employed not only to rest, fallow and manure the land, but to provide land and grass for animals within the settlement's boundaries. This latter point is important, since with extensive pasture or waste it would not have been necessary to alternate arable with pasture in a rotation system; the arable could have been continuously cropped and manured and the animals could

have been accommodated elsewhere. This type of Midland field system has been well studied and examples are numerous: Middleton on the Wolds and Wold Newton in the East Riding of Yorkshire, Chellington in Bedfordshire, Padbury in Buckinghamshire, Elford in Staffordshire, and so on.

Whatever the earliest arrangements of fields, furlongs and strips might have been, by the time we get detailed descriptions in documents and clear views from maps, this system had become very complex, with numerous fields, combinations of strips into single ownership and elaborate rotation arrangements. Most townships, even within the Midland system, had their own variations on this general theme. At Milton under Wychwood in Oxfordshire, for example, there were open fields with strips, but there was also an area of meadow, heath and downland (*Fig. 84*).

Field evidence

Fieldwork and examination of air photographs in these areas of former common fields will often show vast areas (or formerly vast areas where recent ploughing has been intensive) of ridge and furrow earthworks. There have been many spurious explanations of how and why this was formed (including attempts to increase the surface area of a field!), but it now seems that in most areas it indicates former arable and that it serves both to drain the land, particularly on heavy clays, and to demarcate ownership of strips by the provision of ditches and furrows. Maurice Beresford was able to show that ridge and furrow is connected to the strip system in the open fields, even though there was not a direct correlation of ridge to strip, several ridges usually making up one holding.

In such common field areas, the ridge and furrow is characteristically long, wide, high-backed and reversed S in plan – the aratral curve. Much discussion has taken place on how this was formed and worked. These arguments have centred on whether it came about by the action of the plough or was constructed by hand, and whether the plough would maintain the shape, or whether the reversed S came about through

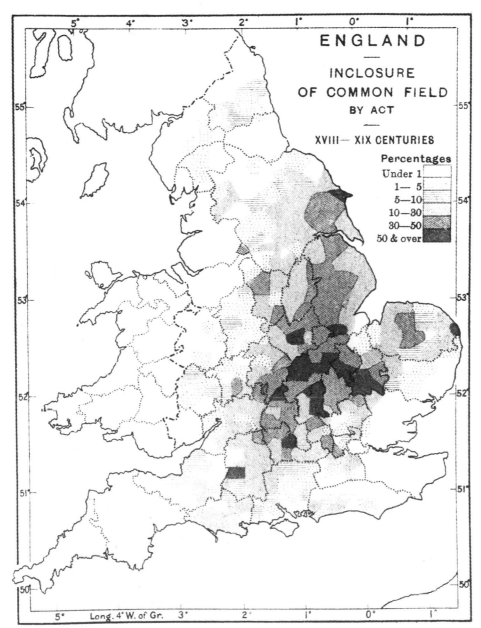

72 *Map of England showing enclosure of common field in the eighteenth and nineteenth centuries. While being a very old map, this still shows best the main areas of common open field arable remaining to be enclosed up to the late nineteenth century. Notice that such enclosure extended into West Somerset, the Welsh Borders, Sussex, East Anglia, and as far north as Northumberland. The main concentration is, however, in Northamptonshire, Leicestershire, Buckinghamshire and Cambridgeshire. (From E. C. K. Gonner* Common Land and Enclosure, *1912)*

continuous ploughing. This question is not yet resolved, but some hand-and-spade construction may have been involved, while ploughing with heavy medieval ploughs would have maintained the profile.

Not all areas of ridge and furrow, however, are like the large medieval earthworks. At present at least five types can be recognised, each different and apparently representing other periods and field systems. The earliest ridge and furrow to be recognised so far is at

Hen Domen in Powys and Gwithian in Cornwall. The latter was buried in a sand-blow in pre-medieval times, whereas the former was covered by the earthworks of a castle built in 1070, or thereabouts, after it had been abandoned as arable for some time, had become overgrown and been used as a hunting area; it could thus be of tenth-century date or earlier. Both areas have narrow, very slight and irregular ridges, and similar examples have been found elsewhere (on the Somerset

73 *Air photograph of ridge and furrow earthworks, Husband's Bosworth in Leicestershire. This picture shows the characteristic earthworks of ridge and furrow with the ridges of variable width, length and orientation, although invariably reversed 'S' in outline. Notice how the earthworks are cut by the railway and overlain by the field boundaries. (Copyright Cambridge University Committee for Aerial Photography AEV19, 31st May 1962)*

farmsteads are indicated by scatters of pottery sherds across the parish. There may be more, since, although the north-east area of the parish is clearly a blank, the north-west is still under pasture – covered in medieval ridge and furrow. It is only the change from pasture to arable since the 1960s that has revealed the sites of these early medieval farms, which were formerly covered by later medieval ridge and furrow. The present, slightly shrunken, village developed around the road junction west of the Manor Court, probably from the thirteenth century onwards. We seem to have at Frocester a late Saxon/early medieval settlement pattern of scattered farms and an isolated minster church, much like we have already seen elsewhere. Only in the thirteenth century does a more nucleated village appear.

Something important happened in the early medieval period at Frocester, and Mr Edward Price, who has done most of the detailed fieldwork in this area, has found important evidence of field system changes in excavating the Roman villa south of the farm. The villa site was not overploughed for centuries, but all around its site are the scratch marks of the pointed ploughs in use until the thirteenth century. Then there was not only a change in headland position and type of ploughing, but also in type of ploughshare, all suggesting perhaps a re-allocation or re-arrangement of fields. This evidence suggests important changes in fields as well as settlements in the early Middle Ages – in this case the thirteenth century. The villa was overploughed; the ridges and furrows were wider and more prominent.

uplands, for example), often apparently of early medieval date and associated with infield/outfield systems. Secondly, there is the classic ridge and furrow already described. In at least one example, at Frocester in Gloucestershire, we seem to have a transition from the earlier narrow to the later wider ridges, in this case associated with settlement changes and the obliteration of Roman villa earthworks.

The case study of Frocester, Gloucestershire

The Frocester area probably began in late prehistoric times as farmland dependent on the nearby hillfort of Uleybury. In Roman times there were at least three villas in the vicinity, including one under the church of St Peter and another next to the medieval manor belonging to Gloucester Abbey. By late Saxon times there was a minster church at St Peter's and, from the eleventh to thirteenth centuries, at least eight separate

74 *The formation and use of ridge and furrow. The medieval plough, as shown in the Luttrell Psalter, consisted of the beam supporting a coulter which cut the sod vertically, a share cutting horizontally and a mouldboard which turned the soil over. The ploughteam consisted of oxen in pairs (up to eight) with the plough, ploughman and a man (or boy) to encourage the team of oxen.*

The common fields were ploughed in strips by such teams and, since the mouldboard threw the soil to the right, the team had to work clockwise around the strip to maintain a ridge of soil (A). The ploughteam could be of considerable length, and problems could develop in getting the plough to the end of the strip (B). The team could be trampling the crop in the adjacent furlong. The solution was to turn the team at the end of the strip on to the headland, while still pulling the plough, before turning back down the strip (C). In theory, the team could be turned to the left or the right. Ridge and furrow in reversed S form (E) seems universal rather than that shown in D. The reason may be that, with the plough already throwing soil to the right, there would have been too many forces acting on the ploughman if the team also moved to the right (D). At least in E the pull of the plough to the right is somewhat compensated for by the team turning to the left. It is easy enough to turn the team on the headland in either case.

No doubt some experimentation by archaeologists would help to indicate if the hypothesis shown here for the use of ridge and furrow is likely to be correct.

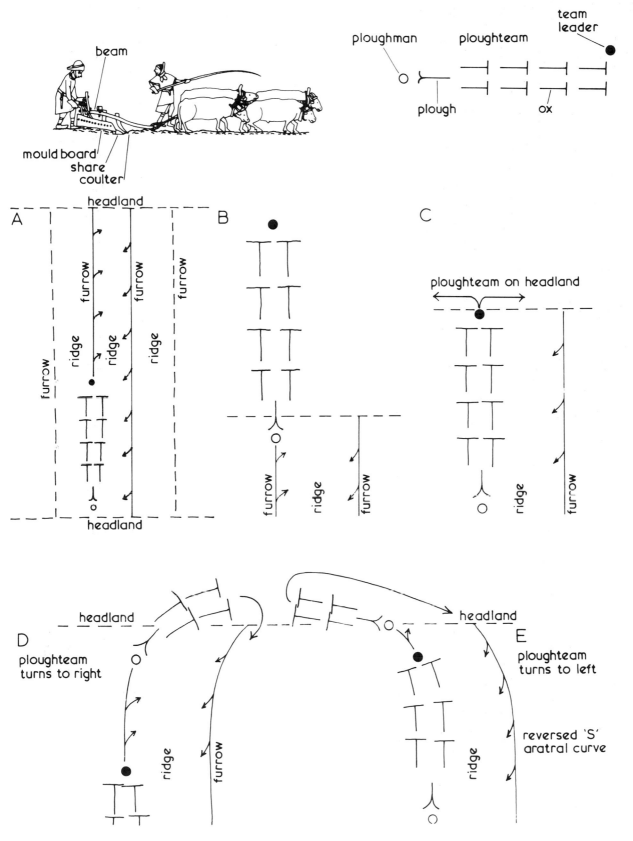

beam

ploughman ploughteam team leader

plough ox

mould board
share
coulter

A headland

furrow furrow furrow

ridge ridge ridge

furrow

furrow

headland

B

furrow ridge furrow

C

ploughteam on headland

ridge furrow

D
ploughteam
turns to right

headland

ridge furrow

E
ploughteam
turns to left

reversed 'S'
aratral curve

ridge

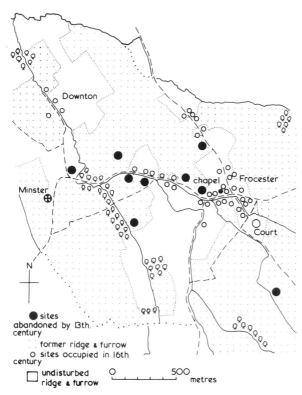

● sites
abandoned by 13th.
century

former ridge & furrow
○ sites occupied in 16th.
century

□ undisturbed
ridge & furrow

0   500
                          metres

75 *Medieval settlement in Frocester, Gloucestershire. The abandonment of many farmsteads and the development of the village at Frocester seem to have been associated with alterations in the fields, including the development of larger scale ridge and furrow (After E. Price, with permission)*

At Frocester in the Middle Ages there was an undeveloped open field system; up to 60 landholders shared strips in 12 open fields, some of which may have been cleared from woodland (as at Nockholte – Oak Wood). Their pasture, however, was held individually and there was an increasing tendency towards the sixteenth century for strips in the open fields to be enclosed. There was very little meadowland, although some of the former arable in low-lying situations may have reverted to pasture after the fourteenth century, but what there was was held in strips (*doles*) or small embanked enclosures down by the streams. In one area the pressure of arable land use in the early Middle Ages can be seen clearly: ordinary ridge and furrow on gentle slopes merges gradually into a series of strip lynchets on the steep slopes below the Cotswolds. This demonstrates, as at Mere in Wiltshire and South Cadbury in Somerset, that strip lynchets are merely strips in the open fields, in this case the Upfield of Frocester, transferred to steeper slopes.

A third type of ridge and furrow can be seen in areas not ploughed and developed until the eighteenth and nineteenth centuries, when horse ploughing and the

use of more elaborate machinery, including steam ploughs, produced narrow, low, but very regular ridges. There is not usually any problem in recognising these late regular earthworks.

Then there are two oddities. The spade-built and -worked lazybeds of the north and west often look like ridge and furrow on air photographs, but the heaped nature of the ridges and the fact that they run together forming a reticulated mass shows them to be different. There are also the low-lying, low ridges of areas like the Somerset Levels (*Fig. 48*). These were clearly intended as drainage earthworks principally (as in part was ridge and furrow), but such areas were used for arable, as is shown by records and the implications of plough teams for such areas in 1086. As we have already seen, watermeadows also resemble ridge and furrow, although their purpose was quite different.

ORIGINS OF OPEN FIELD SYSTEMS

It is very much easier to say how common fields were extinguished than to say how open field systems came into existence. A few common fields still survive in a debased form, so the system is not entirely extinct; the famous examples are Laxton in Nottinghamshire, Braunton in Devon, Portland in Dorset and Soham in Cambridgeshire. Generally speaking, however, enclosure from the Middle Ages onwards was gradual and piecemeal by agreement among the tenants, culminating in the enclosure acts of the eighteenth and nineteenth centuries which extinguished such systems to produce our more familiar landscapes; this will be discussed later.

We can, at the moment, envisage four or five possible origins or models for how such systems might have developed, although these are only theoretical concepts. The first is a racial or ethnic model, first put forward by H.L. Gray when he attempted to show how field systems varied across the country, and seemed to reflect what was thought of the origins of settlements in those areas. Thus, as villages were thought to be Saxon, and assumed to have common fields, so it was reasoned that common fields must have been a Saxon introduction from north Europe. We now know that common field systems did not exist in the country of origin of the settlers at that time, so this idea is no longer tenable. Similarly, it was assumed that the Celtic population remained in the west, where a predominantly enclosed and individual field system was found. All these ideas were modified by C.S. and C.S. Orwin in what we might call a colonisation model. They argued that Saxon settlers clearing woodland and establishing settlements would have had to work together, and hence a communal field system would develop. Further assarting, adding more land, would also take place communally and the spoils would be shared out, but we have already seen that, by late Roman times, not much woodland needed to be cleared and settlements probably had a more continuous life than has previously been thought.

In fact, there must be some element of colonisation in the development of field systems, but it probably took place later, in the pre-Norman period, and from a different basis. With farming, people are always driven by a persistence of the agricultural year. If crops are not planted and animals supervised, there is no harvest and people starve and die. What happens at the top of the hierarchy is unimportant: kings, popes and rulers can change, whole political structures can alter, but if the peasants do not plant, tend and harvest crops, then life cannot go on. What we must envisage, then, is a case of land always being cultivated right through from prehistoric to medieval times. It may not be the same areas, although good quality land would always be farmed. As populations fell, some land would be abandoned, to be recolonised later when there were more mouths to feed.

The actual areas used in medieval and prehistoric times will be the same in some places and we should be able to see prehistoric and medieval fields mixed up together. This idea of a continuity model leads us to one of the most difficult problems in the history of the

English landscape – how and whether the pattern of so-called Celtic fields was developed into the system of medieval open fields and common field systems seen over much of the country by the late Middle Ages. Celtic or prehistoric fields, as we have seen, formed a regular rectilinear pattern of small square fields with, in places, prominent lynchets and clearly defined access ways. Much of the medieval field pattern consisted of open fields made up of blocks of strips, often in the form of ridge and furrow bundled together into furlongs.

How did the one change into the other, as it surely must have done over much of Britain? We might expect to find the pattern of small square Celtic fields developed into long fields and strip systems by overploughing baulks and lynchets, but the evidence is very elusive both in the field and on air photographs. The problem was stated by Peter Fowler and Christopher Taylor in 1978, but few examples have been cited which illustrate the changeover. Air photographs of the Upper Thames Valley imply, in a very few cases, medieval field systems being incorporated into pre-existing patterns of prehistoric and Romano-British ditches, and other examples have been demonstrated in Tormarton in Avon, Garrow Tor in Cornwall and perhaps Malham and Grassington in Yorkshire.

BLEADON
Early fields

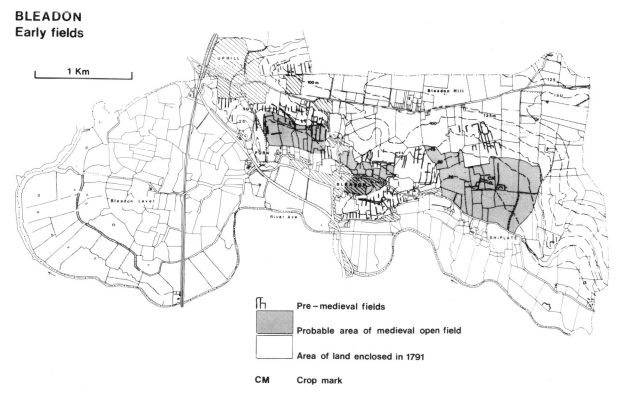

Pre-medieval fields

Probable area of medieval open field

Area of land enclosed in 1791

CM   Crop mark

76 *Fields at Bleadon in Avon. The whole area above the Levels was probably formerly divided up by early boundaries into fields. These have been obliterated in the open field areas but a number of strip boundaries in the medieval fields seem to reflect the earlier field arrangements. (After Rob Iles, with permission)*

Bleadon

A very clear example of this incorporation, however, exists at Bleadon, now in Avon (formerly in Somerset), on the west end of the Mendips near Weston Super Mare. The present parish has three clearly defined zones of land with upland on the Mendip top, *sidelands* and lowlying floodable meadows and hams along the River Axe. On the sidelands there are extensive and well-preserved areas of Celtic fields in a zone which has been permanent pasture for many centuries. On the top the area is now ploughed, but enough remains to show Celtic fields in this area, as in other parts of the top of Mendip. Behind Bleadon village and near Shiplate hamlet there were formerly two small areas of medieval open fields. A particularly detailed thirteenth-century custumal describes the working of land in the parish, and the earliest maps show strips in these areas. The lowland bowls of land behind Bleadon and Shiplate contain the best land in the parish – deep rich loams made up of hillwash, above the wetland of the levels. These areas are sheltered from the west and south-west winds and open to the sun from the south.

On the ground, the area around Bleadon village displays a number of earthworks, some well preserved and others almost ploughed out. With the help of air photographs these can be plotted on a map and shown to represent further areas of prehistoric fields below the surviving portions and overlain by the later strips of the medieval open fields. Indeed, it is clear that the strips nearest the village have been formed by overploughing the cross-banks demarcating the square fields to form long thin strip fields.

This example illustrates a number of points which we might expect to find in the landscape, but which are rarely detected. Firstly, there is a well preserved and extensive prehistoric/Romano-British field system surviving as earthworks in permanent pasture. Secondly, this can be seen to extend into the area of best land in the parish, coming down, in fact, to the edge of the levels and also on to the dry plateau top of the Mendips. Thirdly, the later fields fit into the earlier pattern, implying perhaps some continuity of land use and adaptation rather than replacement of the earlier system. If this can be seen at Bleadon, why cannot it be seen elsewhere? Work at Deerhurst in Gloucestershire failed to provide convincing evidence, but such a state of affairs must exist, logically, in many places. Perhaps we are seeing the evidence without appreciating it. Near to Bleadon it is possible that parts of the parishes of Christon, Uphill and Cheddar may have the same sort of features. It may be that the south-west, with its intensive early land use evolving into not so intensive, but nevertheless full-developed medieval field systems provides ideal circumstances to appreciate the changeover. In the Midlands, certainly, the impression is of all earlier evidence swept away by intensive medieval land use.

Such an impression may, however, be wrong if the model suggested by Harold Fox proves to be accurate. We can call this an evolutionary model, since it assumes gradual and developing complexity from relatively simple, earlier systems. It builds very much on the ideas of Joan Thirsk, who tried to distinguish the essential elements of the common field system and to see when and how these combined and developed into what can be seen most clearly in the well-documented and well-mapped immediate post-medieval period. She distinguished four essential characteristics of the fully-developed Midland system of common fields:

1 Arable and meadow divided into strips among the cultivators, each of whom may occupy a number of strips scattered about the fields.

2 Arable and meadow thrown open for common pasture by the stock of the cultivators after harvest and in fallow times.

3 Common pasturage of waste with rights to gather timber, turf, etc.

4 The ordering of all these activities regulated by an assembly of the cultivators – generally the manorial court.

Two of these characteristics are recorded relatively early on. Common pasturage goes back to the earliest documents, and strips in arable fields are attested in the laws of King Ine of Wessex (compiled between AD 688–694). Common grazing after fallow and communally agreed crop rotations and management appear later. Joan Thirsk concludes: 'with some assurance, then, we can point to the twelfth and the first half of the thirteenth centuries as possibly the crucial ones in the development of village-organized common-field systems', the earliest case of regulated cropping by a whole village being Cotes in Lincolnshire, dated 1156–7, and the first unmistakeable statement about commoning by a whole village, Stanbridge and Tilsworth in Bedfordshire, from 1240. This period represents the time from which documents are becoming more generally available, so it may not represent the beginnings of the system (as we have seen with reference to villages) but merely the first documentary references.

Harold Fox has extended the argument and suggested that, as with villages, we should probably look for a late Saxon origin for the full system, possibly in the ninth or tenth centuries. He suggests that on large estates, with an intermixed economy between hamlets, each settlement would probably have provided for its own subsistence needs from a simple infield/outfield system, using the infield for its crops and the outfield as extensive pasture for its animals. Some hamlets would have provided special commodities depending on their topographical situation, and would thus have rendered sheep, cattle or cereals to the caput of the estate; sometimes this would be reflected in their place names (*Fig. 11*). With the break-up of these early units, as has been discussed, it became necessary for each hamlet to provide all its own needs from its own lands. Although not initially a problem, as the population grew and more land was taken into cultivation, the limits to the land would eventually be reached and, in the absence of extensive land elsewhere, the pasturage, eliminated to provide new areas of arable, would have to be provided by occasionally fallowing some arable for the animals.

This is an attractive model showing the complexity of the Midland system developing alongside population increase and the development of the village form of settlement from the late Saxon period onwards. It suggests evolution from simpler beginnings and implies that all stages of change, from simple to complex, should be found in the landscape at different times: this is, in fact, what is seen.

Finally, there is a fifth model of development, where sudden change takes place and a whole new system is created or deliberately planned. This may, of course, have happened anyway, as every new field system has to have a first year following the decision to change. However, planned field systems can be seen most clearly in a number of northern examples, in Yorkshire in particular. For the Holderness area, Mary Harvey has shown exceptionally even layouts of fields with long strips, very regularly arranged in furlongs associated with apparently unplanned villages. It is difficult to imagine that such fields were not deliberately planned and the impression is of the same regularity which is implied in the 'sun-division' (*solskifte*) arrangement of strips recognised in Scandinavia and increasingly in northern England. In this system the arrangement of the strips in the open fields reflects the arrangement of the homesteads along the village street – neighbours in the street were also neighbours in the fields. Again, it is difficult not to think of deliberate planning behind such a system. The incidence of sun-division and its full implications have still to be worked out, but it seems to have been widespread and may reflect a distant memory to the deliberate creation of common field systems from earlier types of field systems.

If such an evolutionary development of field systems is likely, with deliberate creation of some of the more complex or regular systems later on, it ought to be possible to recognise all the stages of development from primitive examples through to the complex common field examples already mentioned. This does, indeed, seem to be the case. In many areas there are hamlets which have shared arable strips and meadow, but independently-held pasture in enclosed fields, with common waste and woodland elsewhere. The variety is total and the local researcher should accept that this is the case. He should try to explain the system at a particular time, and then consider earlier arrangements, if this is possible, and how more recent patterns emerged. It is no longer necessary to try to understand the fields of any particular settlement as a fully-fledged common field system, with all the strips and furlongs in the open fields and a fully-developed court system to regulate the activities. All sorts of variation are possible.

At Hanbury in Worcestershire (*Fig. 58*) the arable was worked and regulated in common, and so was the meadow, but all the other types of land were held independently by farmers, some of whom lived along a street (not really a village), while others lived in isolated farms across the landscape. At Marden in Herefordshire, a group of hamlets farmed much of the parish in common, but June Sheppard suggested that the furlongs with their strips had evolved from core areas, with more arable strips being added, presumably from pasture and waste, as time passed. At Wheldrake she was able to show that the common fields developed relatively late from an earlier enclosed open field around the village. This is reflected in a surviving *turf dyke* which surrounds the land immediately adjacent to the village. Later common open fields were developed beyond.

Brian Roberts, in his study of the village of Cockfield in Durham, has suggested that the planned row of farmsteads north of the village green replaced a hamlet located near to the surviving farm of the manor house. This earlier hamlet had an oval infield surrounded by a large bank attached to it. It is not clear how the later field system developed from this.

What, then, did the earlier or original field systems look like? We have already seen in the discussion of land use what, in theory, the system should be. It should have arable close at hand, pasture, waste and wood some way off, and meadowland available. Alan Baker and Robin Butlin, in summarising their enormous survey of field systems in Britain, were in no doubt: 'on theoretical grounds, it is possible to consider what form one might expect these early field systems to have taken and on an empirical basis to examine to what extent the surviving evidence and interpretations provide confirmation of these expectations. Both lines of enquiry converge towards the view that an early form of settlement and agrarian organisation was the *hamlet* and its associated *infield-outfield* system'. They suggest that a small group of farmsteads, held by farmers who were related, would form the settlement, while nearby lay the intensively cultivated, well manured and continuously cropped infield, perhaps divided into strips between individuals – open but not

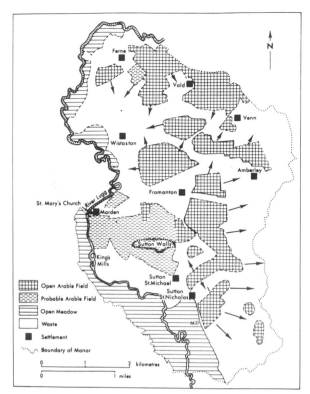

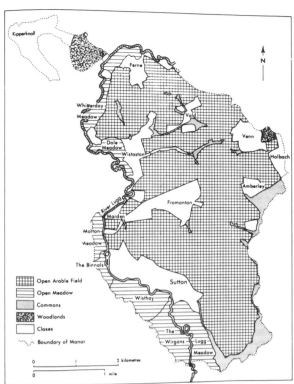

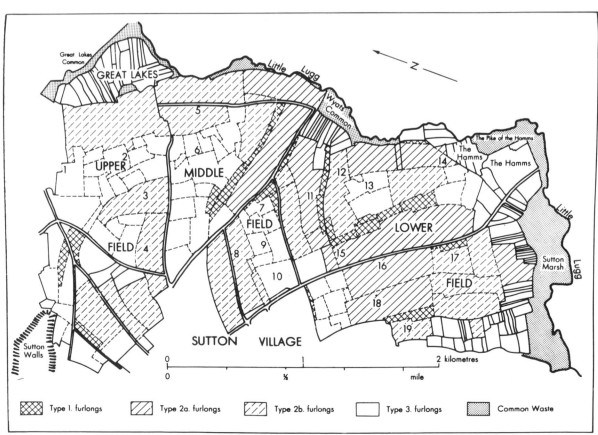

77 *The development of fields at Marden in Herefordshire. June Sheppard suggests that the extensive areas of open field arable evident in AD 1300 (right) were developed from core areas attached to hamlets in the eleventh century (left). In some cases the expansion of arable at the expense of waste seems to be reflected in the pattern of strips in the open fields (below). Types 2a and 2b furlongs may represent original regular blocks of arable, with types 1 and 3 being infilled later on. (After June Sheppard, with permission)*

78 *The turf dyke at Wheldrake in Yorkshire. June Sheppard suggests that the common open fields of this village developed from an infield close in to the settlement. This was demarcated by a 'turf dyke', a massive field bank which can still be traced around much of the village. (After June Sheppard, with permission)*

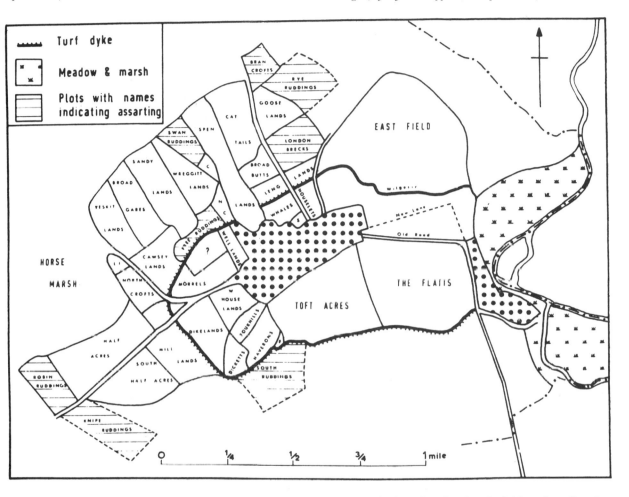

held in common. In the outfield, plots of land would be brought into cultivation from time to time and then abandoned. Thus, short periods of two to eight years cultivation would be followed by six to 25 years of fallow pasture.

Aspects of this system were very widespread. Finberg, writing in 1969, said there was evidence of it in Northumberland, Cumberland, Sherwood Forest, Warwickshire, Norfolk and the East Riding of Yorkshire, while Clapham said 'There can be little doubt that, if we knew medieval England completely, we should meet plenty of it'; Professors Beresford and St Joseph describe an example at Carburton in Nottinghamshire.

The difficulty for the local fieldworker lies in recognising infield/outfield in the local area when there have been so many subsequent changes. Place names like –field in a non-common-field area might help, as might innox or similar words, where 'its sense is clear; it is used in the thirteenth and fourteenth centuries of land temporarily enclosed from the fallow and put under cultivation ... it is in the counties of Wiltshire, Oxfordshire, Gloucestershire and Somersetshire that this word ... is most common'. 'Oldfield' or 'Oldland' names might also indicate earlier infields. It is possible that chemical analysis of fields might show up where the infield was; if it was permanently manured, the phosphate content should be much higher than the

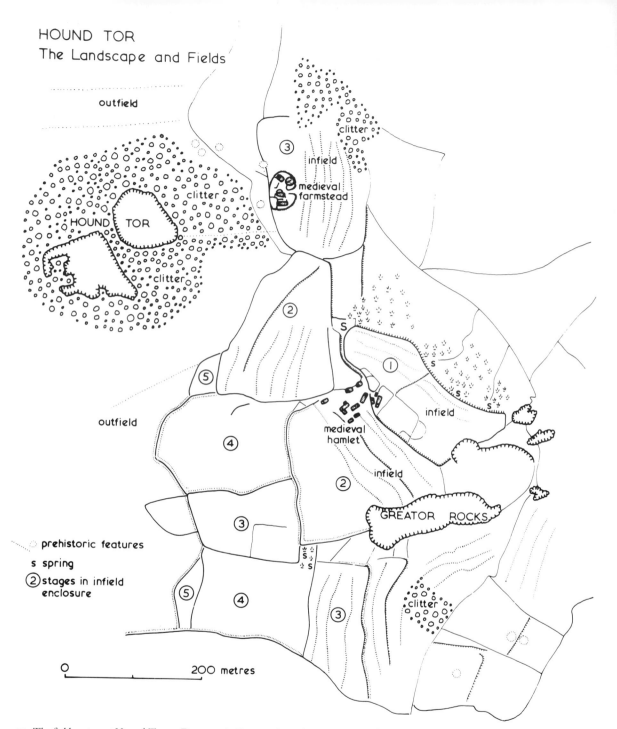

HOUND TOR
The Landscape and Fields

outfield

clitter

infield

medieval
farmstead

③

clitter

HOUND TOR

clitter

②

s

⑤

①

infield

outfield

④

medieval
hamlet

s

s

s

②

infield

③

GREATOR ROCKS

⋯ ○ prehistoric features

s spring

②stages in infield
enclosure

⑤

④

s
s
s

③

clitter

O   200 metres

79 *The field system at Hound Tor on Dartmoor in Devon. Around the medieval settlement (see Fig. 47) enclosures defined by stone walls and 'corn ditches' indicate the infield, which has slight terraces and traces of narrow, slight ridge and furrow. To the east is a wooded valley with springs. To the west are granite tors and extensive upland pasture – the outfield. There was some nineteenth-century farming here but the land seems to have been abandoned for arable farming in the fourteenth century. (After Medieval Village Research Group, with permission)*

unmanured outfield. Frequently, however, later agricultural practices will have rendered this approach unreliable.

Hound Tor

The settlement at Hound Tor on Dartmoor seems to be the sort of place where such an analysis might work, since the site has been little disturbed since the fourteenth century when the settlement was abandoned (*Fig. 47*). We have already seen that this deserted hamlet may represent an early, but typical, form of settlement, and in many ways its field system conforms to what we might expect of a basic infield/outfield system. Around the three or four farm complexes lie several areas of vague strips and terraces demarcated by large embanked and walled boundaries with ditches beyond. These are called 'corn ditches' locally, and seem to be the division between the infield and the outfield. The latter consists of the large areas of rough pasture with tors and granite boulders scattered about, while below are steeper slopes with springs and open woodland. The main site faces east and is thus sheltered from prevailing winds. The subsidiary medieval farm site, Hound Tor II, also has a corn ditch.

These sites are high and marginal, being at 360 metres (1150 feet) above sea level, and this led Guy Beresford to suggest that they were abandoned for largely climatic reasons. There are, however, other sites in the south-west with the same sort of infield/outfield systems which continued in use to the nineteenth century at least. Examples include Bagley (Luccombe in Somerset), Holmoor (Exford in Somerset), Babeny (Dartmoor in Devon) and Leaze (Bodmin Moor in Cornwall). The question must remain, however, of how we can recognise the earliest phases of our fields in a heavily utilised countryside, and whether the model of Hound Tor is really applicable generally, even in pre-common field stages of development in the late Saxon period. Only much more detailed local research will eventually reveal the answers.

ENCLOSURE

The field systems discussed so far will seem strange to most people, since we are used to seeing an enclosed landscape of hedged and walled fields. How this landscape came about is much easier to understand, because it is well documented and a great deal of research has already been undertaken. It is important to realise that there are two main types of enclosure, one further sub-divided into two. We are usually dealing either with the enclosure of former open and common arable lands (*Fig. 72*), or the enclosure of waste, pasture or common (*Fig. 82*). With the former, the enclosure can have taken place either in a piecemeal fashion, over a long period, and generally in a haphazard, unplanned and unsystematic way, or as a result of a specific or general Act of Parliament. For the former – enclosure by 'agreement' (although 'disagreement' might be more appropriate, since there must have been much haggling over how it was done and who had what) – there may be few, if any, documents or maps, and the landscape is probably the best and most reliable source. With the latter, commissioners were appointed, sur-

veys carried out, maps drawn and detailed allocations made (*Fig. 84*).

Areas of early enclosure from arable frequently have patterns of fields and roads reflecting the pre-existing strip patterns. Fields are long and narrow, as at Brassington in Derbyshire, often still with areas of ridge and furrow inside, and hedges are reversed S in shape. Even where all else has been removed, these hedge shapes will show former arable areas and enclosure directly from the strips. Sometimes cropmarks or parchmarks show up the earlier patterns, as at Deerhurst in Gloucestershire or Worton in Oxon. The road pattern also reflects the earlier arrangement, with lanes following thick hedges and turning at right angles across former headlands. The farmsteads of such areas often remain in the villages or hamlets, but, where they have been resited on the farm fields, their architecture often reflects the original date of construction. Thus, all over the West Country there are sixteenth- and seventeenth-century farm buildings, for example Saite Farm (Batcombe in Somerset), with good architectural details reflecting the date of enclosure and resiting of farmsteads.

By contrast, areas enclosed by an Act of Parliament have very regular patterns of roads and field boundaries. Where earlier patterns can be distinguished, they have often been totally ignored by the commissioners drawing up the new landscape on a map. Field boundaries are straight and direct, and the fields enclosed are generally square or rectangular (*Fig. 80*). Roads too are often straight, frequently re-aligned older trackways, and have wide margins, measured and defined in the award. Examples are numerous, since thousands of enclosure Acts, awards and maps were made. In this way, large areas of the East Midlands (Leicestershire, Northamptonshire, Bedfordshire, Oxfordshire, and so on) were created in their present form in the eighteenth and nineteenth centuries and the farmsteads built out on the new land reflect these dates in their names, such as Quebec House, Hanover Farm, Bunker Hill Farm and Jericho Lodge, and in their architectural materials and style.

Areas of forest, pasture and waste had always been enclosed from at least late Saxon times. Over much of the country, the patterns of irregular hedges, winding lanes and scattered farms reflect this process of piecemeal fencing or hedging of an area to make fields. Where trees were felled and the roots dug out, *assarts* were created (from the French *essarter* – to grub up – and reflected in field names like 'sarts' or 'serts'). The farmsteads created either have late medieval architectural details (as do many in the former Arden Forest of Warwickshire) or their names and/or documentary records show that they were in existence by the twelfth or thirteenth century, at least.

This process of piecemeal enclosure of waste and the

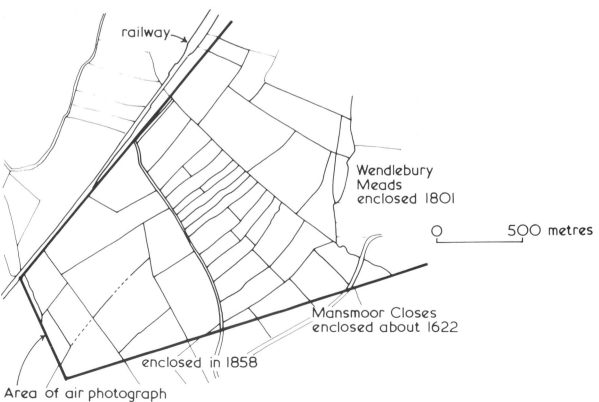

80 *(left) Different types of enclosure at Charlton on Otmoor in Oxfordshire. All over this air photograph can be seen traces of medieval arable strips in the form of ridge and furrow. In the middle distance they survive as earthworks between the hedges of Mansmoor Closes which were probably enclosed, by agreement, shortly before 1622. In the foreground the regular field boundaries indicate enclosure by Parliamentary Commissioners (in 1858) of former common field arable: the ridge and furrow is largely ploughed out. In the distance, Wendlebury Meads, a former area of meadowland, was enclosed in 1801. (Air photography by Trevor Rowley, reproduced with permission)*

81 *Areas of England without common or common field. Gonner's maps of the ends of the sixteenth and seventeenth centuries to a large extent reflect areas of the country which were enclosed early, before Parliamentary Acts of Enclosure (see Fig. 72). Some of these areas were enclosed into small fields in the Middle Ages (if not earlier) but others were the result of enclosure by agreement in the Tudor and subsequent periods. (From E. C. K. Gonner Common Land and Enclosure, 1912)*

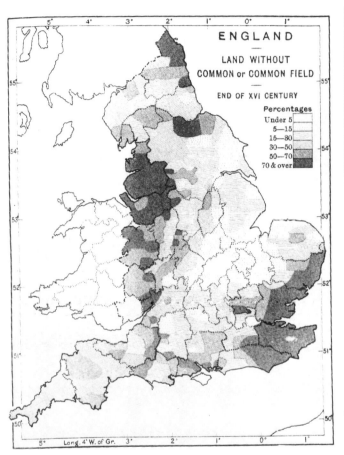

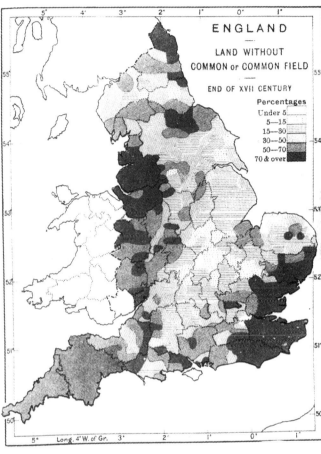

creation of holdings held in severalty – every farmer having a discrete separate holding – continued right through to the eighteenth century. By around 1800, however, there were still large areas of unenclosed pasture, wood pasture and woodland in former royal forests, and wild open upland areas used for seasonal pasture. During the first half of the nineteenth century, most of these areas were enclosed, allotted, and divided up and new farmsteads created. Vast areas lost the appearance they had had for hundreds of years and very quickly assumed the appearance we see today and which we think of as natural. In Somerset, the landscapes of the Mendips, the Black Downs, the Brendon Hills and the old Neroche and Exmoor Forests were all created at this time. Elsewhere, the forests of Peak in Derbyshire, Needwood in Staffordshire and Wychwood in Oxfordshire were all enclosed, and extensive areas of Lancashire were 'improved'.

In these former wooded and wood pasture areas, the landscape can still be distinctive with a high incidence of old oaks and pollarded trees. Hedges may be thick and rich in species, even though the field boundaries are straight and the roads run direct between wide verges from one old forest gate to another. The farms, again, are distinctive by their names and architectural styles.

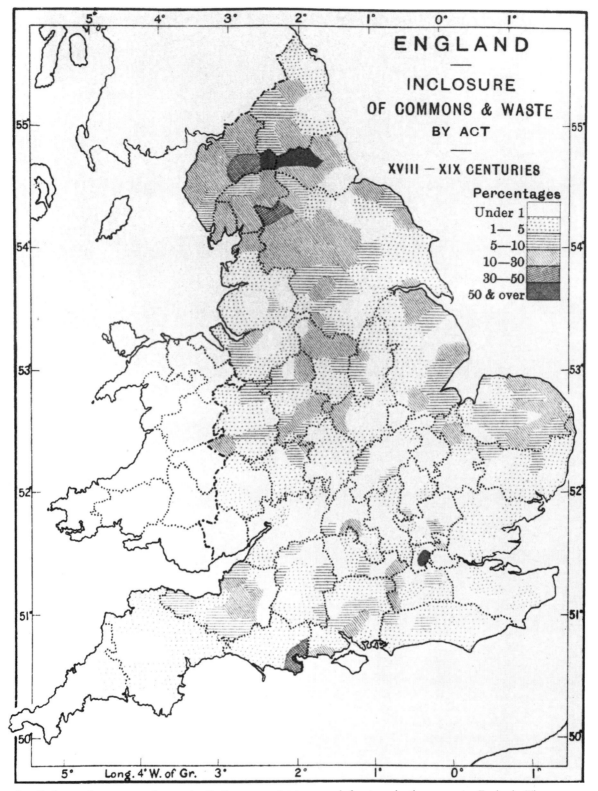

82 *Enclosure of commons and waste by Parliamentary Act in England. To a large extent Gonner's map represents Parliamentary enclosure of former commons, wastes and the upland pastures of old royal forests and other areas in England. These areas were principally pasture and were not the important arable areas. (From E. C. K. Gonner* Common Land and Enclosure, *1912)*

THE FOREST OF NEROCHE
19th CENTURY ENCLOSURE

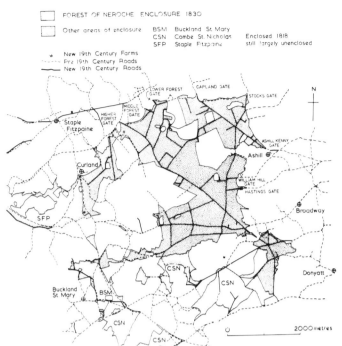

FOREST OF NEROCHE ENCLOSURE 1830

Other areas of enclosure   BSM   Buckland St Mary   Enclosed 1818
                      CSN   Combe St. Nicholas   still largely unenclosed
                      SFP   Staple Fitzpaine

     New 19th Century Farms
     Pre 19th Century Roads
     New 19th Century Roads

83 *The enclosure of the Forest of Neroche in Somerset. The landscape of the former royal forest of Neroche, south-east of Taunton in Somerset, demonstrates the effect of Parliamentary enclosure of a vast common area. In 1800–1810 the common was surrounded by piecemeal medieval assarting and small-scale seventeenth-century enclosures. Roads ran irregularly across this common and there were numerous squatter settlements on it and around the edges. The enclosure of 1830 divided up the area into regular closes and encouraged the development of a regular planned road network.*

THE FOREST OF NEROCHE
circa 1800-1810

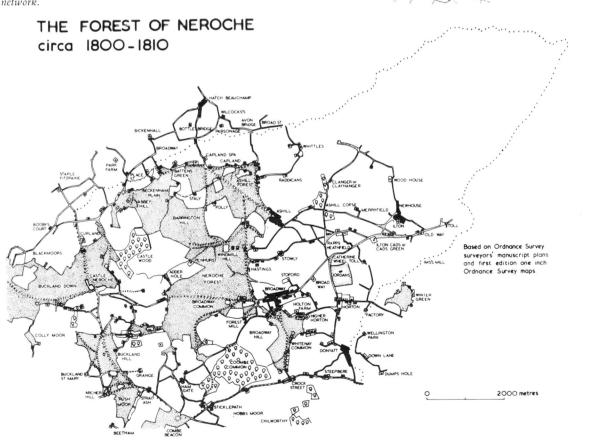

Based on Ordnance Survey surveyors' manuscript plans and first edition one inch Ordnance Survey maps

The straight walls and roads of the uplands with the shelter belts around 'model' farmsteads are also characteristic.

Milton under Wychwood

This village and parish in Oxfordshire represents many of the points discussed here. The open fields were not enclosed until after 1850, so there is a good tithe map showing the strips and furlongs in the common fields and an enclosure map of 1850 showing the old arrangement and the proposed new enclosed landscape. After that date, the fields were enclosed with hedges and stone walls. Bits of the parish mixed up with the adjacent parish of Shipton under Wychwood were rationalised, and the old pattern of irregular lanes replaced by straight new roads between wide hedges. Eventually, new farmsteads were moved out on to the former open fields to work their land more directly, for example High Lodge Farm and Springhill Farm. But enclosure went far beyond this. The former meadowland which had been divided into lots at the north end of the parish by the River Evenlode was enclosed, the heathland nearby was enclosed and Heath

Farm established on it, and the downland on the Cotswold fringe to the south was also enclosed. What had been a fine large green at the north end of the village was reduced to less than a quarter of its former size and, as a final measure, the opportunity was taken to straighten out all the streams to prevent flooding.

The impact of enclosure and attendant developments in a parish could be drastic and result in landscapes which condition our aesthetic appreciation of the places themselves today. Milton is not attractive and has been extensively developed with new estates, shops, schools, etc. It is not a conservation area and is not on the tourist routes, yet it is typical of thousands of parishes in how and when its landscape developed.

Hedge dating

Following suggestions by Max Hooper, it looked likely that, some years ago, the number of woody species might be used to indicate the age of a particular hedge and that this could be used to work out the stages of enclosure in an area. The biological reasoning behind this was never satisfactorily explained, but many studies, in the east of England particularly,

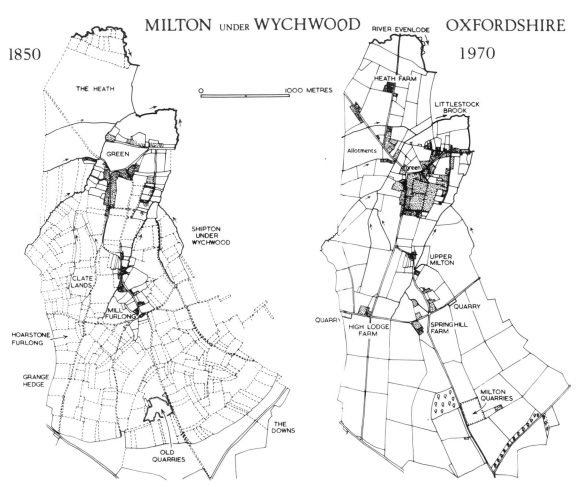

MILTON under WYCHWOOD   RIVER EVENLODE   OXFORDSHIRE

1850   1970

THE HEATH

0   1000 METRES

GREEN

SHIPTON UNDER WYCHWOOD

CLATE LANDS

MILL FURLONG

HOARSTONE FURLONG

GRANGE HEDGE

THE DOWNS

OLD QUARRIES

HEATH FARM

LITTLESTOCK BROOK

Allotments

Green

UPPER MILTON

QUARRY

QUARRY

HIGH LODGE FARM

SPRINGHILL FARM

MILTON QUARRIES

seemed to suggest a close correlation between the number of species and the date the hedge was planted.

In the west, such a method really does not seem to work at all. It is not possible to rely on the number of species and expect an accurate date, although certain species such as spindle and wayfaring tree do tend to occur only in known older hedges, while younger hedges tend to have hawthorn, blackthorn and elder. Where dates of enclosure are known, species counts can be made and compared.

There are two important points to be made here. Since there does not seem to be a direct correlation between numbers of species and date in many instances, it is much more important to work out the date of enclosure from documents and maps, and then look at the actual hedge and assess not only the number but also the type of species represented. Secondly, enclosure in more recent times has been closely related to the activities of nurserymen supplying shrubs at the time of the enclosure. John Harvey has already done important research into early nurseries. In Somerset, there were few nurserymen even in the nineteenth century, and so enclosure in Neroche Forest seems to have involved digging up shrubs in the woods – hedges begin with eight to ten species! In the east of the country, nurserymen were very active in supplying thousands of *quicksets* (hawthorns) for hedges at the time of enclosure in the eighteenth and nineteenth centuries, and so hedges here generally have only one or two species.

84 *The enclosure of Milton under Wychwood in Oxfordshire. Before the enclosure of 1850 there were areas of arable (in strips), downland (i.e. upland pasture), heath (lowland pasture) and meadow, in doles by the river. After enclosure, new fields were laid out, new farms built and a new road network created. The green was made smaller and even the streams were straightened.*

11

Communications — the links between

We have now examined settlements, the landscape around them, the important places in that landscape, and the administrative framework within which all these features were arranged. It now remains only to examine the physical links between all these elements – the communication pattern. In this chapter we shall look at land transport particularly , but we should not forget that, in the past, water often provided a more convenient and usually a cheaper means of moving bulky goods – river, estuarine and coastal communication was of greater importance in earlier times.

We shall not deal in this chapter with the development and use of either the canal or the railway network. These are mainly developments of the eighteenth and nineteenth centuries; they do not represent insurmountable problems of definition or explanation in the landscape and there is abundant literature on their origin, development and use. Similarly, later road developments will be only cursorily discussed. Turnpike roads have not yet received adequate attention as features in the landscape and there is no one suitable text book about their topographical development. The eighteenth- and nineteenth-century military roads in the north will also not be discussed, and neither will Roman roads, for which there is abundant literature.

A great deal of rubbish has been written in the past about roads, particularly Roman roads and ridge-ways. It has been all too easy in the long winter evenings to sit down in an easy chair in front of the fire with a 1-inch (now 1:50000) Ordnance Survey map and draw in straight sections of roads, paths and parish boundaries, and suggest possible and probable road links across the landscape. Little attention is paid to why a particular road might have gone this way or that, what it was used for and which settlements it was linking.

Our main task as parish survey researchers and field archaeologists is to try to understand what the existing patterns of communication mean. We want to know when the pattern came into existence, how it has evolved, changed and been adapted, and why some

parts of it have become derelict. Most importantly, we want to know what purposes the network served at different dates. In this respect, identifying the *functional* role will prove, as with other landscape features, the most fruitful line of enquiry.

Communication in the past, before the age of telephones and television, implied people or goods moving about in the landscape. Therefore, we need to know why there was this movement – the reasons for travel and the movement of goods and commodities from one place to another. Clearly identifiable reasons can be found very easily. Goods, cattle, agricultural produce, stone, wood, timber, and a host of other materials were moved from their place of production to a place of use or consumption. This movement could be via a market or fair, or it could be straight from producer to consumer, particularly if the same person or organisation owned or controlled each end of the link. Oliver Rackham has shown, in his classic study of Hayley Wood, how wood and timber moved about the landscape both within estates in the same ownership and between estates, from land with wood to woodless consumers. In order to understand anything of the movement of goods and commodities in the past, therefore, we must not only see which materials are being moved, but we must look at the way they were moved (by waggon, water, on foot), the amount of movement, and, particularly, we must identify the source and the destination.

Moving goods was always more difficult, although flocks and herds could walk, of course. The latter needed relatively wide, flat and direct routes if travel over any distance was not to be problematical, with plenty of herbage so they could graze *en route*. Other commodities could be moved by waggon and cart or by pack animals on land, or by water. Pack animals must have been very important in the past and a familiar sight in the landscape, as they could use the same routes as foot travellers and horsemen; their great flexibility, together with little investment in expensive equipment like waggons, meant they were very popular. The actual width of many known medieval

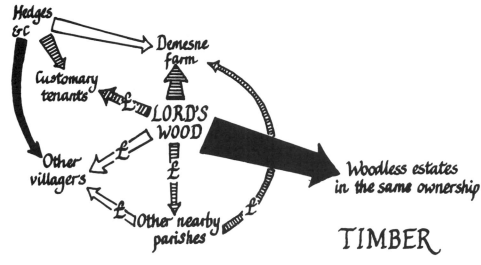

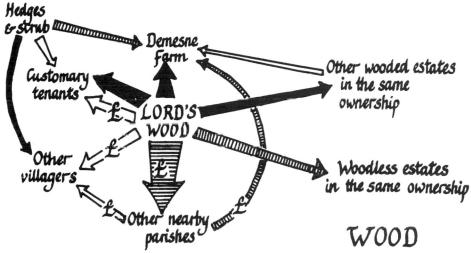

85 *Movements of timber and wood in the medieval countryside. Oliver Rackham's diagrams show the complex movements of wood and timber in the Middle Ages, and imply much use of medieval roads. (After Oliver Rackham, with permission)*

roads in villages and elsewhere, together with the numerous narrow 'pack horse' bridges, particularly in the West Country and the north, shows their former extensive use. St Ives in Cornwall is reputed not to have seen a wheeled vehicle until the early nineteenth century – all goods were carried by pack animal or taken by sea around the coast. Much could be moved in this way and we must imagine lanes full of beasts bearing firewood, cereals, milled flour, vegetables and fodder, as well as our conventional image of donkeys laden with wool packs.

Carts (two-wheeled) and waggons (four-wheeled) were also used; manuscript illustrations make this clear and, for certain goods in lowland Britain away from rivers large enough for transport, there was probably no alternative, particularly if the roads were adequate. Nevertheless, carts and waggons were expensive items and we must not imagine that there were many of them. In the sixteenth century the Prior of Worcester, William More, spent a lot of time and money having a new farm waggon built and it was clearly not an everyday event, nor was it cheap.

Water transport, where it was available, was cheaper and easier to use for moving bulky loads. We tend to forget in our highly motorised society how important even the smallest rivers were for transport in the past. Small boats and barges could bring goods well up river inland. The Thames is very small at Cricklade in Wiltshire today, but it was navigable that far in the past, and the Severn was used well up river beyond Shrewsbury in Shropshire. In the nineteenth century, coal was still brought to Ilchester in Somerset up the river Yeo, which is now little more than a ditch. Little research has been carried out on this aspect, although

86 *The abandoned harbour at Lilstock in Somerset. The entrance to the nineteenth-century harbour from the sea is now blocked by a* *bank of pebbles. Stone walls still line the dock and the remains of the harbour gates can be seen.*

famous vessels such as Thames Sailing Barges and Severn Trows are well known.

Two aspects probably dictated whether rivers could be navigated. Firstly, the sorts of vessels in use – their size, draught, and so on. How far, for example, could a coastal or sea-going vessel of Saxon or medieval times penetrate inland up river before the load would need to be transferred to a shallower draught vessel? Vessel size would be important and, in general, sea-going vessels became larger. This factor alone meant that they could not get as far inland. However, a second factor may have been of even greater importance: it seems likely that rivers may have become less usable over time anyway, especially if they carried more and more silt washed off arable land. The area of arable land would have been expanding until the early fourteenth century and so we would expect to find more run-off of soil after heavy rains and in the winter from late Saxon times onwards. Did this in fact affect river disposition, silting and regime? Moreover, did this, together with vessel size, affect the use of inland ports? Many rivers may have had more abraided courses in pre-medieval times. Did river control, particularly the canalising of rivers into one main channel, mean that access was

maintained? These and other questions would all merit future local research.

The same sort of problems relate to coastal communication. As well as a host of river jetties and transhipment points, almost any small cove, beach or inlet around the coast would have been used in earlier times for the loading and unloading of goods. In Somerset, Minehead was once an important port, with links to Ireland, and along the same coast there is the silted-up harbour of Dunster, and the small nineteenth-century harbours at Porlock and Lilstock. At the latter there are the remains of a stone-built jetty and locked harbour, together with several ruined buildings. It would be impossible to get a vessel of any size into this now, but coal and corn were formerly imported, while limestone and lime went out from the limekiln on the quay.

People moved about for a great variety of reasons, but the same general aspects outlined above still apply. The administration of estates, the links between holdings of a barony or between monastic estates, would all have occasioned movement of officials. The king and his retinue were regularly on the move, visiting estates and landowners, administering royal estates, and issuing documents and charters from particular royal castles and other centres. The administration of justice involved movement, and, as we have seen, hundred meetings, baronial courts, markets and fairs all involved people crossing the landscape. We tend to forget also the social aspects — visiting relatives and friends in nearby villages and towns. Visits to shrines, churches and monasteries on saints' days often involved many people; organised long-distance tours or pilgrimages are evident in many parts of Europe, with well-defined routes coming into existence.

How, then, was all this movement carried out? On land, of course, people either walked or they rode on horseback (or donkey, or pony), and so roads did not need to be wide and considerations such as how straight or steep they were did not have great importance. At all times the steeper slopes and boggy ground would have been avoided and as much travel as possible would have been done in a direct line on the level and when it was dry underfoot. Later on, some people travelled by litter or coach and more attention to particular routes was then important. Steep inclines, in particular, would be difficult, as would ground liable to be muddy after rain. We know relatively little about vehicles in earlier periods, particularly those for transporting people, although there are a few manuscript drawings.

SOURCES OF INFORMATION

Some of the problems and ideas about communication have now been outlined, but where can we get further information about early routes? Excavation in general is of little use in this area of enquiry, although it can produce the evidence of goods and commodities being moved about in the landscape which can best demonstrate trading links, and, by implication, the routes used. Most early roads were not 'constructed' as such; their surfaces wore down and hence any directly associated datable material is usually either eroded or out of context. The study of early ships, however, can be useful and much has been learnt about changing vessel technology from the remains of quays and jetties found in excavations.

Fieldwork is immensely useful in any study of early routes. Abandoned routes can be recognised as holloways — the characteristic worn-down lanes with steep sides which are common on medieval sites and can often be traced up hillsides and through woods. On steep hillsides, numerous holloway routes may be seen and here, as elsewhere, alternative lines often exist — as one lane became boggy or impassable, another was opened up. Frequently, a multitude of tracks developed, as at Walkers Hill near Alton and Posten Hill near Marlborough, both in Wiltshire, or Twyford Down in Hampshire. Elsewhere, terraced ways, partly cut into

the slope on the uphill side and built-up on the downhill side, also remain. In a few cases raised roadways can be seen which must have been in some way constructed. There are cambered roads, for example, in the deserted villages of Fresden and Sheldon in Wiltshire, and there was a similar case at a deserted village site in Odstock parish in Somerset. Other earthworks appear as causewayed roads where side ditches have been dug to drain an area. Numerous ditched *drove* or access ways can be seen in the wet lowlands of Somerset, particularly along the coastal clay belt, and many of Romano-British date formerly existed in the Fens of eastern England.

The fieldworker should be aware also of causeways which have gone out of use and may remain as prominent earthworks. Several Roman bridge abutments have been recognised in this way (for example, Hunwich Gill and Stockley Gill in Durham), and there is an unfinished abandoned eighteenth-century turnpike road in Worcestershire — the abortive Pershore Road which was completed in Birmingham — running across several meadows near the villages of Flyford Flavell and Naunton Beauchamp as a massive embankment.

So far, we have been discussing abandoned or relic features in the landscape, but most of the present pattern of lanes and paths is medieval, if not earlier, in date. We should, therefore, look at the total picture of roads, lanes and paths in use today in our area of study, in addition to any abandoned holloways and tracks, to get a complete picture of communication over a long period. Where this has been done, as for example at Hanbury in Worcestershire (*Fig. 58*) (by Stephen Bassett and Christopher Dyer), the density of routes and the degree of access to land is very great.

Documents can help in reconstructing earlier road patterns, and, of course, place names (together with field and local names) provide further references. There are numerous local names referring to roads and paths, of which *herepath*, or 'army road', is the most obvious. A study of any parish will reveal names of ridgeways and old paths, as well as possible 'streets' suggesting Roman roads. In Warwickshire, Hobs Ditch names near Henley in Arden were found, on excavation, to indicate a Roman road.

'Way' names merit closer attention, since early village names are not generally called after roads. However, Broadway in Somerset lies on a wide long-distance route traceable across south Somerset into Devon, down the Blackdown Hills ridgeway. Before the successful draining of the Levels to the north this would have been the most direct dry-land route to the West Country.

More common, however, are field and place names with —ford as a suffix — a crossing place through a stream or river. Usually this was where particular local

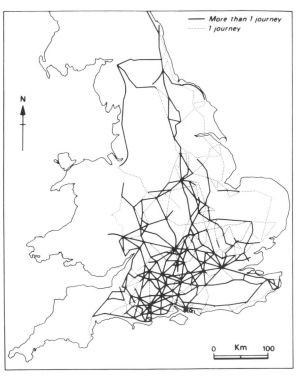

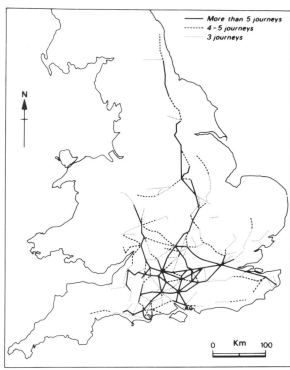

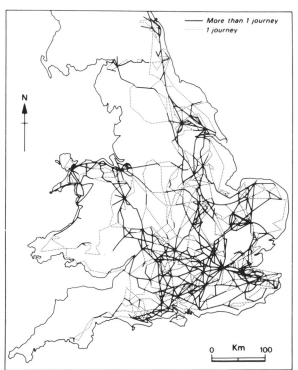

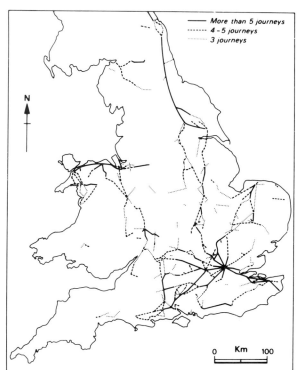

87 *The itineraries of King John and Edward I. Such maps show the travels of medieval kings and imply which roads and routes were most heavily used. The map, top left, shows all the journeys of King John in Britain, while top right shows routes travelled three times or more. Bottom left shows Edward I's travel. Notice how much he travelled in Wales (and also Scotland – not shown). Bottom right shows routes used three times or more during his reign. (After Brian Paul Hindle Medieval Roads [Shire], with permission)*

topographical features produced a hard bed which could be easily waded. Place-name evidence is difficult, as has already been discussed, but such names do clearly tell us something of an area, if only that at that point a route crossed a stream or river. Generally, such places should be seen in a local or regional context and seen together with an assessment of local route ways. In south-east Somerset, for example (*Fig. 90*), there are only two –ford village names, Mudford and Spark-ford; both are significant, as the crossing points of local routes over the Rivers Yeo and Cam respectively.

Maps provide abundant information about early routes, but there are few medieval maps of Britain. The Matthew Paris Map of 1250 shows only one route, Dover to Newcastle, but the Gough Map of about 1360 shows many roads radiating out from London. Thus, by the fourteenth century, the two major elements of British land transport are already established – the dominance of London as the centre of the network and the importance of the later Great North Road. National and county maps become increasingly available from the sixteenth century onwards. Many show roads, but perhaps of greatest significance for major routes is Ogilvy's road book of 1675. This shows in linear strips details of many important roads in the late seventeenth century. Locally, maps become increasingly common from the sixteenth century, with large numbers for the eighteenth and nineteenth centuries. Any particular one may have useful information about local routes.

Finally, the various itineraries are of significance. There are even a few Roman itineraries which tell us something of the situation in late Roman Britain. The Antonine Itinerary of the late third or early fourth century, and the seventh-century Ravenna Cosmography have both been used in this way. Brian Paul Hindle has used the chronicles of medieval kings to reconstruct the most heavily-used royal roads in the Middle Ages and has produced maps for the reigns of John, Edward I and Edward II. Locally, it may be difficult to pick out which road is being used, indeed there may be several alternatives, but nationally the picture is clear. London is the focus, as we would expect, with the route north to York and Newcastle being very dominant. Other major routes run east to Dover and west to Bristol, and in the south-east there is a dense network of roads used by the kings. Few royal visits were made west of Exeter, into Wales, or north of Chester.

From the fifteenth century onwards a host of itineraries become available. William Worcester's itinerary of the fifteenth century and John Leland's of the 1540s are well known, but there are also the travels of Celia Fiennes (1685–1703), Daniel Defoe (1722–1724) and William Cobbett (1822–1830). Each of these people gives information about local top-ography and frequently a description of the country-side around, whether it is enclosed or not, and the existence of particular estates.

There is thus a mass of material available from which to reconstruct and understand early communication links. From documents, maps, air photographs and fieldwork, something of the links in the landscape can be seen. How are we to explain the resulting pattern? It was stated above that we should not study the lines of communication in isolation – this has been the problem with much of the work done in the past. In this book I have been at pains to try to see the landscape as a series of functional units with complex interrelationships. Not only are they complex at one time, but they are constantly changing through time. It is against this background that communications must be seen and, at its most basic, we need to identify the settlements of any period and the reasons why contact was needed between them. From such a stance the complex and sterile arguments about earlier Roman military routes, signalling between hillforts, and much else that has been discussed in the past become irrelevant, especially when faced with the question of why early people needed to do such things.

We can examine communication patterns in the landscape at four different levels – the national (which we shall not discuss further), the provincial (over several counties), the regional (across several parishes), and the local (within a particular territory). At each level different activities were pursued and different contacts needed and created.

Provincial links
Provincial communication has been studied indirectly by a number of people. It can be recognised very early in the prehistoric period with the trade in stone axes. Known stone production sites can be seen all over western Britain, with flint sources in the south-east. Through petrological analysis of stone by thin sectioning, axes found in one place can be traced to sources of stone elsewhere. The implications from this evidence for long-distance contact – or even trade – have only just begun to be considered. Similar developments can be seen with early pottery production. In the Neolithic period, sources of temper for clay were exploited in Cornwall for fine pots used all over southern England; analysis of pottery at Glastonbury in Somerset has shown that, by the Iron Age, outcrops of rock all over the south-west were being used for temper in the clay. Other long-distance links involving iron, stone and luxury goods have been identified at recently-examined sites like Hengistbury Head in Dorset and Danebury in Hampshire.

Such provincial traffic can be identified at all periods. The movement of such items as pottery, salt, iron, exotic stone goods like hones and millstones, and luxury items has always gone on. Much of this material moved from one county to another, from the coast inland (either up rivers or overland), and over long distances. It is more useful to speculate on likely routes between places of production and consumption than just to look at the routes in one locality in isolation. All of this traffic implies that the self-sufficient settlement was a rarity. As Maurice Beresford puts it: 'Assisting in the carriage of the millstones is often found in custumals as an obligation of tenants. In villages remote from suitable stone, the organisation of a supply of millstones presupposes a long-distance trade and transport capable of handling such heavy loads. Thus, every millstone upsets the concept of self-sufficient village economies.'

The implications of the movement of such goods has hardly begun to be considered, particularly, and ironically, for the well-documented medieval and post-medieval periods. Where, for example, did all the millstones produced at Lundy Island or from the Pen Pits near Stourhead in Wiltshire go? Many millstones are known to have been imported from the Forest of Dean via Bridgwater and distributed over Devon, Somerset and Dorset in the sixteenth century. This information is contained in port books and shows Bridgwater as a transhipment point with river and road transport beyond that. There is scope for further work on such documentary sources as port books (and fair books and other little-appreciated sources).

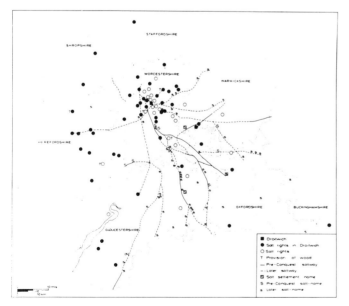

88 *Salt ways from Droitwich in Worcestershire. This map shows the places with salt rights in the brine pits at Droitwich and the named salt ways in the Midland counties. (After Della Hooke 'The Droitwich Salt Industry' in David Brown et al (eds) Anglo-Saxon Studies in Archaeology and History 2, British Archaeological Reports British Series 92 (1981) with permission)*

Similarly, a great deal more petrological analysis of pottery, millstones, and other exotic stones (hones, bricks, stone roofing tiles, and clay tiles) is needed, even for the historic period.

At the provincial level, exchange of goods took place at fairs and the more important markets. It is often difficult to gauge the importance of these in the landscape, but a study of White Down in Somerset shows links with Wiltshire, Devon, Weymouth in Dorset and Llantwit Major in Wales. Horses from Ireland were also frequently traded in the West Country in the seventeenth and eighteenth centuries. Similar but more detailed information comes from the fair books of Taunton Fair and has been studied by Christopher Gerrard (*Fig.19*). Access to such markets and fairs would inevitably be on direct overland routes, and these were probably of great antiquity. It is not difficult to draw attention to these, but it is usually impossible to date accurately a particular ridgeway or long-distance valley road. Even more difficult is the task of assessing the relative importance of coastal and river communications in such traffic.

Two aspects have, however, been studied which show the potential. Firstly, salt produced at Droitwich in Worcestershire and in Cheshire was taken overland to widely-scattered manors which had rights in the brine pits. Local place names incorporating 'salt' or 'saltway' can be used to reconstruct the routes by which the commodity was moved. This trade is documented from the late Saxon period onward, but is probably much older.

Secondly, the dominance of London from the early medieval period onward, if not before, led to distant areas concentrating on cattle production to supply the capital with meat, leather, and other animal products. Wales, the West Country and the north of England, predominantly regions with a long-standing pastoral economy, produced animals which were then walked overland to markets in the south. Such drove roads or driftways have been studied superficially in many areas. Landscape features such as pub names, and the spectacular building at Stockbridge in Hampshire, which has signs outside it in Welsh, can be instanced, and the wide routes with ample grass fodder on the verges can be traced for miles. The Welsh Way in Gloucestershire is such an example, but usually no single route was predominant and a network of these roads must be envisaged.

Regional links

More progress can be made in identifying regional communications. Within any county, at about the hundred level, much communication can be seen within the landscape – access to minsters, caputs, markets, fairs, castles, monasteries, baronial centres, large houses and towns. Regional exchange of goods and the provision of services for places around the main centres should produce a stellar pattern of roads and tracks, and such routes are closely connected with the use of central places, as discussed earlier. In a prehistoric context, these routes can be seen as cropmarks, frequently linking individual farm sites to the more local centres such as hillforts, and in Somerset there are the internationally important timber trackways of the Neolithic and Bronze Ages (*Fig. 5*). These seem to be linking upland settlements with other centres and lowland resources in the Levels themselves.

This latter movement, transhumance over wide areas, results in much of the regional road pattern. Movement of cattle and sheep to upland or lowland seasonal pasture can be instanced in many parts of the country. Somerset has already been mentioned and the links between villages and the Levels have been studied by Michael Williams. Trevor Rowley studied the straker routes on the Clee Hills and a more local example exists in Deerhurst in Gloucestershire – many more could be cited.

Many of these routes wander across country and were used for a variety of purposes. Diversions of well-established old routes, however, did occur. All through the late Saxon and early medieval periods towns were created, as discussed by Maurice Beresford. Frequently, the establishment of a new town was accompanied by the diversion of existing routes into the new market place. This can be seen at Thame in Oxfordshire and Montacute in Somerset, with wider implications for Devizes in Wiltshire. Eleanor Carus-Wilson has shown for Stratford on Avon how a new town can influence the local landscape, although she did not consider the displacement of routes.

The building of some new towns was accompanied by new bridge construction, making redundant many long-established and well-used fords and ferries. The building of Abingdon bridge is cited as an example, since it seems to have led directly to the decline of nearby Dorchester on Thames. In Wiltshire, the building of Harnham bridge at Salisbury has been studied by John Chandler; it contributed to the decline of Wilton, which had been formerly the most important town in the area. Bridges have often been studied as buildings and ancient monuments, but their role as influences in the local communication pattern has apparently been overlooked.

In the same way, the construction of causeways to carry roads over low-lying and boggy areas also had considerable impact on local communications, although medieval roads seem generally not to have been surfaced and little attention was paid to elaborate construction or careful maintenance. The early construction of a clay causeway south of Oxford probably influenced the development of that town, and the same may have happened at Langport in Somerset. A

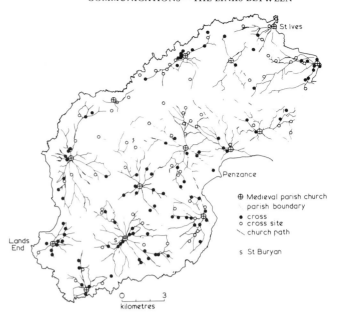

89 *Church paths in West Penwith in Cornwall. These paths, frequently marked by granite crosses, linked outlying farmsteads with the parish church. They provide one of the most obvious links in communication in the landscape. (After I. S. Maxwell Historical Atlas of West Penwith, 1976, with permission)*

spectacular late medieval example is Maud Heaths causeway in Wiltshire, linking villages in a poorly-drained clay area with the market at Chippenham. Foot passengers, at least, could reach the market dry-shod at all times of the year.

Local links

At the local level there was, of course, considerable movement within any land unit, be it parish, township, or tithing. Routes from all settlements or individual farms to the church can often be picked out as 'church paths'. In Cornwall, these are frequently marked by granite crosses, such as the examples seen in St Buryan and elsewhere near Lands End. Most local movement was, however, from farmstead to fields. This is so obvious and has been taken so much for granted that it has hardly ever been studied. Detailed studies of large nucleated villages with extensive open fields have, however, shown that there was a dense network of tracks between blocks of strips and along headlands across the parish. Christopher Taylor instances Stanford, Raunds, Stanwick and Hargrave in Northamptonshire and other examples can be seen at Deerhurst in Gloucestershire (*Fig. 60*) and in south-east Somerset (*Fig. 61*). In an enclosed landscape the density was as great – the example of Hanbury in Worcestershire has already been mentioned (*Fig. 58*). As well as daily access to fields, it was necessary to go less frequently to areas of woodland and the mill.

With enclosure, particularly parliamentary enclosure of an open landscape, new lines of communication were often created, old ones rationalised and some destroyed. Professors Beresford and St Joseph show this dramatically for Padbury in Buckinghamshire and an equally spectacular example can be seen at Milton under Wychwood in Oxfordshire (*Fig. 84*). Along with all the other changes of the eighteenth and nineteenth centuries, road alteration can be seen to be as dramatic as the changes in field and settlement patterns.

Having recorded all this material for an area and sorted out why and when certain routes might be used, there may still remain a problem of explanation. As has been said before, and implied throughout this book, the English landscape is very old and is a palimpsest of features of different dates. We can work out theoretically what our communications might look like at each of the levels we have discussed and see if it relates to the actual patterns on the ground. In many cases it will, but there will be anomalies. Most anomalies will be caused by earlier features still having an influence in a later landscape – inertia again. This is easy to say but difficult to prove. If, however, the predominant road network of an area does not closely relate to the present settlement and land use pattern of a parish, then such an explanation may be likely. In these cases, the evidence might suggest much earlier arrangements in the landscape which had not previously been suspected and for which no evidence other than patterns of roads, paths and boundaries exists. Warwick Rodwell has shown such an example in Essex, where much of the road pattern (and other divisions) seems to be of probable Roman date, while in Somerset, Roger Leech has shown that much of the rural road system was also probably there by Romano-British times. Some of our roads and tracks in the landscape may well be older than we think, and there is probably more prehistory in most landscapes than was formerly imagined.

THE EXAMPLE OF SOUTH-EAST SOMERSET

In the area east of Ilchester there is a bewildering pattern of roads and tracks. The existence of the large hillfort at South Cadbury means that there would have been lanes leading out from this all over its territory in the prehistoric period. The exact area of land attached to this fortified centre is not known, but Ian Burrow suggests a theoretical territory as far as Ilchester, where the land of the next hillfort at Ham Hill began, and northwards to the land of Dundon hillfort.

Similarly, Ilchester would have lain at the centre of a region. We can see the new straight Roman roads laid out with military precision running north, south-west, south and south-east from the town, and a further

possibility is the road east towards Wiltshire. These roads cut across the landscape apparently ignoring the underlying pattern of roads and tracks. Are these earlier then than the Roman roads?

All over this region there is a dense scatter of medieval settlements, surviving as modern villages, hamlets and farmsteads, partially deserted or shrunken, or completely deserted (as at Nether Adber). From field and air photograph evidence the contemporary landscape of these settlements can be reconstructed with areas of arable/pasture, meadowland along the rivers, ancient woodland, and a few areas of upland pasture. Most of the roads, lanes and paths in existence now must have related to the links between these settlements and these areas of different land use. We might expect, therefore, a stellar pattern with paths running out from the settlements to their fields within the territory of each settlement, and these can be defined. Because there are earlier patterns relating to the late prehistoric and Roman periods, we should expect some roads and lanes relating to them still to be in this landscape, either as relict features or surviving in use. Since Ilchester was also the local administrative and marketing centre for this region from the late Saxon period onwards, each settlement should in fact have a direct link with it. Both South Cadbury and later Ilchester were also of more than local significance in their heyday, so more direct long-distance overland routes are also to be expected.

We can thus develop a theoretical framework for the region, against which we can examine the real situation. Do the present and reconstructed past lines of communication fit in with this? Even a cursory examination will show that it does not. There is, in general, a set of north-south and east-west alignments both of the roads and parish and field boundaries which even now appears in places to be very inconvenient to the medieval settlements. This can be seen particularly at Limington, Little Marston, Nether Adber and Chilthorne Domer. The expected pattern is not really in evidence.

Secondly, there are a number of major lines across the landscape which were not anticipated – the present A303 is one which cuts across the parishes and their roads. This is probably a pre-Roman trackway linking up with the dry overland routes across the limestone and chalk to the north and north-east of South Cadbury. Similarly, the route south of South Cadbury is probably a long-distance route, as predicted. Three further alignments deserve consideration – the two angled sections near Rimpton/Marston Magna and that on the east side of Queen Camel. These cut across all other alignments and seem inexplicable at the moment. The other alignment, marked by roads and boundaries, runs in a great arc centred on Ilchester 3–5 kilometres (2–3 miles) away. This is respected by

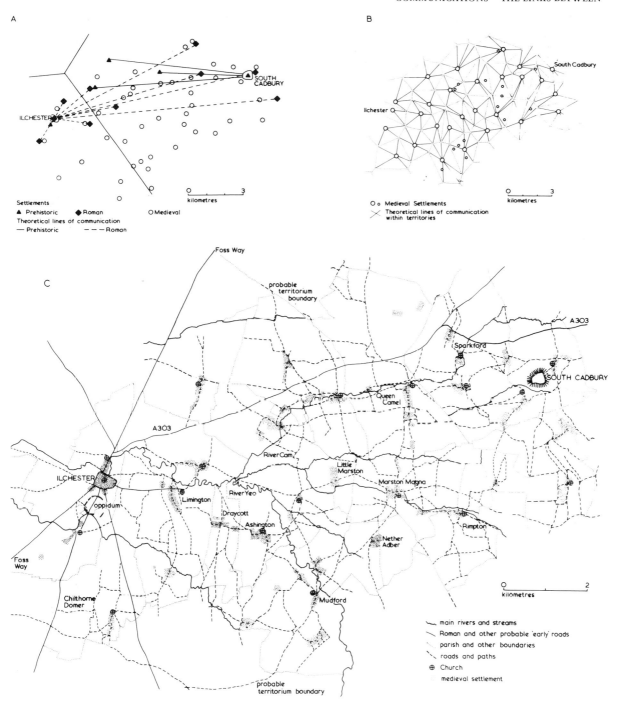

90 *The communication pattern in south-east Somerset. The first map shows the known prehistoric and Roman sites in the region (A). In the later prehistoric period there were important hillforts at South Cadbury, Ham Hill (off to the west) and Dundon (to the north). The straight lines define the theoretical territories (Theissen polygons) of these hillforts. Within these territories little is known of the contemporary settlements, so not much can be suggested of the roads and tracks. At the end of the prehistoric period an oppidum was developed at Ilchester to be succeeded by the Roman town itself, the centre of a region with a number of known sites; there must be others to be found. By the medieval period large numbers of settlements can be identified (B). The theoretical territories attached to these can be suggested (again by Theissen polygons) and within these there should be stellar patterns of roads and tracks running out from each settlement to the borders of its territory.*

The actual situation is very different (C) with many straight and curved road alignments apparently running in awkward courses and directions. The pattern of territorial units (shown as parish, estate, manor and tithing boundaries) is not as expected, and within them the expected stellar pattern of lanes is not evident.

147

many other features and must be a very early line in this landscape. It cannot be proved (probably ever) but it could be a *territorium* boundary for Ilchester's town land in the Roman period.

Finally, let us consider the general underlying pattern of this area. As has been stated, it runs north-south east-west and persistent alignments can be seen across the lands of Adber, Limington, Draycot and Ashington. These lines could represent earlier roads associated with, for example, a Roman field system, or they could be older. With reave systems of late Bronze Age being found on Dartmoor, and earlier overall alignments in such areas of Wessex and Essex being discussed, this underlying pattern could very likely be of prehistoric date. It must be emphasised, however, that this is unproven, and perhaps unprovable.

This particular example has perhaps shown something of the way a pattern of roads, lanes and tracks can be examined in an area. Only by examining settlements of different dates, likely lines between them and related land uses can much progress be made. Other features like field and parish boundaries need to be included to help to expand the range of possibilities examined. Even then, there will always be anomalies which at present defy explanation. Much, however, is likely to emerge of previously unsuspected elements, as in this example.

12

What does it all mean?

In this chapter we shall try to assess what we now know about the way the landscape has developed, what problems remain, and which useful pieces of research will help to solve these problems and perhaps indicate areas and topics where more intensive effort is needed to solve difficulties of interpretation and understanding in the landscape.

Following on from Christopher Taylor's three points – the great age of the man-made landscape, its complexity, and the amount of change within it – we can now suggest the major phases through which the development of the landscape seems to have passed (*Fig. 92*). Such a 'model' will inevitably be simplistic, generalised, and will need to be changed and refined as work progresses. It is offered here as a subject for discussion and not as a fixed, solidly-cast idea; it should certainly not be regarded as a new dogma to replace the old. Let us look at this model in some detail, beginning with the two most important factors – population and its relationship to open land.

POPULATION

Whether the population is rising or falling, and at what rate, and what the demographic structure is at any one time are all fundamental to the impact of people on the landscape. Without improvements in technology, more mouths to feed has always meant more land under cultivation and thus greater impact on waste and woodland resources. Conversely, a falling population should lead to some areas, probably less fertile and less productive, being abandoned and the regeneration of woodland over former fields.

Perhaps the most difficult aspect to assess for any area is the population size at any time. The larger number of early sites now known, the evidence of clearance from pollen analysis and other environmental evidence, and the results of air survey all suggest higher populations and denser concentrations of people in the past than was formerly thought. There are no figures indicating population size available before the eleventh century, and it is not until the nineteenth century that anything

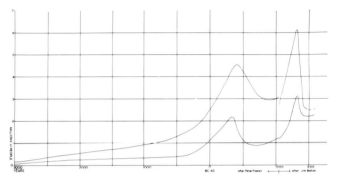

91 *Population in Britain 3000 BC AD 1500; the two lines represent the likely maximum and minimum levels. (After Peter Fowler and Jim Bolton, with permission)*

approaching reliability is reached. Nevertheless, some authors have ventured to put forward figures for various periods. Jim Bolton, for example, argues that a figure of six to seven million is more likely for the population of England in the pre-Black Death period (early fourteenth century) than the conventionally accepted two to three million, which itself is higher than formerly accepted by historians.

Peter Fowler, in looking at the evidence for the late prehistoric and Roman periods, suggests a population of up to five million in the late Roman period, falling back to three to four million in the eighth century. His graph suggests one million or less by the late Bronze Age (*c.*1000 BC), but, on the evidence of the landscape, this could be an underestimate. We can thus suggest a general population rise from late prehistory onwards, with noticeable increases in the Roman period and in the late Saxon/early medieval period (and possibly in the late Bronze Age). The greatest rise, of course, has been from the sixteenth century until the present day. There were significant declines at the end of the Roman period and in the late fourteenth and fifteenth centuries.

PREHISTORIC PERIODS and HISTORIC EVENTS	4000	3000	2000	1000	BC—O—AD	1000
	NEOLITHIC TECHNOLOGY		BRONZE AGE TECHNOLOGY		IRON AGE TECHNOLOGY / ROMAN 43–410	SAXON Alfred / MEDIEVAL / Black Death 1066 1348 / Dissolution 1535
POPULATION	General Population rise?			General Population rise	Fall / Rising	Drastic Fall / Rapid rise
FOREST/OPEN LAND RATIO	Forest Cover / Sporadic Clearance		Major Clearance	Increasing intensive land use and cultivation	Land abandonment / New woodland / Colonisation	Fully developed landscape / Managed Woodland
SETTLEMENTS	Little evidence of settlements	Isolated settlements of single or small groups of buildings		Farmsteads and hamlets	villas some evidence of villages	farmsteads villages develop / farms many villages collapse
FIELD SYSTEMS	Introduction of agriculture and husbandry	unenclosed field plots and extensive grassland		enclosed rectilinear fields		enclosed fields open common fields / enclosure
FOCAL PLACES	None known	Causewayed enclosures Long barrows	Henges Round barrows	earliest hillforts	Hillforts Oppida Shrines and Temples / Roman cities and towns	Towns refounded Monasteries Fairs and markets / New Towns Castles / Full urbanisation
LANDSCAPE STAGES	Full forest cover	Sporadic clearance / RITUAL LANDSCAPE		CELTIC LANDSCAPE		MEDIEVAL LANDSCAPE / modern landscape

92 An outline of the stages of landscape development and how they are related to conventional prehistoric periods, population dynamics, the areas of forest and types of archaeological monuments. This diagram should be regarded as a basis for discussion and further research and not as a definitive statement of developments over the last 7000 years.

FOREST AND LAND USE

Against the background of these demographic changes, environmental evidence shows increasing and more permanent forest clearance and the creation of open land, particularly from the second millennium onwards. By the late prehistoric and Roman periods the landscape was probably as clear of wildwood as in the early fourteenth century. In the centuries after the Roman period there was clearly widespread forest regeneration and it is this woodland which the documents and place-name evidence tells us was being cleared in the late Saxon and early medieval periods. It is worth wondering how many earlier such regenerations and reclearances there had been.

CLIMATE

As little as 1°C (1.8°F) average change in temperature can have a marked effect on the way people are able to use the landscape, particularly in upland areas. Similarly, increases or decreases in rainfall can make some areas difficult to manage. In a predominantly subsistence economy this can make life very difficult and even lead to starvation if crops fail and livestock dies. In a more commercial market-orientated economy, such marginal areas may not be able to compete with lower, dryer or more fertile areas in terms of production, or to raise capital from the sale of produce in order to buy in food and other essentials from other areas.

It is always difficult to be certain of the effects that slight climatic changes might have had, but a great deal of research has been undertaken and the general climatic background over thousands of years in pre-history is generally understood, with marked changes in weather in the historic period also outlined. The climate seems to have become warmer and milder from about 10,000 BC, with first tundra vegetation and then birch and pine woodland eventually giving way to mixed oak forest. The increasing warmth reached its optimum c.3000 BC, to be followed by gradually cooler and wetter weather by the Iron Age, except for a warmer and drier spell in the late Bronze Age. It was probably relatively warmer and drier in the late Saxon/early medieval period, followed by mini ice ages in the fourteenth century and the period from the sixteenth to the nineteenth centuries.

TECHNOLOGY

An assessment of the technological level of people (or what they could achieve with the knowledge and equipment at their disposal) at any particular point in time is very difficult to achieve. The archaeological record does not help in this since implements, machinery and tools in use before the eighteenth century have rarely survived. The problem can be demonstrated by the lack of any complete ploughs or ards surviving from the medieval and earlier periods, as shown by Sian Rees. In addition, early agricultural techniques and practices are little understood; for example, the complex processes associated with grain production alone are invariably not recognisable on archaeological sites, as demonstrated by Gordon Hilman.

Yet improvements in crop types, farming practices and processing can have a great impact on the way land is used and how many people can be supported on it. Outline figures are beginning to be discussed by both prehistoric archaeologists (Mercer, 1981) and medieval historians (Bolton, 1980), and they are frequently given for the early historic period (Cobbett). We might expect the introduction of manuring with farmyard waste and a second, winter, cropping to have led to an increase in crop production and hence population numbers. However, we might also expect greater erosion of soil after frost and rain due to the fields being ploughed and standing almost bare in winter, leading also to changes in river and stream regimes. In addition, different types of plough and the introduction of other farm implements might lead to greater or more efficient production. More research is needed on this topic before much can be said with confidence.

SETTLEMENT AND LAND USE

Looked at against this background of natural and technological changes, what can we say about how people lived, what sort of settlements they inhabited, and what field systems they employed (*Fig. 92*)? For most periods, we can now suggest that the dominant type of settlement has been the farmstead and hamlet with enclosed fields. It is more difficult to see the dynamic changes involved – although this becomes easier for the historical, and particularly the recent, periods – but certain familiar and well-studied aspects such as villages and the common field system can now be seen as atypical. One of the main problems is to explain how, when and why villages developed; of equal significance, and probably intimately connected with this problem, is to understand how common field agriculture evolved from earlier systems. A whole range of problems is encapsulated in these statements.

For any area under study we need to explain the changing settlement pattern. The current model of dispersed settlement agglomerating to nucleated villages and then changing to the farmsteads we see in the present landscape needs to be examined and discussed for many areas. We need to explain how much of the dispersed settlement pattern is 'original', i.e. pre-Norman or even pre-Roman, and how much is the

result of more recent developments. We should also ask perhaps *when* did the present settlement pattern originate as we see it in the landscape and on recent maps, and *what* are the stages through which it has passed. We must ascertain whether the pattern was ever in the form of nucleated groups of farmsteads working the land in common, rather than dispersed farms across the landscape working the holdings individually, in severalty. In other words, when have farms been grouped into hamlets and villages, and when have they been dispersed over the landscape?

In studies of land use, much can be learned from fieldwork and documents about the field systems of the Middle Ages; there is a vast amount of literature as well as many primary documents and maps on enclosure in the post-medieval period. Yet we still do not understand the origin of the common field patterns, manifested in strips and as ridge and furrow in the landscape. We should ask when and how these patterns and arrangements emerged and how they are related, functionally as well as topographically, to the earlier patterns of squarish or rectangular prehistoric fields. Are such systems related to the infield/outfield arrangements, and which was more common? Before these questions can be answered we must learn to recognise traces of infield/outfield systems in the landscape.

Even if little can be said of this change for most parishes, much can often be deduced of overall land use patterns in earlier times – provided we bear in mind how much people have influenced the landscape, how much 'natural' change is occurring all the time, and that earlier landscapes are often buried from view. The ratio of arable land to pasture is fundamental to land use and varies with changing economic circumstances. Periods of predominantly arable production and pastoralism need to be defined and what effects these may have had on settlements. In any case, we need to allow for distant resources such as pasture, woodland and waste.

FOCAL PLACES AND ESTATES

We have already seen that there is a hierarchy of places in the landscape and not everywhere is of equal importance. Glanville Jones has taught us how to look at early estate arrangements, to recognise large blocks of land in discrete ownership and, within these, to look for the caput or head place and the subsidiary units(*Fig. 11*) Our parish or area of study does not and did not exist in isolation – it was part of a larger arrangement, a complex system of interlinked places. We can often see this clearly from the sixteenth century onwards, and we may be able to learn much from the Middle Ages if the documents are available.

If we are interested in origins, the earlier arrangements have to be elucidated, bearing in mind that the structure of estates changes through time. Hundredal arrangements may help us to see earlier estates, particularly on ecclesiastical estates belonging to bishops or early monasteries. *Domesday Book* may tell us something of the distribution of estates belonging to particular owners in 1086. Perhaps the place under study was a royal caput in the seventh or eighth centuries or a hundredal manor in the eleventh century, or it may have had a castle, monastery or great house in the Middle Ages or later. It may be possible to reconstruct the estates dependent on it if this was the case. From an ecclesiastical point of view, we should ask whether it had a minster or mother church or merely a proprietary church or chapel of ease to somewhere more important. The church, that most studied but least understood of landscape features, often provides abundant clues to these landscape relationships in its size, building periods and degree of elaboration.

PARISH HISTORIES AND PARISH SURVEYS

Most of the research on the English landscape has been carried out by people looking at individual parishes. Frequently, such research has been dull or of little interest to the landscape historian, as was mentioned in Chapter 1. More recently, however, a number of researchers have made their parish studies more landscape orientated and have attempted to explain what can be seen around them as well as the history behind it. This movement began after the Second World War, with groups of people under the direction of Victor Skipp and others looking at areas around Birmingham in an attempt to explain the framework of the suburbs. I have no doubt that their research was not the first, nor indeed the finest, but it is typical of attempts, more common now in the mid 1980s, to try to explain from documents and maps, and to a lesser extent from fieldwork, why a particular parish looks like it does.

Parish surveys, however, developed specifically as a tool of archaeologists. Faced with increasing destruction and disturbance of known archaeological sites, and the realisation that there must be many more features to be located, archaeologists set up projects involving fieldwork and simple documentary research. The results have been spectacular. Research in Cornwall, where parish surveys really started under the auspices of the Cornwall Archaeology Society, has shown how many barrows and early settlements remained to be located and catalogued even in that well-researched county. Around Bristol, the work of the Bristol and Avon Archaeological Research Group has proved almost as spectacular, and work is well in hand in other counties like Oxfordshire and Devon. In some parts of the country the work has not only

concentrated on the location and recording of features – everything from prehistoric flint scatters to pill boxes – but some attempt is also being made to highlight landscape changes, with attention being paid to hedge patterns and areas of woodland. Some of the recent surveys from Somerset, such as those conducted in the parishes of Wambrook and Luxborough, show this approach well.

A further development which deserves mention, because its potential for understanding developments in the landscape is so great, is that of research conducted by farmers on their own land. The farmer's intimate knowledge of his land, together with his constant attention to it and the fact that he can take decisions about what to do with it (including whether to excavate it archaeologically or not) mean that potentially, if he has an interest in field archaeology, a great deal can be found out. The fact that decades, or even generations, can be spent examining relatively small areas of land, rather than the short transient research projects carried out by most of us, means that probably all those data which can be retrieved and recorded will be.

It is, of course, not known how much of this work is going on – and generally it has only emerged when a particular farmer's efforts have been combined with those of an archaeologist; even less has, as yet, been published. Yet several examples will suffice to show what can be achieved. Eddie Price's work on Frocester in Gloucestershire has already been mentioned (*Fig. 75*). This has lasted for several decades and his sons are now interested and involved as well. Some of his research has already been mentioned, but sites of all periods have been located, from early prehistory to medieval times. In Norfolk the long researches of John Owles on Witton have recently been published by Andrew Lawson in a fine monograph. On Cranborne Chase, Richard Bradley of Reading University is working with Martin Green, a local farmer, on a reassessment of Pitt Rivers' sites and new fieldwork in the area. Not far away, Barry Cunliffe has for years been working with John Budden on the Chalton area of Hampshire. Of all the work discussed so far, this last piece of research has reached a point at which phases of landscape development are now being suggested. Barry Cunliffe has tried to show not only what the landscape might have looked like around Chalton at the following dates – 7000–2500 BC, 2500–1000 BC, 1000–0 BC, AD 0–500, AD 500–1000, AD 1000–1500 – but also what changes have taken place in settlement form and siting over this long period. His diagram shows not only nucleated and dispersed settlements, but changes of site, desertions, shifts and shrinkages over a 2000–year period (*Fig. 49*). This study is a model of what is needed for all areas.

Two final points need to be emphasised in our

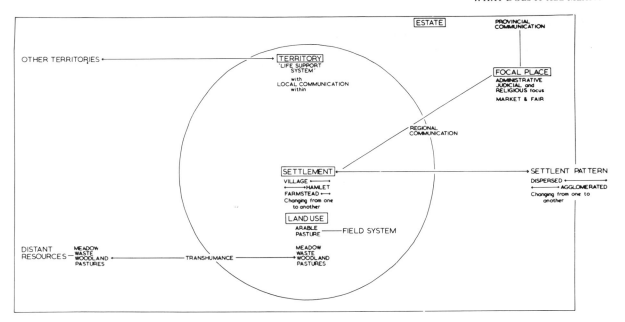

93 *A settlement in its landscape. This diagram is a development of Figs. 1 and 51, and it attempts to show simply some of the complex relationships in the landscape which have been discussed in this book. Like Fig. 92, it should be regarded as a basis for discussion and further research rather than a definitive statement. It is not intended to apply to any particular period.*

endeavours to study and understand the landscape. Firstly, it has been stressed all through this book that we need to, indeed we must, look at the landscape at any period as a complex working system which has many interlinked aspects, each dependent on the others, and all subject to change: the landscape is a dynamic and evolving system like much else in nature. I have tried to isolate certain elements from this and discuss the ways in which they have altered, the factors influencing the changes, and when and why such developments may have occurred. Much of this has been patchy; there is a great deal we still do not know and, conceptually, our approaches to how we study the landscape are still developing.

94 *A prehistoric craftsman and a medieval peasant. People like these laboured to create the landscape as we see it today. With all our attention to details we can easily forget the efforts of millions of ordinary people over thousands of years. (By permission of Nick Tweddle of Somerset County Museum and the President and Fellows of Corpus Christi College, Oxford)*

Because of the complexity of the landscape, the elements within it, how it is changing, and the forces at work within it, we need a model on which to base what we already know and to help us isolate areas of ignorance and to structure our future research. Fig. 93 is offered as a first step: it attempts to show a settlement at any period from prehistory to the nineteenth century in relation to other settlements in the area, local and distant land uses, the larger estate structure, local focal places and distant centres, and the communication links between all of these. Something of potential change is indicated within it, but on the two-dimensional page this is difficult! If nothing else, such a model can act as a check-list for any local study, so that, in accounting for each item in the diagram, attention can be drawn to items and features which at first sight do not appear to be of significance.

Finally, there is man, or more correctly men, women and children. It is all too easy to become so embroiled with earthworks, air photographs, maps, documents, potsherds, and hedges, that we lose sight of what it is all about. One criticism, sometimes valid, of the archaeologist (and recently of the landscape archaeologist) is that he has lost sight of the people in the mass of data collected: I hope this is not true. I keep as my vision the late thirteenth-century peasant, sitting by his fire, drying his boots and cooking his supper (the activity for February [!] from Corpus Christi College, Oxford, manuscript 285), and the prehistoric man building the Sweet Track. They must speak for the millions like them, from prehistory right through to our own time. It was their kind who not only dug the ditches and constructed the buildings, but who for generations felled woodland, ploughed land and harvested crops. We must not lose sight of them and of their labours. Our studies must be of *people* in the landscape, how they have lived, worked, died and worshipped over millennia. Unless we appreciate this, we are not looking at the real forces in the landscape, and our own relationship with it will be the poorer.

Bibliography and references

Introduction

The most important book on the general theme, though very much out of date in the early chapters, is still:

W. G. HOSKINS *The Making of the English Landscape* (Hodder and Stoughton, 1955 plus reprints)

Other very relevant studies are:

M. W. BERESFORD *History on the Ground* (Lutterworth, London, 1957; reprinted Alan Sutton, Gloucester, 1984)

MICHAEL ASTON and TREVOR ROWLEY *Landscape Archaeology – An Introduction to Fieldwork Techniques on Post-Roman Landscapes* (David and Charles, 1974).

ALAN BAKER and J. B. HARLEY (eds) *Man Made the Land* (David and Charles, 1973)

H. C. DARBY (ed) *A New Historical Geography of England Before 1600/After 1600* (2 vols, Cambridge University Press, 1973 and 1976)

W. G. HOSKINS *Fieldwork in Local History* (Faber and Faber, 1967)

W. G. HOSKINS *Local History in England* (Longmans, 1959)

RICHARD MUIR Shell Guide to *Reading the Landscape* (Michael Joseph, 1981)

There are also relevant chapters in:

ALAN ROGERS (ed) *Group Projects in Local History* (Dawson, Folkestone, 1977)

ALAN ROGERS and TREVOR ROWLEY (eds) *Landscapes and Documents* (Bedford Square Press, London, 1974)

Important recent articles include:

CHRISTOPHER TAYLOR 'The Making of the English Landscape – 25 years on' *The Local Historian* Vol. 14 No. 4 (1980)

MICHAEL ASTON 'The Making of the English Landscape – the next 25 years' *The Local Historian* Vol. 15 No. 6 (1983)

1 – How do we know what we know?

Good introductions to *archaeology* include:

PETER FOWLER *Approaches to Archaeology* (A. & C. Black, 1977)

DAVID MILES *An Introduction to Archaeology* (Hyperion, Ward Lock, London, 1978)

KEVIN GREENE *Archaeology: An Introduction* (Batsford, 1983)

General *fieldwork* is covered in:

ERIC S. WOOD *Collins Field Guide to Archaeology* (Collins, 1963 and later editions)

ORDNANCE SURVEY *Field Archaeology* (HMSO 1963 and later editions)

W. G. HOSKINS *Fieldwork in Local History* (Faber and Faber, 1967)

CHRISTOPHER TAYLOR *Fieldwork in Medieval Archaeology* (Batsford, 1974)

MICHAEL ASTON and TREVOR ROWLEY *Landscape Archaeology: An Introduction to Fieldwork Techniques on Post-Roman Landscapes* (David and Charles, 1974)

More specifically:

JOHN M. STEANE and BRIAN F. DIX *Peopling Past Landscapes – A Handbook Introducing Archaeological Fieldwork Techniques in Rural Areas* (CBA 1978)

P. J. FASHAM, R. T. SCHADLA HALL, S. J. SHENNAN and P. J. BATES *Fieldwalking for Archaeologists* (Hampshire Field Club and Archaeological Society 1980)

GLENN FOARD 'Systematic Fieldwalking and the Investigation of Saxon Settlement in Northamptonshire' *World Archaeology* Vol. 9 No. 3 (1978) pp. 357–374

For *air photographs* and *aerial photography* see:

D. R. WILSON (ed) *Aerial Reconnaissance for Archaeology* CBA Research Report No. 12 (1975)

G. S. MAXWELL (ed) *The Impact of Aerial Reconnaissance on Archaeology* CBA Research Report No. 49 (1983)

D. R. WILSON *Air Photo Interpretation for Archaeologists* (Batsford, 1982)

M. W. BERESFORD and J. K. ST JOSEPH *Medieval England: An Aerial Survey* (Cambridge University Press, 1979)

S. S. FRERE and J. K. ST JOSEPH *Roman Britain From The Air* (Cambridge University Press, 1983)

RICHARD MUIR *History From the Air* (Michael Joseph, 1983)

COLIN PLATT *Medieval Britain From the Air* (Guild Publishing, London, 1984)

For *maps* see:

J. B. HARLEY *Maps for the Local Historian – A Guide to the British Sources* (Standing Conference for Local History, 1972)

J. B. HARLEY and C. W. PHILLIPS *The Historians Guide to Ordnance Survey Maps* (Standing Conference for Local History, 1964)

H. P. R. FINBERG and V. H. T. SKIPP *Local History: Objectives and Pursuit* (David and Charles, 1967)

W. G. HOSKINS *Local History in England* (Longman 1959)

ALAN ROGERS (ed) *Group Projects in Local History* (Dawson, Folkestone, 1977)

JOHN WEST *Village Records* (Macmillan, 1962)

W. B. STEPHENS *Sources for English Local History* (Cambridge University Press, 1973)

ALAN ROGERS (ed) *Approaches to Local History* (Longman, 2nd edition, 1977)

R. W. DUNNING *Local History for Beginners* (Phillimore Chichester, 1980)

PHILIP RIDEN *Local History: A Handbook for Beginners* (Batsford, 1983)

Recent important research on *place names* is contained in county volumes published by the English Place Names Society. See also:

MARGARET GELLING *Signposts to the Past: Place Names and the History of England* (Dent, 1978)

MARGARET GELLING *Place Names in the Landscape* (Dent, 1984)

Climate

ANTHONY HARDING *Climatic Change in Later Prehistory* (Edinburgh University Press, 1982)

M. L. PARRY *Climatic Change, Agriculture and Settlement* (Dawson, Folkestone, 1978)

C. D. SMITH and MARTIN PARRY (eds) *Consequences of Climatic Change* (Dept. of Geography, University of Nottingham, 1981).

Environment

JOHN G. EVANS *The Environment of Early Man in the British Isles* (Elek, 1975)

IAN SIMMONS and MICHAEL TOOLEY (eds) *The Environment in British Prehistory* (Duckworth, 1981)

MARTIN JONES and GEOFFREY DIMBLEBY (eds) *The Environment of Man: The Iron Age to the Anglo-Saxon Period* British Archaeological Reports, British Series 87 (Oxford, 1981)

J. G. EVANS, SUSAN LIMBREY and HENRY CLEERE *The Effect of Man on The Landscape: The Highland Zone* CBA Research Report No. 11 (London, 1975)

SUSAN LIMBREY and J. G. EVANS (eds) *The Effect of Man on the Landscape: The Lowland Zone* CBA Research Report No. 21 (London, 1978)

G. W. DIMBLEBY *The Development of British Heathlands and Their Soils* Oxford Forestry Memoirs No. 23 (Clarendon Press, Oxford, 1962)

WINIFRED PENNINGTON *The History of British Vegetation* (English University Press, London, 1974)

SIR HARRY GODWIN *History of the British Flora: A Factual Basis for Phytogeography* (Cambridge University Press, 2nd edition, 1975)

D. WALKER and R. G. WEST (eds) *Studies in the Vegetational History of the British Isles* (Cambridge University Press, 1970)

OLIVER RACKHAM *Trees and Woodland in the British Landscape* (Dent, 1976)

OLIVER RACKHAM *Ancient Woodland: its History, Vegetation and Uses in England* (Edward Arnold, 1980)

2 – Early landscapes

General books on *prehistory*:

RICHARD BRADLEY *The Prehistoric Settlement of Britain* (Routledge and Kegan Paul, 1978)

COLIN RENFREW (ed) *British Prehistory: A New Outline* (Duckworth, 1974)

COLIN RENFREW *Before Civilization: the Radio Carbon Revolution and Prehistoric Europe* (Penguin, 1973)

J. V. S. MEGAW and D. D. A. SIMPSON (eds) *Introduction to British Prehistory* (Leicester University Press, 1979)

For the *environment* see:

IAN SIMMONS and MICHAEL TOOLEY *The Environment in British Prehistory* (Duckworth, 1981)

For the *earliest periods*:

J. GRAHAM and D. CLARKE *Star Carr: a Case Study in Bio-archaeology* (Addison-Wesley Modular Publications, 1972)

CHRISTOPHER NORMAN 'Mesolithic Hunter-Gatherers 9000–4000 BC' in M. Aston and I. Burrow (eds) *The Archaeology of Somerset* (Somerset County Council, Taunton, 1982)

ROGER JACOBI 'Ice Age Cave Dwellers 12000–9000 BC' in M. Aston and I. Burrow (eds) *The Archaeology of Somerset* (Somerset County Council, Taunton, 1982)

R. M. JACOBI 'The Environment of Man at Cheddar 11–10000 Years Ago' in *Somerset Archaeology and Natural History* Vol. 126 (1982)

JOAN TAYLOR and REBECCA SMART 'An Investigation of Surface Concentrations: Priddy 1977' in *Bristol and Avon Archaeology* Vol. 2 (1983)

PAUL MELLARS 'Ungulate Populations, Economic Patterns, and the Mesolithic Landscape' in J. G. Evans, Susan Limbrey and Henry Cleere (1975)

R. M. JACOBI 'Population and Landscape in Mesolithic Lowland Britain' in S. Limbrey and J. G. Evans (eds) (1978)

For *axes* see:

SONIA COLE *The Neolithic Revolution* (British Museum – Natural History, 1963)

T. H. MCKCLOUGH and W. A. CUMMINS *Stone Axe Studies* CBA Research Report No. 23 (London, 1979)

For *soil changes* see:

SUSAN LIMBREY *Soil Science and Archaeology* (Academic Press, London, 1975)

JOHN EVANS *The Environment of Early Man in the British Isles* (Elek, London, 1975)

G. W. DIMBLEBY *The Development of British Heathlands and Their Soils* Oxford Forestry Memoirs No. 23 (Clarendon Press, Oxford, 1962)

MARTIN BELL 'Valley Sediments and Environmental Change' in M. Jones and G. Dimbleby (eds) (1981)

MARTIN BELL 'Valley Sediments as Evidence of Prehistoric Land Use on the South Downs' in *Proceedings of the Prehistoric Society* Vol. 49 (1983) pp. 119–50

For *territories* see:

G. BARKER and G. WEBLEY 'Causewayed Camps and Early Neolithic Economies in Central Southern England' in *Proceedings of the Prehistoric Society* Vol. 44 (1978) pp. 161–86

R. MERCER *Hambledon Hill: A Neolithic Landscape* (Edinburgh University Press, 1980)

D. A. SPRATT 'Prehistoric Boundaries on the North Yorkshire Moors' in Graeme Barker (ed) *Prehistoric Communities in Northern England: Essays in Economic and Social Reconstruction* (University of Sheffield, 1981)

For *models* see:

D. L. CLARKE (ed) *Models In Archaeology* (Methuen, 1972)

RICHARD CHORLEY and PETER HAGGETT *Socio-Economic Models in Geography* (Parts I and III of Models in Geography) (Methuen, 1968)

For the *Somerset Levels* see:

J. M. COLES and B. J. ORME *Prehistory of the Somerset Levels* Somerset Levels Project (1980) and *Somerset Levels Papers* 1–10 (1975–1984, continuing)

For *Dartmoor* see:

VALERIE MAXFIELD (ed) *Prehistoric Dartmoor in its Context* (Devon Archaeological Society, 1979)

ANDREW FLEMING 'The Prehistoric Landscape of Dartmoor Part 1 South Dartmoor' in *Proceedings of the Prehistoric Society* 44 (1978) pp. 97–123

ANDREW FLEMING 'The Prehistoric Landscape of Dartmoor Part 2 North and East Dartmoor' in *Proceedings of the Prehistoric Society* 49 (1983) pp. 195–241

ANDREW FLEMING 'The Dartmoor Reaves: Boundary Patterns and Behaviour Patterns in the Second Millennium BC' in *Proceedings of the Devon Archaeological Society* 37 (1979) pp. 115–30

G. J. WAINWRIGHT and K. SMITH 'The South Dartmoor Project 1976–79' in V. Maxfield (ed) (1979)

For *early land allotment* see:

H. C. BOWEN and P. J. FOWLER (eds) *Early Land Allotment* British Archaeological Reports 48 (1978)

D. N. RILEY *Early Landscape from the Air: Studies of Crop Marks in South Yorkshire and North Nottinghamshire* (University of Sheffield, 1980)

For *river valleys* and *cropmarks* see:

GRAHAM WEBSTER and BRIAN HOBLEY 'Aerial Reconnaissance over the Warwickshire Avon' *Archaeological Journal* 121 (1964)

also Avon Severn Valleys Research Project Annual Reports 1 (1963) to 5 (1968) Council for British Archaeology Regional Group 8

ALAN HUNT 'Archaeology in the Avon and Severn Valleys – a Review' *West Midlands Archaeology* No. 25 (1982)

For the *Thames Valley* see:

DON BENSON and DAVID MILES *The Upper Thames Valley: An Archaeological Survey of the River Gravels* (Oxfordshire Archaeological Unit, 1974)

TIMOTHY GATES *The Middle Thames Valley: An Archaeological Survey of the River Gravels* (Berkshire Archaeological Committee, 1975)

ROGER LEECH *The Upper Thames Valley in Gloucestershire and Wiltshire: An Archaeological Survey of the River Gravels* (Committee for Rescue Archaeology in Avon, Gloucestershire, and Somerset, Bristol, 1977)

For the *Iron Age* see:

PETER FOWLER *The Farming of Prehistoric Britain* (Cambridge University Press, 1983)

ROGER MERCER (ed) *Farming Practice in British Prehistory* (Edinburgh University Press, 1981)

BARRY CUNLIFFE and TREVOR ROWLEY (eds) *Lowland Iron Age Communities in Europe* British Archaeological Reports International Series (Supplementary) 48 (Oxford, 1978)

BARRY CUNLIFFE *Iron Age Communities* (Longman, 1974)

For *Roman landscapes* see:

DAVID MILES (ed) *The Romano-British Countryside – Studies in Rural Settlement and Economy* British Archaeological Reports 103 (Oxford, 1982)

PETER CLACK and SUSANNE HASELGROVE (eds) *Rural Settlement in the Roman North* CBA Group 3 (Durham University, 1982)

S. S. FRERE and J. K. S. ST JOSEPH *Roman Britain from the Air* (Cambridge University Press, 1983)

SARAH WOOL *Fundus and Manerium: a Study of Continuity and Survival in Gloucestershire from Roman to Medieval Times* unpublished PhD Thesis (Bristol University, 1982)

ANN ELLISON and JOHN HARRISS 'Settlement and Land Use in the Prehistory and Early History of Southern England: a Study Based on Locational Models' in D. L. Clarke (ed) *Models in Archaeology* (Methuen, 1972) pp. 911–62

C. W. PHILLIPS (ed) *The Fenland in Roman Times* Royal Geographical Society Research Series 5 (1970)

For a general account of settlement development all through the prehistoric period (and beyond) see:

CHRISTOPHER TAYLOR *Village and Farmstead: A History of Rural Settlement in England* (George Philip, 1983)

3– Estates and boundaries

H. P. R. FINBERG *Roman and Saxon Withington: A Study in Continuity* Leicester University, Department of English Local History Occasional Paper No. 8 (1955)

P. H. SAWYER *From Roman Britain to Norman England* (Methuen, 1978)

JUNE A. SHEPPARD 'The Origin and Evolution of Field and Settlement Patterns in the Herefordshire Manor of Marden' Department of Geography, Queen Mary College, University of London, Occasional Papers No. 15 (1979)

GLANVILLE JONES 'Settlement Patterns in Anglo-Saxon England' *Antiquity* XXXV (1961). This article discusses the basic idea of caputs and then relates them particularly to earlier hillforts as well as the possibility of earlier origins. There is frequent reference to the early Welsh arrangements.

GLANVILLE JONES 'Early Territorial Organization in England and Wales' *Geografiska Annaler* XLIII (1961). This article discusses continuity and the arrangements in 'Celtic' society and there is much discussion on the make-up of the multiple estate. Examples from Wales and Yorkshire are cited, together with a discussion of place names.

GLANVILLE JONES 'Basic Patterns of Settlement Distribution in Northern England' *Advancement of Science* Vol. 18 No. 72 (1961). Based on the north, and especially Yorkshire, this article seeks to show great continuity and inequality in society from prehistoric to medieval times. It discusses place names and characteristics of the multiple estates. There are many Yorkshire examples.

GLANVILLE JONES 'Multiple Estates and Early Settlement' in P. H. Sawyer (ed) *English Medieval Settlement* (Edward Arnold, London, 1979). This article discusses the *Book of Iorwerth* and its theoretical estate organisation for Wales in the thirteenth century, together with the examples of Aberffraw in Anglesey, Malling in Sussex and Burghshire in Yorkshire. There is much about the functioning of a multiple estate.

R. W. DUNNING 'The Origins of Nether Stowey' *Somerset Archaeology and Natural History* 125 (1981) pp. 124–6

B. K. DAVISON 'Castle Neroche: An Abandoned Norman Fortress in South Somerset' *Somerset Archaeology and Natural History* 116 (1972) pp. 16–58

C. J. BOND 'The Estates of Evesham Abbey: A Preliminary Survey of Their Medieval Topography' *Vale of Evesham Historical Society Research Papers* Vol. IV (1973) pp. 1–61

C. J. BOND 'The Reconstruction of the Medieval Landscape: The Estates of Abingdon Abbey' *Landscape History* (1979) pp. 59–75

SUSANNA WADE-MARTINS *A Great Estate at Work: The Holkham Estate and its Inhabitants in the Nineteenth Century* (Cambridge University Press, 1980)

See also the important but difficult essay by CHARLES PHYTHIAN-ADAMS 'Continuity, Fields and Fission: The Making of a Midland Parish' (Claybrooke in Leicestershire) Leicester University, Department of English Local History Occasional Papers 3rd Series No. 4 (1978)

For *Anglo-Saxon charters* see:

P. H. SAWYER *Anglo-Saxon Charters: An Annotated List and Bibliography* Royal Historical Society Guides and Handbooks No. 8 (1968)

Regional volumes:

H. P. R. FINBERG 'The Early Charters of Devon and Cornwall' Leicester University, Department of English Local History Occasional Papers No. 2 (1953)

C. R. HART *The Early Charters of Northern England and the North Midlands* (Leicester University Press, 1975)

CYRIL HART 'The Early Charters of Essex: The Saxon Period' and 'The Early Charters of Essex: The Norman Period' Leicester University Department of English Local History Occasional Papers Nos. 10 & 11 (both 1957)

H. P. R. FINBERG *The Early Charters of Wessex* (Leicester University Press, 1964)

C. R. HART *The Early Charters of Eastern England* (Leicester University Press, 1966)

H. P. R. FINBERG *The Early Charters of the West Midlands* (Leicester University Press, 1961)

See also *English Place Names Society* volumes for particular counties, and:

M. GELLING *Signposts to the Past* (Dent, 1978) – especially Chapter 8, Boundaries and Meeting Places.

M. GELLING *Place Names in the Landscape* (Dent, 1984)

D. BONNEY 'Early Boundaries in Wessex' in P. J. Fowler (ed) *Archaeology and the Landscape* (John Baker, London, 1972)

D. BONNEY 'Early Boundaries and Estates in Southern England' in P. H. Sawyer (ed) *English Medieval Settlement* (Edward Arnold, 1979)

For *origins of parishes*, i.e. ecclesiastical land units, see:

G. W. O. ADDLESHAW *The Beginnings of the Parochial System* University of York, Borthwick Institute of Historical Research, St Anthony's Hall No. 3 (1953)

G. W. O. ADDLESHAW *The Development of the Parochial System from Charlemagne (768–814) to Urban II (1088–1099)* University of York, Borthwick Institute of Historical Research, St Anthony's Hall No. 6 (1954)

F. G. ALDSWORTH 'Parish Bounds on Record' *The Local Historian* Vol. 15 No. 1 (1982)

4 – Status in the landscape

For *geographical* work see:

J. A. EVERSON and B. P. FITZGERALD *Settlement Patterns* (Longman, 1969)

M. G. BRADFORD and W. A. KENT *Human Geography Theories and Their Applications* (Oxford University Press, 1977)

RICHARD J. CHORLEY and PETER HAGGET (eds) *Socio-Economic Models in Geography* (Methuen, 1967)

MICHAEL CHISHOLM *Rural Settlement and Land Use* 3rd edition (Hutchinson, 1979)

For *focal places* see:

M. ASTON 'Post-Roman Central Places in Somerset' in E. Grant (ed) *Archaeology and the Concept of Centrality* (1985)

For *earlier sites* see:

BARRY CUNLIFFE and TREVOR ROWLEY (eds) *Oppida: The Beginnings of Urbanism in Barbarian Europe* British Archaeological Reports Supplementary Series 11 (Oxford, 1976)

R. BRADLEY and A. ELLISON *Ramshill: A Bronze Age Defended Enclosure and its Landscape* British Archaeological Reports 19 (Oxford, 1975)

IAN BURROW *Hillforts and Hill-top Settlement in Somerset in the First to Eighth Centuries AD* British Archaeological Reports British Series 91 (Oxford, 1981)

PHILIP RAHTZ *The Saxon and Medieval Palaces at Cheddar* British Archaeological Reports British Series 65 (Oxford, 1979)

BRIAN HOPE TAYLOR *Yeavering: An Anglo-British Centre of Early Northumbria* (HMSO, London, 1977)

DEREK RENN *Norman Castles in Britain* (John Baker, London, 1968)

DAVID KNOWLES and R. NEVILLE HADCOCK *Medieval Religious Houses: England and Wales* (Longman, 1971)

SUSANNA WADE-MARTINS *A Great Estate at Work: The Holkham Estate and its Inhabitants in the Nineteenth Century* (Cambridge University Press, 1980)

BRIAN K. DAVISON 'Castle Neroche: An Abandoned Norman Fortress in South Somerset' *Somerset Archaeology and Natural History* 116 (1972) pp. 16–58

For *monastic estates*

C. JAMES BOND The Estates of Evesham Abbey: A Preliminary Survey of Their Medieval Topography' *Vale of Evesham Historical Society Research Papers* Vol. IV (1973) pp. 1–61

C. JAMES BOND 'The Reconstruction of the Medieval Landscape: The Estates of Abingdon Abbey' *Landscape History* (1979) pp. 59–75

JOHN BLAIR 'The Surrey Endowments of Lewes Priory Before 1200' *Surrey Archaeological Collections* Vol. LXXII (1980) pp. 97–126

MARJORIE MORGAN *The English Lands of the Abbey of Bec* (Clarendon Press, Oxford, 1946)

R. A. DONKIN *The Cistercians: Studies in the Geography of Medieval England and Wales* (Pontifical Institute of Medieval Studies, Toronto, 1978)

F. M. PAGE *The Estates of Crowland Abbey: A Study in Manorial Organisation* (Cambridge University Press, 1934)

SANDRA RABAN *The Estates of Thorney and Crowland: A Study in Medieval Monastic Land Tenure* University of Cambridge, Department of Land Economy Occasional Papers No. 7 (1977)

S. F. HOCKEY *Quarr Abbey and its Lands 1132–1631* (Leicester University Press, 1970)

BARBARA HARVEY *Westminster Abbey and its Estates in the Middle Ages* (Clarendon Press, Oxford, 1977)

CHRISTOPHER DYER *Lords and Peasants in a Changing Society: The Estates of the Bishopric of Worcester 680–1540* (Cambridge University Press, 1980)

For *hundreds* see:

H. M. CAM *The Hundred and the Hundred Rolls* (Methuen, 1930)

O. S. ANDERSON *The English Hundred Names* (Lund, 1934)

O. S. ANDERSON *The English Hundred Names; The South-Western Counties* (Lund and Leipzig, 1939)

For *exchange* see:

T. K. EARLE and J. E. ERICSON *Exchange Systems in Prehistory* (Academic Press, 1977)

RICHARD HODGES *Dark Age Economics: The Origins of Towns and Trade AD 600–1000* (Duckworth, 1982)

R. H. BRITNELL 'English Markets and Royal Administration Before 1200' *Economic History Review* 2nd series Vol. 21 No. 2 (1978)

R. H. BRITNELL The Proliferation of Markets in England 1200–1349' *Economic History Review* 2nd series Vol. 34 No. 2 (1981)

Also, *markets* in various counties are discussed in:

B. E. COATES 'The Origin and Distribution of Markets and Fairs in Medieval Derbyshire' *Derbyshire Archaeological Journal* 85 (1965) pp. 95–111

G. H. TUPLING 'The Origin of Markets and Fairs in Medieval Lancashire' *Transactions of Lancashire and Cheshire Antiquarian Society* 49 (1933) pp. 75–94

J. H. HAMER 'Trading at St White Down Fair 1637–1649' *Somerset Archaeology and Natural History* 112 (1968) pp. 61–70

A particularly useful study for showing *exchange systems* in the Middle Ages is:

STEPHEN MOORHOUSE 'Documentary Evidence and its Potential for Understanding the Inland Movement of Medieval Pottery' *Medieval Ceramics* Vol. 7 (1983) pp. 45–87

For *ecclesiastical aspects* see:

H. M. and J. TAYLOR *Anglo-Saxon Architecture* Vols. 1–3 (Cambridge University Press, 1965–1978)

MARGARET DEANSLEY *The Pre-Conquest Church in England* (A. & C. Black, 1961)

DELLA HOOKE *Anglo-Saxon Landscapes of the West Midlands: the Charter Evidence* British Archaeological Reports British Series 95 (Oxford, 1981)

COLIN PLATT *The Parish Churches of Medieval England* (Secker and Warburg, 1981)

M. ASTON 'Post-Roman Central Places in Somerset' in E. Grant (ed) (1985)

M. D. ANDERSON *History and Imagery in British Churches* (John Murray, 1971)

RICHARD MORRIS *The Church in British Archaeology* Council for British Archaeology Research Report No. 47 (1983)

PETER ADDYMAN and RICHARD MORRIS *The Archaeological Study of Churches* Council for British Archaeology Research Report No. 13 (1976)

J. H. BETTEY *Church & Community: The Parish Church in English Life* (Moonraker, Bradford on Avon, 1979)

W. RODWELL *The Archaeology of the English Church* (Batsford, 1981)

5 – Deserted villages and after

M. W. BERESFORD *The Lost Villages of England* (Luttermouth, London, 1954, reprint Alan Sutton, Gloucester, 1983)

W. G. HOSKINS 'Seven Deserted Village Sites in Leicestershire' *Transactions of the Leicestershire Archaeological Society* XXII (1944–45) pp. 241–64

M. W. BERESFORD 'The Deserted Villages of Warwickshire' *Transactions of the Birmingham Archaeological Society* LXVI for 1945 (1950) pp. 49–106

Recent research includes:

C. C. TAYLOR *Village and Farmstead: A History of Rural Settlement in England* (George Philip, 1983)

R. MUIR *The Lost Villages of Britain* (1982)

R. T. ROWLEY and J. WOOD *Deserted Villages* (Shire Archaeology, Aylesbury, 1982)

K. J. ALLISON, M. W. BERESFORD and J. G. HURST 'The Deserted Villages of Oxfordshire' Leicester University, Department of English Local History Occasional Papers XVII (1965) pp. 1–47

K. J. ALLISON, M. W. BERESFORD and J. G. HURST 'The Deserted Villages of Northamptonshire' Leicester University, Department of English Local History Occasional Papers XVIII (1966) pp. 1–48

C. C. DYER 'Deserted Medieval Villages in the West Midlands' *Economic History Review* 2nd series Vol. XXXV No. 1 (Feb 1982)

For *Cistercian desertions* see:

R. A. DONKIN *The Cistercians: Studies in the Geography of Medieval England and Wales* (Pontifical Institute of Medieval Studies, Toronto, 1978)

For *finding* deserted villages see:

M. ASTON and R. T. ROWLEY *Landscape Archaeology: An Introduction to Fieldwork Techniques on Post-Roman Landscapes* (David and Charles, 1974)

C. TAYLOR *Fieldwork in Medieval Archaeology* (Batsford, 1974)

Case studies:

M. ASTON 'Gardens and Earthworks at Hardington and Low Ham, Somerset' *Somerset Archaeology and Natural History* 122 (1978) pp. 11–28

H. THORPE 'The Lord and the Landscape, Illustrated Through the Changing Fortunes of a Warwickshire Parish, Wormleighton' *Transactions of the Birmingham and Warwickshire Archaeological Society* 80 (1965) pp. 38–77

M. ASTON 'Deserted Settlements in Mudford Parish, Yeovil' *Somerset Archaeology and Natural History* Vol. 121 (1977) pp. 41–53

C. J. BOND 'Deserted Medieval Villages in Warwickshire and Worcestershire' in T. R. Slater and P. J. Jarvis (eds) *Field and Forest: An Historical Geography of Warwickshire and Worcestershire* (Geo Books, Norwich, 1982)

Wharram Percy:

JOHN HURST (general editor) *Wharram: A Study of Settlement on the Yorkshire Wolds* Vol. 1 (1979) Society for Medieval Archaeology Monograph No. 8

M. W. BERESFORD and J. G. HURST 'Wharram Percy: A Case Study in Microtopography' in P. H. Sawyer (ed) *Medieval English Settlement* (Edward Arnold, 1979). This account can now be seen to be wrong in parts.

The most up-to-date accounts are:

J. G. HURST 'The topography of Warram Percy Village' in B. K. Roberts and R. E. Glasscock *Villages, Fields and Frontiers* British Archaeological Reports International Series 185 Oxford 1983)

J. G. HURST 'The Wharram Research Project Results to 1983' *Medieval Archaeology* XXVIII (1984) pp. 77–111

Understanding of the site increases, however, year by year.
Saxon settlements:

S. E. WEST 'The Anglo-Saxon Village of West Stow: An Interim Report of the Excavations 1965–68' *Medieval Archaeology* XIII (1969) pp. 1–20

P. V. ADDYMAN and D. LEIGH 'The Anglo-Saxon Village at Chalton, Hampshire: Second Interim Report' *Medieval Archaeology* XVII (1973) pp. 1–25

MARTIN MILLETT with SIMON JAMES 'Excavations at Cowdery's Down, Basingstoke, Hampshire 1978–81' *The Archaeological Journal* 140 (1983) pp. 151–279

S. LOSCO-BRADLEY and H. M. WHEELER 'Anglo-Saxon Settlement in the Trent Valley: Some Aspects' in Margaret Faull (ed) *Studies in Late Anglo-Saxon Settlement* (Oxford University Department for External Studies, Oxford, 1984)

See also:

P. J. FOWLER 'Agriculture and Rural Settlement' pp. 23–48

P. A. RAHTZ 'Buildings and Rural Settlement' pp. 49–98; both in D. Wilson (ed) *The Archaeology of Anglo-Saxon England* (Cambridge University Press, 1976)

For *Raunds* see:

G. E. CADMAN 'Raunds 1977–1983: An Excavation Summary' *Medieval Archaeology* XXVII (1983) pp. 107–22

GRAHAM CADMAN and GLEN FOARD 'Raunds: Manorial and Village Origins' in Margaret Faull (ed) (1984)

6 – Surviving villages

For all settlement studies, the following are useful:

C. TAYLOR *Village and Farmstead: A History of Rural Settlement in England* (George Philip, 1983)

B. K. ROBERTS *Rural Settlement in Britain* (Dawson, Folkestone, 1977)

TREVOR ROWLEY *Villages in the Landscape* (Dent, 1978)

M. W. BERESFORD *New Towns of the Middle Ages: Town Plantation in England, Wales and Gascony* (Lutterworth, London, 1967)

M. R. G. CONZEN 'Alnwick, Northumberland: A Study in Town-Plan Analysis' *Institute of British Geographers* No. 27 (1960)

M. R. G. CONZEN 'The Use of Town Plans in the Study of Urban History' in H. J. Dyos (ed) *The Study of Urban History* (Edward Arnold, 1968)

For detailed *village* and *village planning* studies:

JUNE SHEPPARD 'Pre-enclosure Field and Settlement Patterns in an English Township – Wheldrake, near York' *Geografiska Annaler* 48 (1966) pp. 59–77

PAMELA ALLERSTON 'English Village Development: Findings from the Pickering District of North Yorkshire' *Institute of British Geographers Transactions* 51 (1970) pp. 95–109

BRIAN ROBERTS 'The Regulated Village in Northern England: Some Problems and Questions' *Geographica Polonica* 38 (1978) pp. 245–52

BRIAN ROBERTS 'The Anatomy of the Village: Observation and Extrapolation' *Landscape History* Vol. 4 (1982) pp. 11–20

BRIAN ROBERTS 'The Study of Village Plans' *Local Historian* Vol. 9 No. 5 (Feb 1971) pp. 233–41

BRIAN ROBERTS *The Green Villages of County Durham: A Study in Historical Geography* Durham County Library Local History Publication No. 12 (1977)

JUNE SHEPPARD 'Metrological Analysis of Regular Village Plans In Yorkshire' *Agricultural History Review* 22 (1974) pp. 118–35

JUNE SHEPPARD 'Medieval Village Planning in Northern England: Some Evidence from Yorkshire' *Journal of Historical Geography* 2 (1976) pp. 3–20

M. W. BERESFORD and J. HURST *Deserted Medieval Villages* (Lutterworth, London, 1971)

BRIAN ROBERTS *Village Plans* Shire Archaeology Aylesbury 27 (1982)

C. TAYLOR 'Polyfocal Settlement and the English Village' *Medieval Archaeology* XXI (1977) pp. 189–93

J. RAVENSDALE *Liable to Floods: Village Landscape on the Edge of the Fens AD 450–1850* (Cambridge University Press, 1974) especially 'Village Patterns', pp. 121–50

CECILY HOWELL *Land, Family and Inheritance in Transition: Kibworth Harcourt 1280–1700* (Cambridge University Press, 1983) especially Chapter 7, 'Village Morphology and Buildings'

J. E. B. GOVER, ALLEN MAWER and F. M. STENTON *The Place Names of Wiltshire* English Place Name Society Vol. XVI (1939, reprinted 1970)

PETER WADE-MARTINS 'The Origins of Rural Settlement in East Anglia' in P. J. Fowler (ed) *Recent Work in Rural Archaeology* (Moonraker, Bradford on Avon, 1975)

PETER WADE-MARTINS 'Fieldwork and Excavation on Village Sites in Launditch Hundred, Norfolk' *East Anglian Archaeology* 10 (1980)

The most recent study with current ideas is:

DELLA HOOKE (ed) *Medieval Villages: A Review of Current Work* (Oxford University Committee for Archaeology, 1985)

7 – Farms and hamlets

For the *general background*, see especially:

C. TAYLOR *Village and Farmstead* (George Philip, 1983) Chapter 10

B. K. ROBERTS *Rural Settlement in Britain* (Dawson, Folkestone, 1977) Chapter 6

For *place names* see:

JOHN McNEAL DODGSHON 'The Significance of the Distribution of the English Place-name in '-ingas','-inga' in South-East England' *Medieval Archaeology* X (1966) pp. 1–14

MARGARET GELLING *Signposts to the Past* (Dent, 1978)

For *farmstead* studies:

R. L. S. BRUCE-MITFORD 'A Dark Age Settlement at Mawgan Porth, Cornwall' in R. L. S. Bruce-Mitford (ed) *Recent Archaeological Excavations in Britain* (Routledge and Kegan Paul, 1956)

A. KING 'Gauber High Pasture, Ribblehead – An Interim Report' in R. A. Hall (ed) *Viking Age York and the North* Council for British Archaeology Research Report No. 27 (1978)

D. COGGINS, K. J. FAIRLESS and C. E. BATEY 'Simy Folds: An Early Medieval Settlement Site in Upper Teesdale' *Medieval Archaeology* 27 (1983) pp. 1–26

W. G. HOSKINS 'The Highland Zone in Domesday Book' in *Provincial England* (Macmillan, 1965)

R. LEECH 'Roman Town and Countryside' in M. Aston and I. Burrow (eds) *The Archaeology of Somerset* (Somerset County Council, Taunton, 1982)

M. ASTON 'Deserted Farmsteads on Exmoor and the Lay Subsidy of 1327 in West Somerset' *Somerset Archaeology and Natural History* 127 (1983) pp. 71–104

ANGUS J. L. WINCHESTER 'Deserted Farmstead Sites at Miterdale Head, Eskdale' *Transactions, Cumberland and Westmorland Antiquarian and Archaeological Society* 79 (1979) pp. 150–5

CATHERINE D. LINEHAN 'Deserted Sites and Rabbit Warrens on Dartmoor, Devon' *Medieval Archaeology* X (1966) pp. 113–44

GUY BERESFORD 'Three Deserted Medieval Settlements on Dartmoor: A Report on the Late E. Marie Minter's Excavations' *Medieval Archaeology* XXIII (1979) pp. 98–158

HAROLD FOX 'Contraction: Desertion and Dwindling of Dispersed Settlement in a Devon Parish' in *Medieval Village Research Group* 31 Annual Report (1983) pp. 40–2

HARALD UHLIG 'Old Hamlets with Infield and Outfield Systems in Western and Central Europe' *Geografiska Annaler* Vol. XLIII (1961) pp. 285–312

For *colonisation* see:

PETER SAWYER 'Medieval English Settlement: New Interpretation' in Peter Sawyer (ed) *English Medieval Settlement* (Edward Arnold, 1979)

R. A. DONKIN 'Changes in the Early Middle Ages' in H. C. Darby (ed) *A New Historical Geography of England Before 1600* (Cambridge University Press, 1973)

MICHAEL WILLIAMS 'Marshland and Waste' in L. Cantor (ed) *The Medieval English Landscape* (Croom Helm, London, 1982)

BRIAN ROBERTS 'A Study of Medieval Colonisation in the Forest of Arden, Warwickshire' *Agricultural History Review* XVI (1968) pp. 101–13

BRIAN ROBERTS 'The Historical Geography of Moated Homesteads: The Forest of Arden, Warwickshire' *Transactions of the Birmingham and Warwickshire Archaeological Society* 88 (1976–77) pp. 61–70

R. A. DONKIN *The Cistercians: Studies in the Geography of Medieval England and Wales* (Pontifical Institute of Medieval Studies, Toronto, 1978) especially Chapters 2 and 4

M. WILLIAMS *The Draining of the Somerset Levels* (Cambridge University Press, 1970)

For *settlement evolution* studies:

B. CUNLIFFE 'Saxon and Medieval Settlement Pattern in the Region of Chalton, Hampshire' *Medieval Archaeology* XVI (1972) pp. 1–12

PETER DREWETT *et al* 'The Archaeology of Bullock Down, Eastbourne, East Sussex: The Development of a Landscape' *Sussex Archaeological Society* Monograph 1 (1982) especially Chapter XI

Brian Roberts has written much on settlement development and his ideas are summarised in:

B. K. ROBERTS 'The Anatomy of the Village: Observation and Extrapolation' *Landscape History* 4 (1982) pp. 11–20

8 – Sites and patterns

The best general study is:

MICHAEL CHISHOLM *Rural Settlement and Land Use: An Essay in Location* particularly the 3rd edition (Hutchinson, 1979)

For *site catchment analysis* see:

CLAUDIO VITA-FINZI and E. S. HIGGS 'Prehistoric Economy in the Mount Carmel Area of Palestine: Site Catchment Analysis' *Proceedings of the Prehistoric Society* 36 (1970 pp. 1–37

A. ELLISON and J. HARRIS 'Settlement and Land Use in the Prehistory and Early History of Southern England: A Study Based on Locational Models' in D. L. Clarke (ed) *Models in Archaeology* (Methuen, 1972) pp. 911–62

B. J. GARNER 'Models of Urban Geography and Settlement Location' in R. J. Chorley and P. Haggett (eds) *Socio-Economic Models in Geography* (Methuen, 1967) pp. 303–60

Changes in the Post-Roman landscape are discussed in:

CLAUDIO VITA-FINZI *Archaeological Sites in Their Setting* (Thames and Hudson, 1978)

FRED ALDSWORTH and DAVID FREKE *Historic Towns in Sussex: An Archaeological Survey* (Sussex Archaeological Field Unit, 1976)

BARRY CUNLIFFE 'The Evolution of Romney Marsh: A Preliminary Statement' in F. H. Thompson (ed) *Archaeology and Coastal Change* Society of Antiquaries Occasional Paper (New Series) 1 (1980) pp. 37–55

M. W. BERESFORD *The Lost Villages of England* (Lutterworth, London, 1954)

M. W. BERESFORD *New Towns of the Middle Ages* (Lutterworth, London, 1967)

TREVOR ROWLEY (ed) *The Evolution of Marshland Landscapes* Oxford University Department of External Studies, 1981)

H. C. DARBY *The Medieval Fenland* (Cambridge University Press, 1940)

H. C. DARBY *The Draining of the Fens* (Cambridge University Press, 1956) 2nd edition

H. C. DARBY *The Changing Fenland* (Cambridge University Press, 1983)

M. WILLIAMS *The Draining of the Somerset Levels* (Cambridge University Press, 1970)

Settlement patterns are discussed in:

I. HODDER and C. ORTON *Spatial Analysis in Archaeology* (Cambridge University Press, 1976)

J. A. EVERSON and B. P. FITZGERALD *Settlement Patterns* (Longman, 1969)

CHRISTOPHER TAYLOR 'Roman Settlements in the Nene Valley: The Impact of Recent Archaeology' in P. J. Fowler (ed) *Recent Work in Rural Archaeology* (Moonraker, Bradford on Avon, 1975)

ROGER LEECH 'Roman Town and Countryside' in M. Aston and I. Burrow (eds) *The Archaeology of Somerset* (Somerset County Council, Taunton, 1982)

CHRISTOPHER TAYLOR *Village and Farmstead: A History of Rural Settlement in England* (George Philip, 1983)

BRIAN ROBERTS *Rural Settlement in Britain* (Dawson, Folkestone, 1977) especially Chapter 4, 'Patterns of Village Settlement'

9 – Land use

For *animals*, *crops* and *related topics* see:

ROGER MERCER (ed) *Farming Practice in British Prehistory* (Edinburgh University Press, 1981)

For *medieval diet* see:

CHRISTOPHER DYER 'English Diet in the Later Middle Ages' in T. H. Aston, P. R. Coss, C. Dyer and J. Thirsk (eds) *Social Relations and Ideas: Essays in Honour of R. H. Hilton* (Cambridge University Press, 1983)

JOHN HARVEY 'Vegetables in the Middle Ages' *Garden History* Vol. 12 No. 2 (Autumn 1984) pp. 89–99

For *honey* and *hives* see:

EVA CRANE *The Archaeology of Beekeeping* (Duckworth, 1983)

For the use of *distant resources* see:

MICHAEL CHISHOLM *Rural Settlement and Land Use* (Hutchinson, 3rd edition, 1979)

DAVID CLARKE 'A Provisional Model of an Iron Age Society and Its Settlement System' in D. L. Clarke (ed) *Models in Archaeology* (Methuen, 1972)

J. M. COLES and B. J. ORME *Prehistory of the Somerset Levels* Somerset Levels Project (1980)

MICHAEL WILLIAMS *The Draining of the Somerset Levels* (Cambridge University Press, 1970)

For *woodland*:

OLIVER RACKHAM *Trees and Woodland in the British Landscape* (Dent, 1976)

OLIVER RACKHAM *Ancient Woodland: Its History, Vegetation and Uses In England* (Edward Arnold, 1980)

OLIVER RACKHAM *Hayley Wood: Its History and Ecology* (Cambridgeshire and Isle of Ely Naturalists Trust Ltd, 1975)

See also *Somerset Levels Papers* 1 (1975) to 10 (1984) and continuing, especially:

OLIVER RACKHAM 'Neolithic Woodland Management in the Somerset Levels: Garvin's, Walton Heath and Rowland's Tracks' *Somerset Levels Papers* 3 (1977) pp. 65–71

For *royal forests* see Oliver Rackham's books (above, 1976 and 1980) and:

C. R. YOUNG *The Royal Forests of Medieval England* (Leicester University Press, Leicester, 1979)

For *individual forest* studies:

K. P. WITNEY *The Jutish Forest: a study of the Weald of Kent from 450 to 1380 AD* (Athlone Press, London, 1976)

CRISPIN GILL (ed) *Dartmoor: A New Study* (David and Charles, 1970)

EDWARD T. MCDERMOT *A History of the Forest of Exmoor* revised edition (David and Charles, 1973)

L. M. CANTOR 'The Medieval Forests and Chases of Staffordshire' *North Staffs Journal of Field Studies* Vol. 8 (1968)

See also:

L. CANTOR (ed) *The English Medieval Landscape* (Croom Helm, London, 1982)

For *parks* see:

L. M. CANTOR and J. HATHERLEY 'The Medieval Parks of England' *Geography* Vol. 64 (1979) pp. 71–85

L. CANTOR (ed) *The English Medieval Landscape* (Croom Helm, London, 1982) Chapter 3

O. RACKHAM *Trees and Woodland in the British Landscape* (Dent, 1976) Chapter 8

For *commons* see:

W. G. HOSKINS and L. DUDLEY STAMP *The Common Lands of England and Wales* (Collins, 1963)

R. T. ROWLEY 'Clee Forest – A Study in Common Rights' *Transactions of Shropshire Archaeological Society* Vol. LVIII part 1 (1965) pp. 48–67

For *rabbits* see:

JOHN SHEAIL *Rabbits and Their History* (David and Charles, 1972)

R. HANSFORD WORTH *Worth's Dartmoor* (David and Charles, 1967) plates 28–9 and pp. 157–62

M. W. BERESFORD and J. K. S. ST JOSEPH *Medieval England: An Aerial Survey* 2nd edition (Cambridge University Press, 1979) pp. 68–72.

For *duck decoys* see:

SIR RALPH W. F. PAYNE-GALLWEY *The Book of Duck Decoys, their Construction, Management and History* (J. Van Voorst, London, 1886)

For *meadows* and *watermeadows* see:

J. H. BETTEY *Rural Life in Wessex 1500–1900* (Moonraker, Bradford on Avon, 1977)

ERIC KERRIDGE *The Farmers of Old England* (Allen and Unwin, 1973)

NIGEL HARVEY *The Industrial Archaeology of Farming in England and Wales* (Batsford, 1980)

J. H. BETTEY 'Sheep, Enclosures and Watermeadows in Dorset in 16th and 17th Centuries' in M. Havinden (ed) *Husbandry and Marketing in the South West 1500–1800* (Exeter University, 1973)

J. H. BETTEY 'The Development of Water Meadows in Dorset During the 17th Century' *Agricultural History Review* 25 (1977) pp. 37–43

MICHAEL COWAN *Floated Meadows in the Salisbury Area* South Wiltshire Industrial Archaeology Society – Historical Monograph 9 (1982)

C. S. ORWIN and R. J. SELLICK *The Reclamation of Exmoor Forest* (David and Charles, new edition 1970)

10 – Field systems

For the development of ideas see:

H. L. GRAY *English Field Systems* (Harvard University Press, 1915)

C. S. and C. S. ORWIN *The Open Fields* (Clarendon Press, Oxford, 1938)

JOAN THIRSK 'The Common Fields' and 'The Origin of the Common Fields' in R. H. Hilton (ed) *Peasants, Knights and Heretics, Studies in Medieval English Social History* (Cambridge University Press, 1976)

A. R. H. BAKER and R. A. BUTLIN (eds) *Studies of Field Systems in the British Isles* (Cambridge University Press, 1973)

ROBERT A. DODGSHON *The Origin of British Field Systems: An Interpretation* (Academic Press, 1980)

TREVOR ROWLEY (ed) *The Origins of Open Field Agriculture* (Croom Helm, London, 1981)

For specific examples, which are legion, see:

DENNIS R. MILLS (ed) *English Rural Communities: The Impact of a Specialised Economy* (Macmillan, London, 1973)

M. W. BERESFORD and J. K. ST JOSEPH *Medieval England: An Aerial Survey* (Cambridge University Press, 2nd edition, 1979)

The latter discusses the field evidence, as do:

DAVID HALL *Medieval Fields* (Shire Archaeology, Aylesbury, 1982)

CHRISTOPHER TAYLOR *Fields in the English Landscape* (Dent, 1975)

MAURICE BERESFORD 'Ridge and Furrow and the Open Fields' *Economic History Review* 2nd Series Vol. 1 No. 1 (1948) pp. 34–45

P. J. FOWLER 'Agriculture and Rural Settlement' in David Wilson (ed) *The Archaeology of Anglo-Saxon England* (Cambridge University Press, 1976)

P. BARKER and J. LAWSON 'A Pre-Norman Field System at Hen Domen, Montgomery' *Medieval Archaeology* Vol. XV (1971) pp. 58–72

P. FOWLER and A. C. THOMAS 'Arable Field of the Pre-Norman Period at Gwithian' *Cornish Archaeology* 1 (1962) pp. 61–84

For *early fields* see:

H. C. BOWEN and P. J. FOWLER (eds) *Early Land Allotment* British Archaeological Reports 48 (1978). This includes C. TAYLOR and P. FOWLER 'Roman Fields into Medieval Furlongs' pp. 159–62

HAROLD FOX 'Approaches to the Adoption of the Midland System' in T. Rowley (ed) (1981). This is a most important article.

MARY HARVEY 'The Origin of Planned Field Systems in Holderness, Yorkshire' in T. Rowley (ed) (1981)

MARY HARVEY 'The Morphological and Tenurial Structure of a Yorkshire Township – Preston in Holderness 1066–1750' Queen Mary College, London, Occasional Papers in Geography Vol. 13 (1978)

MARY HARVEY 'Regular Field and Tenurial Arrangements in Holderness, Yorkshire' *Journal of Historical Geography* 6 part 1 (1980) pp. 3–16

For *solskifte* or sun division see:

GEORGE C. HOMANS *English Villagers of the 13th Century* (Harvard University, Cambridge, Mass., 1941; reprinted Norton, London, 1973)

SÖLVE GÖRANSSON 'Regular Openfield Pattern in England and Scandinavian Solskifte' *Geografiska Annaler* Vol. XLIII (1961) pp. 80–104

JUNE SHEPPARD 'The Origins and Evolution of Field and Settlement Patterns in the Herefordshire Manor of Marden' Department of Geography, Queen Mary College, London, Occasional Papers No. 15 (1979)

JUNE SHEPPARD 'Pre-Enclosure Field and Settlement Patterns in an English Township, Wheldrake near York' *Geografiska Annaler* Vol. 48 Series B (1966) part 2 pp. 59–77

B. K. ROBERTS 'Townfield Origins: The Case of Cockfield, County Durham' in T. Rowley (ed) (1981)

H. P. R. FINBERG 'The Open Field in Devon' in *West Country Historical Studies* (David and Charles, 1969)

The 'innox' quotation is from:

J. E. B. GOVER, ALLEN MAWER and F. M. STENTON *The Place Names of Wiltshire* (Cambridge University Press, 1939) being English Place-Name Society Vol. XVI (p.134)

For *Hound Tor* see:

GUY BERESFORD 'Three Deserted Medieval Settlements on Dartmoor: A Report on the late E. Marie Minter's Excavations' *Medieval Archaeology* XXIII (1979) pp. 98–158

For *enclosure* see:

E. C. K. GONNER *Common Land and Enclosure* (Macmillan, 1912)

W. E. TATE *The English Village Community and the Enclosure Movements* (Gollancz, 1967)

M. WILLIAMS 'The Enclosure and Reclamation of Waste Land in England and Wales in the 18th and 19th Centuries' *Transactions, Institute of British Geographers* Vol. 51 (1970) pp. 55–69

MICHAEL TURNER *English Parliamentary Enclosure: Its Historical Geography and Economic History* (Dawson, Folkestone, 1980)

GILBERT SLATER *The English Peasantry and the Enclosure of Common Fields* (Constable, 1907) No. 14 Studies in Economics and Political Science

For *hedge dating* see:

W. G. HOSKINS *Fieldwork in Local History* (Faber and Faber, 1967) although the list of species is suspect

E. POLLARD, M. D. HOOPER and N. W. MOORE *Hedges* The New Naturalist (Collins, 1974)

Hedges and Local History (National Council for Social Service, London, 1971)

GEOFFREY HEWLETT 'Stages in the Settlement of a Downland Parish: A Study of the Hedges of Chelsham' *Surrey Archaeological Collections* Vol. LXXII (1980) pp. 91–6. This uses hedges and hedge dating critically with a useful discussion.

JOHN HARVEY *Early Nurserymen* Phillimore, Chichester (1974)

11 – Communications – the links between

A great deal has been said in the past about communications, but little that has been published is any good. There are no good books on early sea and river communications. For roads, the best are:

CHRISTOPHER TAYLOR *Roads and Tracks of Britain* (Dent, 1979)

BRIAN PAUL HINDLE *Medieval Roads* (Shire Archaeology, Aylesbury, 1982) with a very good bibliography

BRIAN PAUL HINDLE 'Roads and Tracks' in L. Cantor (ed) *The English Medieval Landscape* (Croom Helm, London, 1982)

Roman roads

R. W. BAGSHAWE *Roman Roads* (Shire Archaeology, Aylesbury, 1979)

I. D. MARGARY *Roman Roads in Britain* (John Baker, London, 1967)

Medieval roads

M. W. BERESFORD and J. K. S. ST JOSEPH *Medieval England: An Aerial Survey* (Cambridge University Press, 1979) pp. 273–84 'Roads'

C. T. FLOWER 'Public Works in Medieval Law' *Seldon Society* 32 & 40 (1915 and 1923)

H. GOUGH *Itinerary of King Edward the First throughout his reign, AD 1272–1307 exhibiting his movements from time to time, so far as they are recorded ... 2 vols.* (Paisley, Alexander Gardner, 1900)

BRIAN PAUL HINDLE 'The Road Network of Medieval England and Wales' *Journal of Historical Geography* 2 (1976) pp. 207–21

BRIAN PAUL HINDLE 'Seasonal Variations in Travel in Medieval England' *Journal of Transport History* 4 (1978) pp. 170–8

J. A. A. J. JUSSERAND *English Wayfaring Life in the Middle Ages* (Unwin, 1889)

G. H. MARTIN 'Road Travel in the Middle Ages' *Journal of Transport History* 3 (1976) pp. 159–78

F. M. STENTON 'The Road System of Medieval England' *Economic History Review* 7 (1936) pp. 1–21

Medieval maps

BRIAN PAUL HINDLE 'The Towns and Roads of the Gough Map' *The Manchester Geographer* 1 (1980) pp. 35–49

12 – What does it all mean?

C. TAYLOR 'The Making of the English Landscape – 25 Years On' *The Local Historian* Vol. 14 No. 4 (Nov. 1980). A review of what has been learned as has been discussed already. Followed by:

M. ASTON 'The Making of the English Landscape – The Next 25 Years' *The Local Historian* Vol. 15 No. 6 (May 1983)

Population

J. L. BOLTON *The Medieval English Economy 1150–1500* (Dent, 1980) pp. 48–65

P. J. FOWLER *The Farming of Prehistoric Britain* (Cambridge University Press, 1983) pp. 32–6

Forest and land use

JOHN EVANS *The Environment of Early Man in the British Isles* (Elek, London, 1975)

WINIFRED PENNINGTON *The History of British Vegetation* (English Universities Press, London, 1974)

HARRY GODWIN *History of the British Flora* (Cambridge University Press, 1975)

D. WALKER and R. G. WEST (eds) *Studies in the Vegetational History of the British Isles* (Cambridge University Press, 1970)

Climate

H. H. LAMB 'Climate from 1000 BC to 1000 AD' in M. Jones and G. Dimbleby (eds) *The Environment of Man: The Iron Age to the Anglo-Saxon Period* British Archaeological Reports British Series 87 (Oxford, 1981)

C. D. SMITH and M. PARRY (eds) *Consequences of Climatic Change* (Dept. of Geography, University of Nottingham, 1981)

M. L. PARRY (ed) *Climatic Change, Agriculture and Settlement* (Dawson, Folkestone, 1978)

Technology

A difficult area with little written of any use. Peter Reynold's research at Butser has opened our eyes to a range of new possibilities of how much early people were capable of.

P. J. REYNOLDS *Iron Age Farm: The Butser Experiment* (Colonnade, British Museum, 1979)

General accounts and ideas are discussed in:

LYNN WHITE *Medieval Technology and Social Change* (Oxford University Press, 1962)

M. HODGEN *Change and History: A Study of Dated Districts of Technological Innovations in England* (Viking Fund Publications, New York, 1952)

SIAN REES 'Agricultural Tools: Function and Use'; GORDON HILMAN 'Reconstructing Crop Husbandry Practices from Charred Remains of Crops'; and P. ROWLEY-CONWY 'Slash and Burn in the Temperate European Neolithic' all in Roger Mercer (ed) *Farming Practice in British Prehistory* (Edinburgh University Press, 1981)

Index